RALPH NADER CONGRESS PROJECT

WHO RUNS CONGRESS?

By
MARK J. GREEN
JAMES M. FALLOWS
DAVID R. ZWICK

Preface by Robert C. Fellmeth
Introduction by Ralph Nader

A BANTAM / GROSSMAN BOOK

BANTAM BOOKS
TORONTO/NEW YORK/LONDON
A National General Company

GROSSMAN PUBLISHERS
NEW YORK

To the constituents

WHO RUNS CONGRESS?
*A Bantam Book/published jointly with
Grossman Publishers*

Bantam edition published September 1972
2nd printing
3rd printing
4th printing
5th printing

Published simultaneously in the United States and Canada

*Bantam Books are published by Bantam Books, Inc., a National
General company. Its trade-mark, consisting of the words "Bantam
Books" and the portrayal of a bantam, is registered in the United
States Patent Office and in other countries. Marca Registrada.
Bantam Books, Inc., 666 Fifth Avenue, New York, N.Y. 10019.*

PRINTED IN THE UNITED STATES OF AMERICA

Acknowledgments

When one works with a group the size of the Congress Project, it is impossible to thank adequately all those who have contributed. Some, however, warrant special mention. Robert Fellmeth, Joan Claybrook, and Harrison Wellford gave generously of their time and insights as the book progressed. Senate staffer Michael Pertschuk aided us far more than we ever should have expected, but with a quality that we always anticipated. Doug Cassel contributed his ideas generally and chapter 9 specifically; researchers Craig Kubey and Anne Uttermann were always available to ferret out stubbornly elusive facts; and Pauline Postotnik and Elayne Butwinick patiently typed and retyped as we wrote and rewrote. Tom Stewart, our editor (and contributor to chapter 8), prodded and pulled the manuscript, applying his deft touch as he went along. Also, it would be difficult to invent a more encouraging and enthusiastic tandem than publisher Dick Grossman and his aide, Julie Colmore. As well, there is Oscar Dystel, who perceived the public need to understand Congress better and who accordingly helped launch this book. Finally, of course, our appreciation to Ralph Nader, who constantly fed us his ideas and shepherded this book to completion.

MARK J. GREEN
JAMES M. FALLOWS
DAVID R. ZWICK

Washington, D.C.
September, 1972

Contents

Preface

Who Runs Congress? is the first in a projected series of publications to be issued by the Ralph Nader Congress Project. It is intended to raise and explore briefly, in an unpedantic style, the fundamental problems besetting Congress. Yet the issues raised here—campaign funding and the election process, Capitol culture and Capitol crime, lobbying and information, executive preemption of the Congress—are all deserving of separate studies. In works to follow we shall publish profiles of each member of Congress, studies of each congressional committee, studies of special topics, and a handbook for citizen action. Thus, for those seeking a more detailed discussion than any one volume can pretend to accomplish, we refer you to these later elaborations.

The publications of the Congress Project are the result of a year and a half of work. Several hundred citizen volunteers, working in their own communities, systematically interviewed party leaders and district office staff and researched local newspapers and campaign finance records in the fifty states and most of the 435 congressional districts. In June, 1972, some two hundred political scientists, attorneys, economists, journalists, and college and graduate students converged in Washington to complete their focused research on particular profiles, topics, and congressional committees.

The Constitution places Congress, among the three branches of government, closest to the people. Theoretically accountable to the public via elections, the Constitution gave to Congress the authority and responsibility to declare war, impose taxes, allocate the federal budget, and establish federal laws for the general welfare. The abdication or abuse of these powers places responsibility for correction with the one group capable of guaranteeing their proper exercise, the citizenry itself.

ROBERT C. FELLMETH
Project Director
Congress Project

Washington, D.C.
September, 1972

Introduction: Your Stake in Congress
Ralph Nader

This book is about your power, your money, and your Congress. In a democracy, ultimate governmental power is supposed to reside in the people. And in the interest of practicality and expertise, the people delegate much of the daily exercise of this power to elected legislatures, which on the national level means Congress. But delegation requires vigilance, and, lacking vigilance, delegation becomes abdication. One of the objectives of this volume is to make more people care about what they've lost to Congress so that they can take more of it back for the good of themselves, their fellow citizens, and their children. For the people have indeed abdicated their power, their money, and their democratic birthright to Congress. As a result, without the participation of the people, Congress has surrendered its enormous authority and resources to special interest groups, waste, insensitivity, ignorance, and bureaucracy.

Everyone knows what Congress looks like. Many people know that there are 100 senators and 435 representatives, but how many citizens connect their daily lives and hopes with what these 535 legislators do or do not do every day? Not many. Congress is seen as something out there—in Washington, on the television screen—and not closely related to their daily activities. Less than half the adults polled back in 1965 knew the name of their congressman; worse, the 535 members of Congress are of no interest to the vast majority of people they're supposed to represent.

Americans spent more time last year watching the New York Jets and the Dallas Cowboys than thinking, reading, or doing something about Congress. But they also spent far more time worrying about their personal problems—taxes, schools, health, pollution, war, traffic, housing, consumer prices, crime, injustice, poverty, corruption. They worried about a steady slippage in the quality of American life—not about Congress. Yet these are the problems and abuses that Congress has the power to help them with—that is what Congress is *supposed* to be for. As the branch of government that allocates some $250 billion of taxpayers' funds every year, its laws affect the price of meat and gasoline; decide how clean the environment is to be; permit or encourage warfare; feed massive military expenditures; shape huge government bureaucracies (which it alone can create); and affect the size and quality of the economy.

Whatever its impact, Congress has shackled itself with inadequate political campaign laws, archaic rules, the seniority system, secrecy, understaffing, and grossly deficient ways to obtain crucial information. It is what Congress has done to itself, under external prodding, which should be the most immediate base point for citizen focus. It is a Congress which does not lead, but is led, and which continues to relinquish its constitutional authority and leadership role in government. Crushed by the burden of checking and balancing the executive branch, Congress operates nonetheless on a yearly budget equivalent to less than three days' expenditure of the Pentagon.

Congress is the great American default. The popular explanation for this is that it is under the domination of the White House and relentless special interests. There is no question that this is true. Why? Because, in large part, Americans have failed to involve themselves in the activities of Congress, and they have failed to expend the energy to determine the direction these activities should take. Of the three branches of government, the executive and judicial may get away with being insulated from the citizenry, but Congress is potentially the branch most exposed to democratic demand. And so turning Congress around *for* the people is the most practical and immediate priority in improving the executive and judicial branches as well.

The stakes are now so apparent and so mounting that accomplishing this transformation *by* the people must be viewed as an *obligation,* not just a right, of citizenship. This citizenship must be ingrained as part of the daily work of America.

There should be little disagreement over the assertion that ours is a society of unparalleled material wealth and skill, increasingly unable to solve, diminish, or forestall problems to which wealth and skill should be responsive. This gnawing paradox is a signal fact of contemporary American life—one with worldwide repercussions. As our dollar Gross National Product (GNP) zooms upward, our cities are rotting; malnutrition and disease stalk millions of impoverished citizens; pollution is increasing faster than GNP; the narcotics trade eats at the human fiber; government corruption and waste are bursting out all over; bureaucracy has become the opiate of the people; consumer fraud accelerates hand in hand with Big Business domination of the economy and much of government; rank-and-file disgruntlement with labor leadership deepens; and housing, rapid transit, and medical care seem to defy even a focused effort at resolution. At the same time, the law stands mocked or manipulated by the powerful. Consequently, the poor and middle class, who are given little access and less compassion by the legal system, view it with increasing contempt.

When was the last time the press reported that any of the country's major domestic problems had been rolled back? Americans of yesteryear prided themselves as problem solvers. Americans of today seem unable to meet the challenges of growth or to overcome the injustices created by that growth. This is not to say that we have no problem solvers today. Each month, obstacles are overcome in the development of more efficient weapons, of more sophisticated trips into space, and of more facile persuasion of consumers to buy deodorants. And yet there is a peculiar resistance or aversion to solving the problems that adversely affect millions of people as they go about their daily lives. A paralysis grips the land as major institutions, private and public, callously fail to respond to the present crises and needs of the American people. More portentously, risk levels for the future—particularly from technology—are rising, and yet little anticipatory planning is done about it.

If we cannot reduce our spreading crises, with all our wealth and talent, we are entitled to ask: What remains to meet the challenge of achieving the necessary changes? One answer is the U.S. Congress. Like the nerve center of a traffic control system, Congress stands potentially as both reflector and initiator of operational democratic responses and solutions. The word *potentially* is used deliberately—as both an expression of hope and of realistic possibilities—even though Congress in its past and in its present has been a continuous underachiever.

What does the public know of Congress? Not much at all. There is, to be sure, a widespread cynicism about "politicians," along with the feeling that nothing can be done about them beyond mere endurance. At times three major impressions of Congress prevail: that it is something to be manipulated by special interest groups or bureaucracies; that it is something to be ridiculed, or ignored, because it is an ornament; or that it is hopelessly beyond reach.

I disagree on all three counts. The often futile but valiant efforts at internal reform by some congressmen have failed, largely because they were undertaken with little understanding and less participation by citizens. This need not be so. I believe that an institution—which yearly distributes several hundred billion tax dollars; which is possessed of broad constitutional powers to advance the well-being of Americans and, to some degree, the rest of the world; which can assess or air a nation's problems openly; which can secure the information to plan for the future intelligently; and which can be run by the American people—can be the prime lever for change and justice in our country.

Nothing compares with the Congress as the initiating hope of reclaiming America. By reclaiming the Congress, America revolutionizes itself. For in so doing there is a required build-up of citizenship, expertise, and stamina such as this country has never seen. It is the right and duty of every citizen to strive for such development. And it should not have to be the equivalent of reaching for the stars.

Traditionally, the political system in this country has lead Americans to look to the presidency for inspiration and leadership. But the Congress can be an even more effective leader and shaper and receiver of democratic values and action. For some of Washington's old hands, such an aspiration might be taken as a bad joke, if not an explicitly bizarre goal. But it is not as bizarre as it sounds when one considers the number of flexible and decentralized options that are open to Congress. The constitutional authority given to Congress accords it an importance that far transcends the endemic delay and chronic inaction presently woven into its fabric by its insulated surroundings.

The personal stake of every citizen in Congress is obvious. Only Congress takes twenty-five cents out of every dollar earned by the worker, supposedly to achieve a better society. Only Congress can send this country to war or allow the White House to enter unilaterally into a military holocaust. Only Congress can choose to ignore the recognized problems of the future and condone the felt abuses of the present which it exclusively is invested to confront.

Who Runs Congress? shows why Congress is in crisis and offers some initial practical advice on what *you* can do about reclaiming it for American citizens. The rest is up to you—your sense of justice, your faith in people, your energy and imagination. It is your only Congress. If you want to do something about it, you start now. It is the mark of our nation's fingertip potential, unprecedented in world history, that we are a generation of Americans who have to give up so little in order to achieve so much of lasting endurance for the earth's people. Two centuries of delegation have worn their course. It is time to grasp the labors of daily citizenship and assume more closely the responsibility of government.

1

Who Owns Congress?

Congress is the best money can buy.
—Will Rogers

The influence of big money on government has been a theme of critics ever since the founding of the Republic. Were it not for the sordid tales of bribery and pay-offs regularly floating out from behind the Capitol Curtain, scandal columnists would long ago have gone on unemployment compensation. But for all their titillating impact, the crudest forms of bribery are vastly over-shadowed as a corrupting influence by a much more sophisticated and widespread practice. Instead of going into the congressman's pockets, the money is instead put in the campaign coffers for the next (or sometimes the previous) election.

Of course, when a big campaign contribution is given in return for an assurance of receiving special treatment, it doesn't matter what the transaction is called. It's still nothing more than good old-fashioned graft in a very thin disguise. But who needs to extract a promise from a politician if spending enough money at election time can put a "reliable" man into office? Or better yet, if spending enough money at primary election and nominating time can ensure that *all* the surviving candidates by the time the general election rolls around are "reliable." Whether campaign contributions buy an entire election or favored treatment or simply special access to politicians, they are the main reason why the rich men who make them get richer while the average citizen gets what little is left over.

Expensive Merchandise

Part of the problem is inflation. Like meat, congressmen have risen in price. As the cost of U.S.-Prime political influence has soared, casual buyers have fled the market and left it to the truly rich or the corporate purchasers. Expenses weren't always so high. In the election campaign of 1846, friends of Abraham Lincoln collected a fund for his first try for Congress. The $200 they scraped together would barely cover one week's phone bills for a modern candidate. But at the end of the campaign, Lincoln returned $199.25 of it. The rest had gone for his one campaign expense, a barrel of cider for local farm hands.

Honest Abe might have spent the rest of his life chopping rails if he'd tried the same thing much later. The turning point for campaign expenses came with the Civil War. As the newly powerful corporate empires began to buy political favors—and as the politicians of the time showed themselves willing to be bought—competition pushed the prices up. The mounting expense, however, did not curb demand, since the companies saw the hard business advantage of friendly politicians. In 1903, a Standard Oil agent (who was himself a member of Congress), screening a "loan request" from a senator, wrote to the company's vice-president John Archbold, "Do you want to make the investment?"

The return on investments like this was a Congress increasingly populated with men like Senator Boies Penrose. Penrose was a Pennsylvanian, a Republican, and a devoted glutton.* But his deepest allegiance was to the welfare of Corporate America. He explained his philosophy of economy and life to a group of his business beneficiaries: "I believe in a division of labor. You send us to Congress; we pass laws under . . . which

---

* He weighed 350 pounds and kept in condition with meals like the following: one dozen oysters, pots of chicken gumbo, a terrapin stew, two ducks, six kinds of vegetables, a quart of coffee, and several cognacs.

you make money; . . . and out of your profits you further contribute to our campaign funds to send us back again to pass more laws to enable you to make more money." A good operating guideline, he once confided to an associate, was to work on "legislation that meant something to men with real money and let them foot the bill" (as when Archbold of Standard Oil gave him $25,000 on one proven occasion).

Today's politicians can afford neither Penrose's candor nor his appetite, but his mottoes live on. Where does the money go? Before the coming of television as a political tool, most of it went to the old-fashioned paraphernalia of an election—billboard ads and two-cent stamps, campaign workers and envelope lickers, whistle-stop tours and barbecue rallies. Occasionally, of course, it went to buy votes outright. Oklahoma's Senator Fred Harris has fondly recalled his baptism in this old style of campaign spending, in the 1954 Oklahoma election, which found one oil millionaire (Robert Kerr) who held a Senate seat facing another oil millionaire (Roy Turner) who wanted it. Harris, who worked for Turner, says:

> Some [people] wanted to be county or town campaign managers for whichever candidate would pay the most. An unprincipled preacher offered to bargain away supposed influence with his unsuspecting congregation. An Avon saleswoman was willing to consider—for a price—adding a pitch for a candidate to her usual sales promotion to regular-route customers. And there were the ubiquitous importunings of hundreds of poll haulers and hangers-on. They wanted everything from $25,000 to carry a county to a half-pint of whiskey to make the day. From fifty dollars for "gas and expenses" to get to the district church conference, to a thousand dollars to pay back taxes to keep a weekly newspaper publishing. . . .
>
> One young man in the Turner headquarters had as his principal duty running to the Federal Reserve Bank every day as soon as it opened to bring

back a thousand or so dollars in cash to be doled out to those who came in declaring that victory in their counties required a little money "to put on a barbecue" or "to hire some woman to pick up old folks on election day."

But Darwin rules in politics as in nature, and the richest survive. Turner ran out of money midway through the campaign and had to quit. Kerr kept his seat.

If Turner were running his campaign in 1972, the daily money deliveries would have to be closer to ten thousand than to one. As election techniques have risen from barbecues and preacher-bribing to the higher technologies of media advertising, costs have soared. One of the new, and costly, techniques is air travel. Congressmen who languish in Washington learn the truth of out-of-sight, out-of-mind. In election years, congressmen and their staffs spend much of their time in the air between Washington and the home-state voters. One Senate staffer told Haynes Johnson of the *Washington Post* that to mend political fences he averaged twenty-two trips per year, at an annual cost of $10,500. Trips for government affairs can be deducted as business expense, but not campaign junkets. The result? "I can't describe to you what a constant worry that is or how I would go out of my way through this maze or that, trying to cover these bills. The only way to do it was through campaign contributions."

The real thrust behind skyrocketing costs, however, is television advertising. When saturation campaigns of one-minute spots or half-hour specials took over from more primitive, and cheaper, forms of publicity, election funding became a truly big business. As recently as 1952, when Eisenhower first ran for the presidency, the total spent in national election campaigns was "only" $140 million (according to the Citizens Research Foundation). Over the next twelve years, the total rose slowly; in 1964, it was an estimated $200 million. But only four years later, in the 1968 campaigns, the figure had risen by 50 percent, to $300 million. More than any other factor, television was the cause.

The most extreme example of television's effect on campaigns is the 1970 senatorial elections. Of the fifteen major candidates in the seven largest states, eleven were millionaires. The four who were not lost. One of the nonmillionaires was Charles Goodell, the liberal Republican who was trying to hold his seat in New York. Goodell spent $1.3 million in the campaign—more than half of it for television. Goodell raised the money through an executive finance committee. This was a group of fifteen wealthy men who called other wealthy men and asked them to donate between $1,000 and $10,000 apiece. But Goodell still ended up outspent by the opposition and $400,000 in debt. "We were always on the verge of a [TV] blackout because of lack of money," he told reporter Johnson. A TV blackout, as Goodell knew, would mean political death, given the voters' residual ignorance about him, and given his opponents' free-spending ways. The eventual winner, Conservative James Buckley, reported spending $2 million, while Democrat Richard Ottinger invested $4 million in his losing effort.

If the apparent lesson is that money won't necessarily buy victory, it is worth remembering that Ottinger, who had not been widely known in the state, won the Democratic primary almost solely through an overwhelming, expensive television campaign.

As costs have risen to the point where even the millionaires must borrow, so too rises the certainty that politicians must turn to rich special interests for help. President Eisenhower, in an era of what now looks like small-change campaigns, was appalled by the "outrageous costs of getting elected to public office." Later, Robert Kennedy agreed that "we are in danger of creating a situation in which our candidates must be chosen from among the rich [like the Kennedys] . . . or those willing to be beholden to others."

Who "owns" the politicians? A look at campaign fund sources shows two main stockholders, one holding so many shares that it is content to be silent, the other feisty but much weaker. The small shareholder is the organized labor movement. A relative newcomer to big-money politics, unions became an important force in the 1950s. A key starting point was the AFL-CIO's decision to set up a political action arm, the Committee on Political Education (COPE). Federal law bars unions from using their own funds in political campaigns, so committees like COPE serve as a handy and legal conduit for members' contributions. Aside from COPE, the committee list now includes the teamsters' DRIVE, the United Auto Workers' Good Government Fund, and many others. Together, according to Americans for Constitutional Action, they contributed more than $4 million to candidates in the 1970 elections.

While union contributions might potentially be a necessary counterweight to big-business spending, the tactics some unions use to collect their funds give the working class a bad name. One of the more notorious examples is the Seafarers International Union (SIU). The SIU has long been a big giver; in 1968, its 80,000 members came up with more than three times as much campaign money as the 1.4 million United Auto Workers. The money has been put to effective use, too. Much of the more than $600,000 collected that year was spread among friends of the maritime industry in Congress, where it oiled the way for a series of lush subsidies to the U.S. merchant fleet. So far, so good for the SIU. But along the way, there had been technical troubles. In 1970, eight of the union's officers were indicted for making illegal contributions of $40,000. This was allegedly part of a conspiracy involving donations of $750,000 over many years. The source of these huge funds is supposed to be "voluntary" contributions from union members, but grumblers claim that the word is used in a sense no one outside the SIU would recognize. As an aid to voluntarism, some SIU members have said, "goon squads" show up at collection time (a charge denied by union spokesmen). According to Jerry Landauer of the *Wall Street Journal,* the SIU collects from all crewmen on a U.S. ship—including foreigners, whose interest in American politics is presumably slight.

Campaign collectors in the business community are delighted when exploits like the SIU's come to light. To-

gether with the well-publicized contributions from COPE
and DRIVE, the union horror stories are just the thing
to spur businessmen to greater spending sacrifices for
their favorite candidates. It is a tribute to the determination of the fundraisers, and to the businessmen's refusal
to be complacent, that the money still rolls out in response to the union threat. For, as all the available evidence shows, the business world has nothing to worry
about.

It is difficult to total up the business contributions as
exactly as those from labor. Unlike the unions, who
typically trumpet each dollar they collect from the members and pass on to the candidate, business interests
prefer to keep their work largely invisible. A few have
COPE-type committees—such as the American Medical Association's AMPAC (a reported $693,000 in
1970) or the National Association of Manufacturers'
BIPAC ($539,000)—but most shun even that degree
of publicity.

Some rough estimates are available. From extensive
research into Democratic party contributions, reported
in his *Fat Cats and Democrats,* Professor William Domhoff estimates that roughly half the party's money comes
from corporate moneymen (55 percent). The rest
comes from labor (20–25 percent), racketeers and
gangsters (10–15 percent in some metropolitan areas),
and Apple Pie Middle-class Americans (roughly 15
percent). Domhoff says that the Republicans' contributors (who typically outspend their Democratic counter-
parts by 6 to 4 or 7 to 3) are much more heavily
weighted toward industrialists, bankers, and other mo-
guls.* A final estimate comes from Senator Russell
Long, who speaks from long experience on the receiving end. In a speech on the Senate floor in 1967, Long

---

* A few candidates in each party also receive contributions
from citizens', environmental, and peace groups. The amount
of such contributions is small, however, and they are generally
earned by those who have offended the large corporate givers
by taking strong environmental stands, or are given to the
opponents of incumbents with blatantly insensitive records on
these issues.

said, "Most campaign money comes from businessmen. Labor contributions have been greatly exaggerated. It would be my guess that about 95 percent of campaign funds at the congressional level are derived from businessmen. At least 80 percent of this comes from men who could sign a net worth statement exceeding a quarter of a million dollars." In a crucial last sentence, Long added, "Businessmen contribute because the Federal Corrupt Practices Act prohibits businesses from contributing." Like the unions, corporations find troublesome regulations standing between them and the politicians they want to buy. Dodging the rules takes two steps—getting "voluntary" contributions from employees through tactics reminiscent of the SIU, and finding ways to send the money to the right candidate.

Where seafaring men might use a goon squad, Texaco uses an interoffice memorandum. "We must as individual citizens support those candidates who understand and appreciate the validity of our position," intones a letter from Texaco's vice-president for public relations and personnel. It closes with a request that employees contribute $5 per month, or $60 for the entire year. Sterling Drug Inc., applying a means test, asks its 525 executives who earn more than $15,000 per year to give at least one-half of one percent of salary, up to a ceiling of $200. "Specifically, we're asking for a *voluntary* contribution from you," the letter says, "for a political fund to be allocated to those legislators . . . whose . . . election is *important* to our industry and to *Sterling Drug Inc.*" (emphasis in original) The volunteer donor—eager to help his industry's patrons, and curious about the use of his money—might ask the company who the important legislators are. Upholding the best professional traditions of confidentiality, Sterling refuses to tell.

Other corporations, more considerate of their workers, may add "bonuses" to executive paychecks with the understanding that the money will be passed on to a candidate. Still others—like the Union Oil Company and the Cleveland-based defense firm Thompson-Ramos-Woolridge (TRW)—avoid the middleman by simply deducting an arranged amount for "campaign contributions" from the paychecks of cooperating employees. The Public Affairs Council, whose members include two hundred corporate titans, is so struck by the plan that it is working for the day when the nation's thousand biggest companies will all have automatic campaign funding.

A possible flaw in the project is a new federal campaign finance law, which went into effect on April 7, 1972. One of its clauses forbids government contractors to participate "directly or indirectly" in campaigns. The citizen organization Common Cause went to court against TRW, claiming that its deduction plan violates the law, since the company, not the employees, decides where the money will go.* It is not yet clear whether this is an "indirect" participation in campaigns—or how strictly "contractor" will be defined (since nearly all the biggest corporations have some government contracts). But for the moment the law is holding up wider use of automatic funding plans. Once the Justice Department clears the doubt with a legal ruling, the way may be open for the biggest round of political inflation yet.

Clever as these ploys may be, they do not begin to cover the range of deceptions available to the determined business contributor. Another effective ruse is to use a company lawyer as a broker: the company pays him "legal fees," which he then passes on to a grateful politician. More directly, a group can support its candidate by paying him an appropriate honorarium for a good speech (as can any other interest group, for that matter). In 1971, seventy-six senators reported speaking fees totaling $787,433. How much more was paid and received is unknown, since listing the amounts is voluntary. If the businessmen don't want to put up with a speech, their corporation may simply buy large blocs of tickets for $100- or $1,000-per-plate fundraising

---

* In response, TRW dropped its plan temporarily and Common Cause dropped the suit. Another TRW fund, in which the employees get to designate where the money goes, was not challenged by Common Cause.

dinners, which no one but a few lobbyists need even attend.

Payments also come "in kind." Some companies keep men on the payroll to loan as campaign workers to deserving candidates. Boeing, recognizing a politician who had earned its support, did just that for Scoop Jackson during his doomed run for the presidency. Others give special discounts on, or offer free, products ranging from air travel to hotel rooms to printing presses. Companies can donate computer time to a candidate, or take expensive surveys and give away the results. A traditional means of hidden contributions to the national party occurs every four years, when companies buy ads at ludicrously inflated rates in the parties' convention programs.

The effect of these twisting and hidden paths is, as might be expected, to thoroughly deter attempts to find who's sending money to whom. Journalist Walter Pincus (now heading the Nader Congress Project's campaign finance investigations) discovered how tangled the threads could be when, in 1970, he tried to survey campaign reports from eight states and the District of Columbia. At the end of his labors, he had turned up undercover spending programs run by General Electric, U.S. Steel, Procter and Gamble, Union Carbide, and other corporations, totaling more than $1 million. But piecing together the evidence required a detective effort that would do credit to Scotland Yard. To track down one small item—a secret Union Carbide fund of at least $20,000—six researchers had to spend ten weeks looking through reports filed by individual candidates and cross-checking names of hundreds of contributors with lists of corporate executives. Small wonder that few members of the public know what industries are supporting which politicians.

The campaign disclosure laws have not been much help. The scripture of modern politics, the Federal Corrupt Practices Act of 1925, had deficiencies so obvious that Lyndon Johnson called it "more loophole than law." For a start, the law did not even apply to primaries —where so much of the spending goes on, particularly in

one-party states. For everything after the primaries,
Senate candidates were required to file spending reports
with the secretary of the Senate, and House candidates
with the clerk of the House. Just how seriously the law
was taken is indicated by a few of the filed reports. In
his 1968 reelection campaign in South Dakota, George
McGovern's total expenditures were "none." The explanation is that the candidates must only report funds
used with their "knowledge and consent." McGovern's
executive assistant George Cunningham kept McGovern
in blissful ignorance by being "very careful to make sure
that Senator McGovern never sees the campaign re-
ceipts."

Another clause making for hilarity at the public's
expense is the provision that all donors of $100 or more
must list their names and addresses. Witty contributors
get around this by making as many $99.99 donations
as they want to various campaign committees working
for the same candidate. The most important loophole
in the 1925 law, however, was its provision that campaign committees would have to report their contributors only if the committee operated in two or more
states. There was ample office space in the District of
Columbia for thousands of campaign committees, and
none of them had to report their activities. Along with
the cherry trees, another rite of election-year springs in
Washington has been the flowering of campaign committees for candidates all over the country. To choose
two illustrations among the many offered in 1970:
Congressman Thomas O'Neill of Massachusetts, august
chairman of the House Special Subcommittee to Investigate Campaign Expenditures, demonstrated the need
for such an investigation by setting up a dummy committee in the District of Columbia. Similarly, James
Buckley took in $400,000 toward his New York Senate
seat through a series of false-front D.C. committees.
More receptive to the spirit of the law than many dead-
pan candidates, Buckley's staff invented names like
"Committee to Keep a Cop on the Beat," "Neighbors
for Neighborhood Schools," and "Town Meeting Pres-

ervation Society" for their groups. "We made a game of it," staffer David Jones said.

Figuring that even a good joke may get stale after forty-seven years, the public pressured Congress to enact a new law in February, 1972. The Federal Election Campaign Act will take much of the fun and suspense out of old-style campaigning. It extends coverage to financing of primaries, runoff and special elections, party caucuses, and nominating conventions. A candidate can no longer feign ignorance of funds spent by others on his behalf.

But Congress, determined to have the last laugh, relented at the last minute and left in a few amusing provisions. The least subtle of these was the "grace period"—the two-month delay between the bill's passage in February and the date when candidates would first have to report contributions. With a joyous, free-for-all spirit not seen since the Oklahoma Land Rush, candidates from all parties scrambled to pack their campaign chests before the April 7 deadline. Led by the president—whose chief fundraiser, Maurice Stans, openly exhorted businessmen to get their money in on time—many congressmen lost all inhibitions in their eagerness to make the most of the remaining time. The only barrier was fatigue: one lobbyist, hand presumably sore from reaching for his wallet, complained to Arizona Congressman Sam Steiger that he had to attend 162 fundraising parties between February 23 and April 7.

With such freewheeling times behind them, private interests still have to rely in the future on the bill's more restrained loopholes. One, a minor revision of the $99.99 clause, now says that only contributions of "more than" $100 must be reported. Another, which will probably turn out to be the secret contributor's bread and butter, is the evasion known as "earmarking." This means that a contributor sends money to a campaign committee, with instructions that an equal amount of money be passed on to his candidate. Since one committee, such as the Democratic Senatorial Committee, handles contributions for dozens of candidates at one time, the trails become blurred as the money passes through the committee. By making the contribution in two steps—donor to committee, committee to candidate —there is no way of knowing, from the outside, which of the funds coming in are linked to those going out.

The Public Affairs Council's director, Richard Armstrong, has prepared a brief lesson on earmarking for his corporate pupils. In a memo to officials of Humble Oil, GM, IBM, R. J. Reynolds, and others, he told of "another possible dodge":

> For years many corporate committees have contributed political funds through four campaign committees (Republican senatorial, Republican congressional, Democratic senatorial, and Democratic congressional). To some extent this has been a "smoke screen." Customarily, they will "trade checks" with you. (I.e., you want to give $500 to Congressman X's campaign. But you do not want to report it and do not want him to report it. Therefore, you make a contribution to the Congressional Campaign Committee of $500. The Campaign Committee makes out a check to Congressman X. They may even let you deliver it.) So, it may be possible for a political fund to file a report simply saying that it gave equal amounts to each of these four committees. On the surface, it would appear that the fund just wanted to help everyone. Actually, *every nickel could be directed to specific candidates*. [emphasis in original]

Like crooks lugging baskets of dirty money to be washed through legitimate business fronts, the corporations may cleanse their contributions in the purifying waters of the campaign committee. The overseers of this cleansing operation—the committee directors—have indicated that the role does not upset them. "If it isn't illegal, and it isn't," John T. Calkins, director of the Republican National Congressional Committee, told reporter James Polk, "I don't see how we can refuse to do it—swap checks with them."

As if such a sign were needed, Congress has given one

further indication that it did not intend this new law to veer into the realm of seriousness. To enforce the tough new provisions, Congress avoided calling in any outside supervisors or creating a scrupulous watchdog agency. The guardians of the new law will instead be the same old crew that chuckled through the old law: the House clerk, the Senate secretary, and the Justice Department. The clerk and the secretary are both paid employees of Congress; over the years they have surprised absolutely no one by their reluctance to crack down on their masters. If, for unknown reasons, one of them begins to take his job too seriously, Congress can quickly right matters by removing all his staff. Ohio's Wayne Hays, chairman of the House Administration Committee, has already given House clerk W. Pat Jennings a taste of what to expect if he gets too nosy: Jennings asked for thirty-eight staff officials to administer the new law, but Hays gave him nineteen. (Hays took away the clerk's computerized equipment, and he forced a rise in the price the public must pay for copies of the politicians' reports, from ten cents per page to one dollar. Common Cause went to court and got an order reversing the price rise.) Neither Hays nor anyone else has figured out what to do about the clause allowing the public to look at the reports, but they take some comfort in knowing that the public is in a race with the clock. The reports are kept on file and publicly available for only one election term—two years in the House—before they vanish.

There is, of course, a final member of the trio of enforcers: the U.S. Department of Justice. Those who have watched this crack organization at work against ITT and other corporate suspects will not be surprised by its performance in regulating campaign finance. For years, the law was openly and massively violated, yet Justice never acted. Then in 1968, newly elected House clerk W. Pat Jennings surprised everyone by sending over to Attorney General Ramsey Clark a list of violations from the 1968 campaign. Before the list got any further, Clark was out of office, replaced by President Nixon's new attorney general, John Mitchell. Mitchell,

fresh from firsthand experience with campaign contributors during his year as Nixon's campaign manager,
was fascinated by Jennings's list; he and his colleagues
at Justice kept it so close that it seemed to have disappeared. Jennings, slow to get the message, sent other
lists in 1969 and 1971—each time with the same result.
One of the violators himself then tried to help out. A
defeated candidate from Vermont's 1970 House election, Dennis Morrisseau, wrote to Mitchell that he was
deliberately violating the law and asked to be prosecuted.
The merciful Justice Department turned the other cheek.

The new 1972 law has received roughly similar treatment. One day after President Nixon signed it, Ralph
Nader and his action group, Public Citizen, tried to
sting Justice into action by filing a lawsuit demanding
strict enforcement. Their complaint was accompanied
by a ninety-two-page list of hundreds of unprosecuted
campaign finance violations (for example, candidates
who had waited to file until after the election, "thus
defeating the purpose of preelection disclosures," or
who had failed to file reports at all).

The suit is still not decided, but the Justice approach
appears to be. In June, 1972, Common Cause asked
the clerk of the House to investigate ninety-one candidates from Alabama, Indiana, Ohio, Pennsylvania, and
the District of Columbia who had ignored the reporting
requirements of the new law. Shortly afterwards, Common Cause charged that more than two-thirds of California's 1972 congressional candidates had failed to file
correct disclosures before the May primary. As of
September, 1972, the Justice Department has never
prosecuted a single candidate for breaking the campaign
finance laws.

Wise Shoppers

The special interest investors, who would not dream
of pouring their money into dud stocks, are equally
careful when it comes to choosing their legislative port-
folio. A freshman legislator with a seat on a dull committee won't cost much, but won't yield much return,

either. The logical result is that the money goes to the men who rule Congress—the members of the key committees, the party leaders of each of the houses, and those aging powers who have stored up seniority, the committee chairmen. Following this guideline, the political arm of General Foods—the "North Street Good Government Group"—did not squander its money on Armed Services committee members. Instead, it aimed at three men whose influence on questions dear to General Foods equaled that of a hundred other congressmen combined: three powerful members of the House Agriculture Committee. The bankers' group, BankPAC, similarly excludes anyone not on committees which affect the industry.

For congressmen who happen to be in the key positions, this arrangement can ease many of life's problems. Congressman Wayne Aspinall, for example, must theoretically rely on his Colorado constituents to vote him into office again and again. But the money Aspinall uses for his campaigns comes mainly from private interests in other parts of the country. In 1970, for example, 79 percent of the $50,000 Aspinall reported that he spent came from outside his district. The reason is that Aspinall is chairman of the House Interior Committee, and, as such, one of the men who does most to determine the profit rates in the mining, timber, and oil industries. Aware of this, Kennecott Copper sent Aspinall nine separate checks in 1970; Humble Oil mailed seven checks from Texas; and Shell Oil, Martin Marietta, and American Metal Climax and Oil Shale Corporation also chipped in. From Washington, D.C., help came from lobbyists and executives of Union Oil, Atlantic Richfield, Dow Chemical, Burlington Northern Railroad, and the Southern tobacco industry. The hewers of logs, whose hewing depends on regulations Aspinall passes, joined in as well: the Southwest Forest Industries of Phoenix and the Western Wood Products Association of Portland, Oregon, sent funds.

Given the shape of the corporate economy, the importance of government regulations in making rich men richer, and the vulnerability of politicians to financial persuasion, it takes little imagination to see how campaign contributions can influence the activity of Congress.

It used to be that corporations helped their candidates in return for an even larger slice of the government's pie; nowadays many big businessmen find they already have as much as they can decorously eat. Their main concern is to guarantee against shrinkage, and they view their campaign contributions as a kind of insurance policy. As a member of the Senate Finance Committee explained to the *Atlantic*'s Elizabeth Drew, "By and large, the big contributions come from the privileged. They're not asking for any new privileges. Therefore, a man can say, 'Sure, I got a lot of money from the oil companies, but they never asked me for a thing.' That's because what they want is protection of the status quo. . . . By and large, Wall Street gives you money because you're against the war, or for health, but you think long and hard before being against capital gains or depreciation on real estate."

This benign approach may rapidly change if the businessmen see signs of impending danger. In 1955, for example, the Texas oil industry noted that congressional proposals to change the industry's tax subsidies had not been killed as quickly as usual. Anxious to set things right, the president of the Texas oil trade association told his fellows that "it seems only fair to tie a few strings to the contributions we make to political organizations and candidates." When, in 1958, the oil depletion tax loophole was up for its biennial round of criticism in Congress, a staff member of the Democratic senatorial campaign committee went to see some candidates from the Western states. "I was informed that if I could get some of these fellas out West to express their fealty to the golden principle of 27.5 percent [depletion allowance], there might be a pretty good piece of campaign change involved," he later told Ronnie Dugger of the *Texas Observer*.

In each case, the contributions would obviously have a purpose—to get those sympathetic to the oil lobby into Congress and to convince those already there to open their hearts to oil. But the bargain need not be stated that baldly. "Don't kid yourself about the 'no-strings attached' to a contribution," one congressional staffer with long experience in the wilderness of fundraising has said. "There's always a string attached. It may not be a black string, but it's a string, and some day it's going to get pulled."

These invisible links may swell to chainlike dimensions when the contributions pull a candidate out of a predicament like the one Congressman Edward A. Garmatz of Maryland nearly succumbed to in 1966. As primary election time approached, polls showed him doing badly. Then, the Seafarers International Union appeared to rescue him. The $17,000 in publicly reported contributions from the SIU for Garmatz was the largest amount of money any lawmaker got from any reported source. Garmatz sailed through and then returned the favor. He was able to do so through his position as chairman of the Merchant Marine and Fisheries Committee, which doles out the subsidies to the shipping companies that hire the SIU. In 1968, 90 percent of Garmatz's funding came from shipping interests. In 1970, the industry raised a reported $37,000 for him, even though he was unopposed for reelection.

Men in Garmatz's position often point to the old chicken/egg question: Do they do what they do because of the campaign contributions they received? Or do they receive the contributions because they do what they do? As one House staff aide noted, "There are some guys around here who honestly *believe* that industry is getting screwed by the consumers." When contributions make the difference between a career in Congress and another twenty years tending the small-town car dealership or law firm, the answer is that the distinction doesn't really matter. In 1970, six of the many candidates struggling for victory in the congressional primaries of North Carolina, Texas, and Pennsylvania found themselves blessed with contributions from the National Association of Manufacturers (through its political committee, BIPAC). All six went on to win.

BIPAC relies on campaign gifts rather than direct lobbying, because, as its newsletter editor Edward Maher has put it, "if you get the right group down there, you don't have to lobby."

Even when their contributions are not likely to be decisive, contributors often spread money for good will with whoever ends up in office. The more cautious contributors go further and hedge their bets by sprinkling a little good will among all likely near-or-distant winners—provided, of course, that they are "reasonable on the issues" (in the words of one Union Carbide operative). Thus if Tweedledee and Tweedledum are running a close race, a little butter may be applied to both. Even though a congressman is not dominated by any one special interest, his donors expect that he will remember gratefully those who helped him along. After his brief campaign for the presidency had foundered, Ways and Means Committee Chairman Wilbur Mills was $91,000 in debt. In June, 1972, the heads of ten breweries sent contributions of $6,000. This could hardly "buy" Mills, but as Robert A. Schmidt, president of the Olympia Brewing Company, explained, "Being in the brewing industry, you have to play both sides of the street. If they don't know that you contribute, the next thing you know, you might get an extra tax you don't like."

If those good-will contributions succeed in buying nothing else, they inevitably buy that vague but crucial commodity, *access* to an elected official. "We're not trying to buy votes," says a money handler for the oil industry. "We're trying to buy an entrée to talk about our problems." The purchase is usually successful. Politicians make way on their appointment schedules for potential or past contributors. As one congressional aide explained, "I'd always tell the Old Man, 'You don't want to know where it [the money] comes from, but if I tell you to see a guy, you'd better damn well see him.'"

More than dramatic payoffs and scandals, it is this entrée that twists the direction of government policy. Reporter James Polk has described the "fraternal" atmosphere that springs from these cordial talks; politicians naturally begin to "understand" their patrons' problems better than they otherwise might. Few congressmen would admit that they can be "bought," but their protest is like that of a free-living woman who decides she might as well take money for what she enjoys, but insists she is not a prostitute. With their more sympathetic view, they can open up the range of government favors to private interests: subsidies, lucrative contracts, tax exemptions, toothless regulatory laws, restraints on overeager regulating agencies, protective tariffs, foreign policies to protect private investment, domestic policy that stimulates demand. Those who suffer when the favors are passed out—the taxpayers, the purchasers of overpriced goods—never get a chance to sit down with the politicians in the same chummy atmosphere.

The next time you buy a quart of milk, you might reflect on how the alliance of politicians and private interests can affect you. Early in 1971, the dairy industry was demanding that the government raise the guaranteed price it paid farmers for "manufactured milk"—raw milk used to make many dairy products. The increase they wanted would raise retail food prices by hundreds of millions of dollars, at a time when inflation was already rampant. It would also, U.S. Department of Agriculture officials predicted, lead to serious milk surpluses piling up in government warehouses—an extra burden on an already strained federal budget.

Weighing these disadvantages, Secretary of Agriculture Clifford Hardin announced on March 12, 1972, that the price would not go up. Concern for the food budgets of hard-pressed families had apparently persuaded the administration to resist.

But not for long. Dairy representatives swung into action, and by March 25—less than two weeks later—the administration had caved in. Citing "new evidence," Secretary Hardin announced a 6 percent price boost, just what the milkmen had asked for. The cost of the decision to the American eater, who spends one out of every seven food dollars on dairy products, will be an estimated $500 million per year (one cent extra per quart, plus large increases in other dairy prices).

What did the milkmen have going for them that the housewife didn't? They've got a lot of pure homogenized Grade A cash, milked from the housewife in inflated prices. Like the shrewd John Archbold of Standard Oil, they invest their money wisely; by putting it into politics, they earn the legal right to bilk the housewife of more money, a small portion of which they can again invest in politics. The dairymen hit on the tactic several years earlier, when—as William A. Powell, president of Mid-America Dairymen, explained in a letter to one of his organization's members—they learned "that the sincere and soft voice of the dairy farmer is no match for the jingle of hard currencies put in the campaign funds of the politicians by the vegetable fat interests, labor, oil, steel, airlines, and others."

The obvious remedy was to make sure the farmers could match the other jingles with an ample jingle of their own. In their first two years of political fundraising, they put together a war chest of $1 million. More than $500,000 of this they sunk in the congressional elections of 1970. So, in their time of trouble one year later, they could turn to those they had helped. The list was formidable: starting with Speaker Carl Albert and working down through Congressmen W. R. Poage (chairman of the House Agriculture Committee) and Page Belcher (ranking Republican on the committee), key House members could look back on dairy donations. Even though Poage had no opposition for reelection, the dairymen spent $11,500 on a dinner for him and gave $500 apiece to him and Belcher. In the Senate, the dairy groups concentrated on Edmund Muskie, then a front-runner for the presidency, and Hubert Humphrey (member of the Agriculture Committee), Gale McGee (chairman of the Agricultural Appropriations subcommittee), and William Proxmire (the senator from lacteal Wisconsin, and a member of McGee's subcommittee).

The investment paid off. Within a week of Hardin's first announcement, the industry had drafted a bill that would have taken the price decision out of the Agriculture Department's hands by making an increase mandatory. In the House, 116 members—50 of whom had received dairy contributions—jumped on the milk wagon as cosponsors. There were 29 sponsors in the Senate, including consumer advocate Gaylord Nelson. Twelve of these senators had run in 1970—8 of them with dairy contributions.

But another dairy beneficiary, the Nixon administration, beat Congress in making the move. The clincher was the $255,000 the farmers sent to Nixon's election fund to help him make up his mind. Of this, $35,000 was a down payment, funneled into Republican campaign committees only days before Hardin announced the price rise. The rest was paid out in installments, stretching several months past "delivery." The first of these, a $45,000 installment, was paid on April 5, just four days after the new price went into effect.

What happened just before Hardin's turnabout announcement is revealing. The first big contribution was on March 22. It got quick results. The next day, President Nixon invited sixteen dairy and farm representatives to the White House. Their audience with the president—the ultimate in purchased political access—lasted nearly an hour, twice as long as scheduled. The meeting with the president was later described by William Powell, president of the Mid-America Dairymen, in a letter to one of his members:

> We dairymen as a body can be a dominant group. On March 23, 1971, along with nine other dairy farmers, I sat in the Cabinet room of the White House, across the table from the president of the United States, and heard him compliment the dairymen on their marvelous work in consolidating and unifying our industry and our involvement in politics. He said, "You people are my friends, and I appreciate it."

Two days later an order came from the U.S. Department of Agriculture increasing the support price of milk . . . which added from $500 million to $700 million to dairy farmers' milk checks. We dairymen cannot afford to overlook this kind of economic benefit. Whether we like it or not, this is the way the system works.

The only thing unusual about the dairy campaign was the publicity it received. Fresh off the farm, the dairymen at first made the mistake of filing a candid set of financial reports. An amazed Democratic campaign hand told Frank Wright of the *Minneapolis Tribune,* "My God, we've been doing that sort of thing for years, and we've never, never had it reported so publicly." The milkmen's efforts at concealment may have been a bit rough around the edges, but they had learned their basic lesson well: they paid their money and patiently waited for the dividends. The rest of us should think about changing the whole political marketplace.

2

Who Influences Congress?

*Suppose you go to Washington and try to get
at your government. You will always find that
while you are politely listened to, the men really
consulted are the men who have the biggest
stake—the big bankers, the big manufacturers,
the big masters of commerce. . . . The government of the United States at present is a
foster child of special interests.*
— Woodrow Wilson

When the dairy industry was looking for its 1971 price
rise, it had the advantage of having warmed up dozens
of congressmen with campaign contributions. If the
milkmen had done no more, the quart of milk might still
be at its old price. Only through *lobbying*—direct persuasion of legislators—was the industry able to convert
its half-million line of credit with Congress into a half-
billion extra income. The lobbyists who undertake this
friendly persuading are like the special interest's infantry.
At the same time Congress is being bombarded by big
money: the heavy artillery. Both in tandem can be an
impressive display of power; the dairy case is again il-
lustrative.

With the bad news of Agriculture Secretary Hardin's
initial decision not to grant the price increase, six full-
time Washington lobbyists swung into action. In addition to lining up sponsors for the bill they had quickly
drafted, they worked at "getting friendly senators and
representatives to file statements with the Department
of Agriculture supporting our position," as one of them

put it. The number of statements that flowed in was, according to a department source, "very substantial." Meanwhile, letters from co-ops across the country were pouring into both Congress and the White House. Faced with the possibility that Congress might take the decision out of the administration's hands (and reap the obvious financial rewards), the president quickly succumbed.

News of a lobbying coup like the milkmen's understandably leaves the public with a sour taste, but, in its broadest sense, "lobbying" is anything but sinister. A lobbyist is, by definition, anyone who works to influence decisions by public officials—including a concerned citizen who writes his congressman urging a vote on stricter air pollution laws. This right to "petition the Government for a redress of grievances" is firmly grounded in the Constitution's First Amendment. But the way the armies of special interest agents have largely monopolized these guarantees into tools for private government has made "lobbyist" synonymous with corruption, shiftiness, or improper influence.

As might be supposed, the lobbyists first got their name from hanging around in the lobbies of government buildings, waiting to launch their pitch for government favors. By the middle of the nineteenth century, high-paid panhandlers swarming all over Congress prompted James Buchanan to write to Franklin Pierce: "The host of contractors, speculators, stock-jobbers, and lobby members which haunt the halls of Congress all desirous . . . on any and every pretext to get their arms into the public treasury, are sufficient to alarm every friend of the country."

By 1950, lobbyists had so increased their strength in Washington that the House Select Committee on Lobbying Activities declared lobbying "a major industry." There are currently an estimated five thousand or more full-time lobbyists in Washington—ten for each member of Congress—and the lobbying industry continues to grow. One estimate is that eight of every ten of the nation's thousand biggest corporations already have representatives in Washington, and each year at least a dozen new companies set up permanent beachheads in the Capitol.

The power of many lobbyists who have worked in Washington through the years is legendary. Wayne B. Wheeler, the legislative counsel for the Anti-Saloon League during the days of its prohibition successes, "controlled six Congresses, dictated to two presidents . . . and was recognized by friend and foe alike as the most masterful and powerful single individual in the United States," said his administrative assistant, who would watch him maneuver. While no single individual today approaches that power, the combined grip of the various lobbies on Congress remains tight.

Apart from whatever power they may have to generate election-time assistance (financial or otherwise), the lobbies derive their strategic advantage by controlling the flow of information in and out of Congress. By this, lobbyists serve two functions; they take and they give. First, they constitute, in effect, an informal intelligence network that can pick up advance and often confidential information, and use it to good advantage. (When lawyer-lobbyist Thomas Corcoran was asked why he was so successful, he said, "I get my information a few hours ahead of the rest.") Second, they supply Congress with the essential raw material of lawmaking —outside information about problems that Congress is or could be working on. And, as any industrialist can tell you, he who controls the source of supply can control the product. To intelligently regulate the natural-gas industry, to take one example, the government must rely heavily on, of all disinterested observers, the industry and its lobbyists. This reliance by public authority on private interests is a consequence of Congress's weakness. As former New York Congressman Allard Lowenstein complained,

> How much can anyone do with limited staff, and all the mail and what not to cope with? If you aren't independently wealthy, you can't have a staff that is capable of putting things together much beyond what you can come up with from the sources avail-

able to everyone—the executive departments, the
lobbies, the staffs of congressional committees, the
Library of Congress. That's one reason why the
lobbies are so influential. They have people who are
able to spend all their time collecting data on why
pollution is good for River X. What congressmen
can match that?

None can. That's why congressmen so often have to
depend on the superior manpower of the lobbies to suggest solutions to problems, draft legislation, provide the
evidence for it, help develop legislative strategy, persuade the rest of Congress to go along, and even raise
the problems in the first place. With the lobbies' pressure bearing in from all sides, Congress ends up, for the
most part, responding to the heaviest push. It's true, as
Senator John Kennedy once said, that lobbyists are "in
many cases expert technicians and capable of explaining
complex and difficult subjects in a clear, understandable
fashion," which makes them all the more persuasive.
But there is one catch. "Each is biased," as Kennedy
noted. He compared the procedure to "the advocacy of
lawyers in court which has proven so successful in re-
solving judicial controversies." But while organized, special interest lobbies contend, unorganized interests—the
public, the taxpayer, the consumer—typically go un-
represented in the court of Congress. Who, for example,
presented expert data on behalf of the American housewife when the dairymen were ramming through their
price increase in less than two weeks' time? Information-
inundation of Congress by those with a special ax to
grind has created a kangaroo court.

Lobbying's Who's Who

Despite the lobbies' awesome impact on the law, the
public retains only a cloudy picture of who the lobbyists
are and what they do. For the economic interests who
run the lobbies have hidden behind vague, institutional
titles like the Sugar Lobby, the Tobacco Lobby, the
Highway Lobby, etc. The Oil Lobby, generally recog-

nized as the most mammoth of them all, has been most successful in preserving its facelessness. For years, even those congressmen who strongly opposed the industry's many subsidies failed to penetrate its cloak of anonymity. A civil servant with long experience handling the industry explained to Robert Engler, chronicler of the oil industry: "Oil goes after individuals down here. Be general, say 'oil lobby.' That's OK, but let a politician or bureaucrat be specific, name names, and they'll gun for him."

The oil lobby has plenty to gun with. When fully mobilized, oil can send into action lawyers from the most respectable law firms, public relations consultants, numerous ex-government officials, newsmen who serve as "advisers," company executives, corporate legal departments, government officials in several of the executive departments, trade association representatives, and —though only a small fraction of the total—men who actually register as lobbyists. Whenever legislation affecting oil is on the docket, the oilers can easily afford to have a corporate vice-president or similarly impressive official assigned to persuade every member of every relevant committee. If reinforcements should be needed, the industry can call on a vast reserve of sales agents, filling station operators, and other small businessmen. In other words, they are different from you and me.

Presiding over these far-flung legions are the various oil trade associations, most powerful of them the American Petroleum Institute. The API is generally regarded as the spokesman for the "majors"—including Standard Oil of New Jersey, Mobil, Shell, Standard Oil of Indiana, Texaco, Gulf, and Standard Oil of California—although its membership roster runs on to include some 350 other companies. One of the API's subsidiaries, the American Petroleum Industries Committee, has operated in virtually every oil-drenched state capital, augmenting the work of individual oil companies and a formidable array of state and regional trade groups. Organized to the grass-roots level, the industry also has committees with tentacles reaching into local and county governments.

Only brethren of the oil fraternity know how much

API spends; some industry sources placed it at between $5 and $10 million annually, much of it, the API insists, on "research." This goes to support a staff of two hundred, working in Washington, D.C., plus offices in Dallas and New York. Whatever the institute and its companion lobbies spend, the expense is worthwhile. Oilmen have long profited from tax bonanzas and special import benefits—the latter alone transferring, according to a downplayed White House study, at least $5 billion each year from the pockets of consumers and taxpayers to the bank accounts of Big Oil.

Faced with the burden of holding off the public on so many fronts, the oilmen are fortunate to have a number of sympathetic allies. The major oil companies have representatives in such useful groups as the American Merchant Marine Institute (concerned with oil pollution regulations applicable to large tankers) and the Asphalt Institute (member of an umbrella lobbying group, the American Road Builders Association, which backs massive highway construction programs). The American Bar Association, whose Mineral Law section has over the years consisted mainly of lawyers for the oil industry, is only one of many professional groups that have aided oil when danger threatened. The oil lobby can also count friends among several business groups whose boards and committees include oilmen. Prominent among them are the Chamber of Commerce of the United States and the National Association of Manufacturers (NAM).

These organizations are in themselves powerful lobbies. The Chamber of Commerce is one of the nation's leading pressure organizations against laws that would protect the public from fraudulent advertising, defective products, occupational hazards, and related abuses. The Chamber, the NAM, and the American Farm Bureau Federation (an alliance of business leaders and corporate farmers) form the heart of the anticonsumer axis in the nation's capital. Of the three, the NAM has been the most consistently vocal opponent of policies that would restrict its corporate members. NAM's record in the past was dotted with such events as the bribing of several congressmen, publicly admitted in 1913 by association lobbyist Martin M. Mulhall. Mulhall also said that he had paid the chief House page $50 per month for inside information from the cloakrooms and that he had influenced leaders in the House to plant NAM's chosen congressmen on key House committees. The subsequent congressional investigation led to the censure of one congressman—who then resigned—and the exoneration of six others. Thirty-five years later, when Congress finally passed a law to regulate such lobbying excesses, NAM brought the first suit challenging the law's validity.

NAM takes a see-no-evil stance where its members' reputations are concerned. In late 1971, for example, association witnesses blithely told Senator Proxmire's Joint Economic Committee that industry as a whole made only a small contribution to water pollution, and that pollution on the whole was not as bad as it used to be. NAM's unsupported assertions were no match for federal figures showing that industry accounted for four to five times as much water pollution as domestic sewage, and that water pollution was getting worse.

Other key business lobbies now at work:

• The Military Armaments Lobby, which is the instrument of what President Eisenhower famously nicknamed the "military industrial complex." Aside from its powerful connections in Congre , the defense industry relies on ties within the military itself: *Congressional Quarterly* has reported that as of 1960 "more than 1,400 retired officers of the rank of major or higher (including 261 of general or flag rank) were employed by defense contractors."

• The Tobacco Lobby, which has secured some delays but also suffered defeats in the last eight years on the issue of health warnings on packages and in media; yet it still gets government subsidies for both domestic growing and sending its crop abroad.

• The Automobile Lobby, which in the past several years has mushroomed in Washington to fight tougher auto safety standards and air pollution requirements and to push for favorable tax privileges.

• The American Medical Association, lobby for high-priced health, opponents of Medicare before its passage in the 1960s, propagandists for the system which gives U.S. doctors an average annual salary of $42,500. In part through the AMA's lobbying efforts, Americans spent $75 billion for health care in 1971 and watched medical costs rise at a rate double that of cost of living or the Gross National Product. The AMA represents just under half of the country's practicing physicians, a figure which is declining due to dissatisfaction in the profession over the AMA's desultory performance.

Pushing Congress from another ideological vantage point is the Labor Lobby. The lynchpin of labor's effort is the AFL-CIO's lobbying arm, headed by the well-known Andrew J. (Andy) Biemiller. In recent years, labor has been stymied on many strictly "labor" issues, where the unions find themselves without allies, but has had some striking successes as part of coalitions working on broader social issues. The Golden Age of labor's social-progress lobbying was in the mid-1960s, when the Leadership Conference on Civil Rights—an alliance of labor, religious, civic, and civil rights groups, which counted labor as its most powerful member—pushed through civil rights legislation and, finally, over long-time AMA opposition, Medicare. The "liberal-labor" coalition in Congress has also risen to successfully challenge Supreme Court appointments of Nixon nominees Carswell and Haynsworth.

Apart from these successes, labor has continued to pour the bulk of its energies into a few key issues (like the perennial battle to overturn the Taft-Hartley Act), to the relative neglect of others which are worker-related, like (until recently) job safety and consumer protection. Some unions have been stampeded into open opposition to environmental protection proposals as a result of industry-invoked fears of job loss, while others have straddled the fence. In March, 1972, the AFL-CIO undermined a coalition of groups backing stronger water pollution controls in the House by remaining on the sidelines, after the coalition had included an AFL-CIO-initiated measure to protect workers from phony threats of job layoffs. The United Auto Workers (UAW), Steelworkers, Clothing Workers, and the Oil, Chemical, and Atomic Workers (OCAW) did stick with the environmental coalition and, though the bulk of the measures lost, succeeded in passing the worker protection amendment. The UAW and the OCAW are among the few unions which would like the labor lobby to exchange its narrow economic targets for broader social goals.

A relative newcomer to Washington is the lobby for the nation's cities. Scrambling after the more than $43 billion the federal government hands out each year to state and local governments (five times as much as ten years ago), the cities are represented by the National League of Cities/U.S. Conference of Mayors, two organizations that merged in 1969. The state lobbyists have been around for quite a while longer. As of June, 1972, seventeen states had Washington lobbying offices. A recent, central focus of the local-government lobbies has been the revenue-sharing proposals now before Congress. By monitoring daily developments, the city and state lobbies can let their mayors or governors know the right time to make a telephone call to a wavering congressman.

Another group of lobbies aims at government policies rather than federal money. One of the older and more influential of these is the National Rifle Association, spokesman for the nation's rifle and gunowners. After each of the political assassinations of the sixties, it was mainly the NRA that discouraged Congress from passing tough gun control laws. Although a large majority of the public wanted such laws, a large majority of senators understand the kind of focused protest and sanction that organized gun interests can inflict on a politician, as ex-Senator Joseph Tydings learned.

The newest face on the lobbying scene, the environmental and public interest lobbies, began arriving in the late 1960s. Before that time, pressure for the protection of natural resources had come from conservation groups who had to hold back from frequent lobbying to protect

their tax-deductible status. Active environmental/con-
servation lobby groups now include the Sierra Club, the
Citizens Committee on Natural Resources, Zero Population Growth, Environmental Action, Friends of the
Earth, and the Environmental Policy Center. These
groups have applied pressure on environmental issues
as well as on a wider range of public problems.

They tallied their biggest victory in 1971, when
Congress ended the taxpayers' subsidy for the SST.
But efforts by environmentalists beyond merely blocking
bad measures have been less successful. The heavy
defeat of the environmental coalition's move in March,
1972, to toughen the industry-gutted House water pollution bill signaled a hardening opposition to the movement for environmental change. Although ecology is
fashionable in name and concept, converting it into
legislative reality is quite another matter.

Completing this recent list of "public" advocates are
an increasing number of young lawyers who have tried
to counter the private interests' prestigious Washington
lawyer-lobbyist by creating "public interest" law firms.
They undertake court litigation and advocacy before
the state and federal courts, the federal regulatory
agencies, and the Congress. Together, this array of
public lobbyists has been instrumental in the passage
of several new laws: Common Cause led a push for
stronger campaign finance laws and for the 18-year-old
vote; others pushed successfully for auto safety, job
safety, gas pipeline safety, meat and poultry inspection
laws, and the new Independent Consumer Agency.

But as compared to the silent successes of the business
bloc—the oil depletion allowance, procurement cost
overruns, regulatory nonfeasance, which endure unin-
terrupted—the citizens' groups have far to go before
equaling their opponents. One problem is the sheer
overwhelming size of the opposition forces. While special interest groups can keep their agents stationed at
all the important pressure points in Congress, the public
lobbyists are lucky to have among them the equivalent
of a single person working full time on any major issue.

Instead of constant coordinate pressure, the public groups are, for the most part, still limited to crash campaigns on short notice.

Aggravating the manpower shortages are federal tax laws operationally designed to stifle public interest lobbying and to promote that of big business. If a nonprofit group takes up active and significant lobbying, the donations members make are no longer tax-deductible. The Sierra Club was stripped of its tax-deductible status in 1968, while lobbying against Grand Canyon dams. But profit-making businesses can deduct their lobbying costs as a business expense—in effect, subsidizing private lobbies.

The business lobbies have found another way of making the victims bear the cost of their anticonsumer political efforts: by passing it along in the form of higher prices. And finally, when the lobbies for the economic interests succeed, they are further enriched, enabling them to send a bigger lobby back for an even bigger piece of the pie. (This vicious cycle is the modern form of taxation without representation.) The public lobbies receive nothing, even though they may save the taxpayer billions or clean up the poisoned environment or protect the consumer from a food or price increase.

The very nature of public interest work adds another handicap. Every private interest measure—an increase in oil tax loopholes, or a rise in dairy supports—affects the public one way or another. But not every public issue affect all the private interests: the dairy lobby can peacefully sit out a struggle over logging in national forests. The public interest groups, with short funds and sparse staff, must try to guard the whole waterfront, while each special interest can stick to its own special preserve.

To a Congress accustomed to servicing private interest lobbies—who have time, information, and, potentially, campaign money—the public lobbies stand at the back of a long waiting line. One environmental lobbyist recalls waiting outside a closed committee session, surrounded by milling lobbyists from numerous industrial

interests, known and unknown. Seeking stringent pollution control measures, he was heartened when, during
one of the breaks, a congressman walked out and said,
"I got one of yours in." His elation was tempered when
he realized that the same congressman was delivering
what looked like similar good tidings to the other lobbyists clustered in the hall. But the doling out of table
scraps can hardly satisfy those motivated by a kind of
gnawing hunger when there is a feast under way for
others. A former key committee aide in the Senate
described the legislating process this way: "It's like
there's a bushel basket in the middle of the table. Everyone is trying to throw as many of their things into the
barrel as they can." By taking careful aim, the public
interest lobbies have begun to hit the basket with increasing frequency. But for the most part, it's still brimming
over with a variety of special interest plums.

How Lobbies Work

To get as many preferential plums in the basket as
possible, the organized lobbies have developed a variety
of techniques for plying their trade. The following are
two of the most popular:

WINING AND DINING. "I've never known a lobbyist
who wasn't a nice guy," is a familiar refrain. Which is
not at all surprising, for savvy lobbies understand Mc-
Luhan and politics: the context is more important than
the content, and an amiable delivery can camouflage
any bias. To develop a congenial ambience, lobbyists
for the large economic interests come equipped with the
traditional expense accounts to make life more pleasant
for select congressmen. The sweeteners can range from
imported perfumes to friendly poker games to rides in
the Freight Forwarders' air-conditioned yacht. "Certainly, senators and congressmen have been entertained
on a small scale," the Freight Forwarders' Washington
representative Stanley Sommer concedes, "but it's nothing more than a three-hour cruise down the Potomac."

Former Senator Paul Douglas has explained the process:

> The enticer does not generally pay money directly to the public representative. He tries instead, by a series of favors, to put the public official under such a feeling of personal obligation that the latter gradually loses his sense of mission to the public and comes to feel that his first loyalties are to his private benefactors and patrons. . . . Throughout this whole process the official will claim—and may, indeed, believe—that there is no causal connection between the favors he has received and the decision which he makes. He will assert that the favors were given or received on the basis of pure friendship.

To nourish this friendship, the good lobbyist prides himself on knowing where and how to find anything the congressman may desire. A Washington lobbyist told correspondent David Sheridan that he makes discreet arrangements for one congressman who enjoys an occasional lady of the night. Good lobbyists don't forget the staffers, either. "All congressmen have secretaries and aides," says former lobbyist Robert Winter-Berger, "and often these are the people who determine which visitors and mail the congressman sees every day, so they must be included in a lobbyist's budget." Many staffers—like Nick Zapple of the Senate Communications subcommittee, for example—don't have to worry about forgetting their lunch money. The communications companies stand in line to take Zapple out to lunch.

This thoughtfulness eventually makes its point. "You begin to look forward to those three or four lunches a week with the lobbyists at the good restaurants," one committee aide said, "to the $25 bottles of Scotch, the football tickets, the occasional junkets, and if you don't watch out, you get pulled into the lobbyist's frame of reference." Or as Maurice Tobin, who has seen the goodies flow from both directions (as counsel to the

House Public Works Committee and, more recently, as legislative consultant to a number of corporations), summed it up, "Everybody likes freebees."

POLITICAL STOCKBROKERING. Even more than free-bees, politicians like currency in their campaign chests. This is where the gladhanding lobbyists can really win gratitude, respect, and occasionally even fear. Not only do the special interest lobbyists exploit the financial credit already built by their groups, but—so there will be no mistake—they often collect and deliver the funds themselves.

There is a long tradition of lobbyists coming to congressional offices to drop off cash in envelopes, ostensibly for "campaign contributions." Former Representative Richard Ottinger observed the process happen to him, he said in an interview, and he rejected the offer. (Ottinger concluded, from his experience, that a seat on the House Interstate and Foreign Commerce Committee was worth a substantial amount of money.) Congressman Pete McCloskey is convinced that straight cash from lobbyists in the form of campaign contributions is a subterranean corruption of great significance in terms of its influence on the behavior of recipient congressmen. But at least one such recipient disagrees. This congressman willingly took $250 in cash at a Washington bar from an industrial lobbyist, and then turned to a Washington reporter and indignantly protested, "That son of a bitch thinks he can buy me for $250." But he kept the money.

One freelance lobbyist explained that he serves as a "political consultant" to his clients, advising them where to place their election money for greatest effect. Every two years, for example, he reminds certain construction companies to contribute about $4,000 to a key Southern congressman whose committee approves construction of federal hospitals. A well-known clearing house for oil money used to be lobbyist Peter Nyce, who once explained his method of doing business: "I made oil companies ante up for various candidates." When two merchant shipping lines presented nearly $6,000 in illegal campaign contributions to important House and Senate committee members, they chose lobbyists to make the delivery.*

William Whyte, a vice-president for U.S. Steel, coordinates a secret campaign fund which the company collects from its executives. The company found a good use for Whyte early in 1972. Whyte sent a telegram to several congressmen on behalf of U.S. Steel, urging them to support the United States water pollution bill "without any amendments." On the other side were twenty-five civic, farm, labor, and environmental groups who thought the bill perforated by loopholes preferential to industrial polluters. But instead of a secret campaign fund, all the groups managed was a flood of letters pouring in from citizens all over the country. No one who observes this or dozens of other lobbying campaigns will be surprised by former Senator Joseph Clark's evenhanded assessment that the Republican and Democratic campaign finance committees are "prisoners of the lobbies."

The Congress-Lobby Complex

A more subtle form of compensation to the legislator for his labors on behalf of a corporation or lobby organization is the potential of a high-paying job when he retires from Congress, what has been called the "deferred bribe." Not that congressmen *expect* to be out of office in the near future, but the unhappy possibility can never be entirely out of their minds. In fact, later employment in the lobbying sector is a popular career path among retired politicians. They charge higher lobbying fees than others, but their clients know they are worth it. Former members of Congress have a number of

---

* The companies were caught when they tried to deduct the contributions from their tax returns. The largest payments reportedly went to Congressman Garmatz ($1,500) and Senator Warren Magnuson ($1,000). The checks went through a special bank account, a public relations man, and two lobbyists, so the recipients would not know they were illegal contributions from corporations.

built-in advantages as lobbyists. They already know dozens of members and staff, they are schooled in the intricacies of congressional bargaining, and they have lifetime visiting privileges on the floor of the house in which they served. A tasteful Senate custom holds that the senator-lobbyists should not appear on the floor when a measure affecting their client comes up—a custom, however, occasionally honored in the breach. But such excesses are really not necessary, for the normal prerogatives and contacts that former members have are usually more than adequate to make their views known and to convince clients they are worth their keep. Fully 124 former members have registered as lobbyists under the 1946 Lobbying Act; given the widespread noncompliance with that law, more than 124 former members return to Congress to lobby their earlier colleagues.

Nearly every big lobby has at least one (and often more) ex-member of Congress on its staff. The road from the floor of Congress to the lobby is so well worn that only a few of the many examples can be given:

• Frank Ikard was a protégé of House Speaker Sam Rayburn and served with him as congressman from Texas from 1952 to 1961. In 1961, Rayburn died, Ikard resigned, and the American Petroleum Institute got a new lobbyist, one who now heads their Washington office. Ikard said that his change of job was "a question of economics."

• Andrew Biemiller, who, as chief lobbyist for the AFL-CIO, has the money and membership of millions behind him, got his training in legislation as a representative from Wisconsin, serving two terms in the late 1940s.

• Harold Cooley has dealt with sugar for a long time—for sixteen years as Democratic representative from North Carolina and chairman of the House Agriculture Committee (where he was known as the "sugar king"), and more recently as lobbyist for sugar interests in Liberia and Thailand. Joining him in the sugar contingent is a relative novice in sugar questions, former Senator Thomas Kuchel of California. Despite his inexperience, Kuchel has earned $200 per hour as a lobbyist. These men—and others, like Thomas Hale Boggs, Jr., and former Congressman Charles Brown—fight to get their countries' increased shares of the total sugar import quota. The competition first began in earnest when Cuba was disqualified from the contest, and relatively tight import quotas (to keep domestic prices high) mean that countries like Thailand and South Africa have to bid for the best talent in order to obtain the valuable few quotas.

One of the sugar lobbyists—Thomas Hale Boggs, Jr. —illustrates yet another variation on the congressman-as-lobbyist theme. Young Boggs's father, House Majority Leader Hale Boggs, has as much influence in Congress as these other former representatives—if not more. Understanding this, several private interests are reported to have made use of young Boggs's legal services: the Hilton Corporation, the Parvin-Dohman Corporations, the Baltimore Contractors, General Dynamics, General Electric, the Radio Corporation of America, Sperry Rand, and Bell Telephone, among others. Which is not bad for a young lawyer 32 years old.

The revolving door also whirls fast for congressional staffers. The banking lobby, for example, counted no less than five alumni of the Senate Banking, Housing and Urban Affairs Committee's staff among its ranks during its successful 1970 effort to soften a Senate bill to regulate so-called one-bank holding companies, a device which banks can use to take over other industries. The lobbies complete the cultural exchange by placing *their* men on key committee staffs. The American Institute of Merchant Shipping, for example, gets a warm reception from Ralph Casey, chief counsel of the House Committee on Merchant Marine and Fisheries. Casey came to the committee from his previous post as executive vice-president and lobbyist for the institute.

And if there's any difference between a lobbyist and a staffer, the Senate Finance Committee might be hard pressed to say what it is. When the committee was considering changes in oil tax laws as part of the 1969 Tax Reform Act, six lobbyists for the Independent Petroleum

Association were, according to Erwin Kroll in the *New York Times Magazine,* "highly visible among the oilmen who flitted in and out of the back door to the Senate Finance Committee's offices while the committee, in sessions closed to the public, was considering oil provisions." Lobbyist Peter Nyce used to have such a clear pipeline into the Senate Interior and Insular Affairs Committee that he often sat in on closed meetings, was allowed to question other witnesses at hearings, and reportedly wrote two Senate bills on mineral leasing.

Washington Lawyers

When a lobbying assignment calls for the maximum in prestige, legislative strategy, and delicate dealing, as well as inside influence, the men who are often called upon to do the job are Washington lawyers, the aristocrats of lobbying. Lawyer-lobbyists in Washington are often men of liberal persuasions who came to Washington in high posts with a Democratic administration and then stuck around to make the most of their well-developed contacts in government. Among the best known of the Washington lawyers are such luminaries as Thomas ("Tommy the Cork") Corcoran, former New Deal brain truster who has often been retained by gas and airlines clients; Lloyd Cutler, who, as hired lobbyist for General Motors, successfully had the criminal penalties section deleted from the 1966 Automobile Safety Act; and Abe Fortas, Lyndon Johnson's confidant on matters requiring discreet handling. But the archetype of the breed is probably Clark Clifford.

From his prestigious St. Louis law firm, Clifford followed fellow Missourian Harry Truman into the White House in 1945 and remained in Washington to serve, in and out of government, as an adviser to four presidents, most recently as Lyndon Johnson's last secretary of defense. When he opened his own law office in Washington in 1950, it became an instant attraction for clients like Allied Chemical, Grace Lines, Pennsylvania Railroad, Phillips Petroleum, and Standard Oil of California. A Clifford specialty has been helping clients like these wriggle around the laws and regulations he helped pass while he was in government. Most of his energies on their behalf have been directed at the regulatory agencies and the executive departments, but during the leaner Republican administration years, his Democratic friends in Congress have helped him pull through. The time they are believed to have pulled the hardest is in 1962, when he masterminded a plan to get E. I. duPont de Nemours and Company out of hundreds of millions of dollars in income taxes on the sale of a massive block of General Motors stock, ordered by a court divestiture decree. Clifford was the behind-the-scenes general who directed DuPont president Crawford Greenwalt into the offices of key congressmen and put the appropriate words in his mouth. The legislation was passed, DuPont got its multimillion tax break, and Clifford, according to Joseph Goulden, author of *Superlawyer,* got a ten-year retainer of $1 million. Yet Clifford and his Washington-lawyer counterparts typically disavow any connections whatsoever with the trade of lobbying. Until he was appointed secretary of defense in 1968, neither he nor any of the other members of his firm registered. "We did no lobbying and never have." What he is doing is simply keeping his corporate clients "informed on policies and attitudes in government."

Personal Associations

One day in 1926, Pennsylvania Senator David Reed —whose father had been a key member of the Gulf Oil controlling syndicate—went to lunch with the president of the Mid-Continent Oil and Gas Association. The Mid-Continent man told Reed of the heavy burden that drilling costs were forcing on the industry. The senator was so moved by this complaint that he rushed to tell his colleagues on the Senate Finance Committee of the oilmen's desperate plight. Out of that discussion was born the oil depletion allowance.

It was, of course, natural that Reed, one who was raised under the roof of Big Oil, would be dining out with another oilman. Men in Congress obviously have social acquaintances and former, if not present, business acquaintances outside of Congress. That simple fact gives the business lobbies one of their most important conduits into the Congress.

The danger arises because the average congressman is not the average American. Allard Lowenstein has commented that "the House in some ways isn't very representative. There's almost never anyone here under 30. . . . And, of course, there are only nine blacks [in 1969] when proportionately there should be about fifty." This disproportionate representation is even more skewed for women and blue-collar workers. The fact that members of Congress come almost exclusively from professions that serve mostly business clientele or from business itself gives the corporate community a several-step head start over other citizens in making Congress work for them.

Congressmen not only talk to oilmen at lunch but also at the club, the golf course, and at dinner parties—the so-called "social" lobby. The average citizen, who rarely gets to peep in on the posh parties, gets little opportunity to see lobbying operations in action, as they are seldom covered in the news media. One that did make the news occurred in connection with the 1970 lobbying effort of the banking industry on one-bank holding company legislation. The American Bankers Association wrote to the officials of three banks asking them to get in touch immediately with three key members of the House-Senate conference handling the question to ask them to oppose stringent controls. The three members happened also to be large stockholders in the respective banks. The banker who was asked by the association to contact Congressman J. William Stanton of Ohio also happened to have been Stanton's campaign treasurer in the previous election. The Bankers Association letter stressed an important point: "If at all possible, please make your contact in person."

The most powerful recent example of a congressman putting his network of friendly ties to good use was the August, 1972, battle over federal no-fault insurance in the Senate. The idea of a no-fault system (which pays regardless of who is at fault) is essentially to eliminate the necessity for a trial (and trial lawyer) in most cases. But a proposal to eliminate business for lawyers was calculated to dismay the American Trial Lawyers Association (ATLA), whose members earn a good part of their keep by going to court on auto accident cases. ATLA alerted its members, and lawyers in Congress were swamped with calls from old law school classmates.

The ATLA lawyers had more going for them than just classroom ties. "Some of these lawyers earn $80,000 a year fighting auto negligence cases," an aide to one senator told United Press International. "They can be counted on for a contribution of $3,000 or $4,000 or $5,000 to a senator running for reelection. A phone call from one or two can be effective." More than one or two called in. In just a few hours before the vote was taken, one senator told Morton Mintz of the *Washington Post* that he got calls from twenty lawyer friends urging him to help shelve the proposal.

Picking Up Allies

No grass-roots campaign is complete without an attempt to enlist as many supporters as possible among state and local officials, various professional associations, and other groups. State and local agencies are a particularly good place to turn, since they are often firmly allied with dominant local industries. During the NAM's successful campaign to keep the House water pollution bill's loopholes intact, lobbyists for the states were also working to beat back stricter controls. The state insurance commissioners were brought into the battle against no-fault on the side of ATLA, as were other state officials, including Ohio Governor John Gilligan. Gilligan's letter to Ohio's Republican Senator Robert Taft, Jr., pleading for the no-fault bill's defeat in the Senate, showed that Gilligan had apparently been the target of a successful lobbying effort at the local level. The letter cited statistics that matched those in a memorandum put out by Allstate Insurance Company, a strong opponent of national no-fault. The Allstate statistics had been discredited, but Gilligan apparently never got the word. Senator Taft's reply to Gilligan accused the governor of having "uncritically accepted these inaccurate and unsubstantiated statistics from a group with a special interest."

ATLA members' efforts to bring the state officials into their camp went beyond phony statistics. Jack Anderson obtained a copy of a letter written to Nevada Insurance Commissioner Richard Rottman by Howard McKissick, a state legislator who heads ATLA's legislative branch. The McKissick letter denounced the no-fault plan as "a bastardly thing . . . some kind of Communist conspiracy."

The experience in Texas on the no-fault fight points up why government officials make such valuable allies for special interest lobbies. The Texas state insurance board released a study purporting to show that no-fault would increase insurance premiums. (Some insurance companies have already projected cost savings, and one company, Aetna Life and Casualty Company, has promised to write no-fault policies without premium increases in any state.) The Texas study carried all the weight of the state behind it and helped generate almost six hundred anti-no-fault letters in a single week to Texas Senator Lloyd Bentsen.

Going to the "Grass Roots"

Among ATLA's lobbying pressures is a variation on an age-old tactic—"grass-roots" lobbying. Rather than simply buzzing in the legislator's ear in Washington, the aim is to subject him to mass appeals from people back home, or people that supply his campaign money, or simply any people that he cares about.

The oil industry has always excelled at this tactic, particularly when the large companies pool their efforts. In one carefully orchestrated industry effort on the depletion allowance, for example, one oil company asked its stockholders to write to Congress; another worked at mobilizing its retired employees; another aimed at service station operators, a fourth mailed off brochures to its credit card holders. Intent on preserving an impression of spontaneous revolt emanating from the hinterlands, the Washington coordinators of oil's campaigns have on occasion remained conspicuously silent while the letters and requests to testify flooded in.

To help its members put the pressure where it does the most good, Gulf thoughtfully prepares "complete dossiers of all congressmen from the states in which Gulf has an interest. . . . These dossiers will include not only voting records, but everything that will assist Gulf's people in obtaining a more complete understanding of their elected representatives." Armed with their dossiers, the "grass roots" of the corporate lobby are ready to go into action when the trumpet sounds. A particularly loud trumpet call came in March in the form of a letter from National Association of Manufacturers President W. P. Gullander to the presidents of the twenty thousand largest manufacturers in the country. The NAM letter was summoning the troops to battle for weaker water pollution controls. Gullander first frenzied them by asserting that the measure they were fighting would "require the elimination of the discharge of industrial pollutants by 1985," when in fact it did not. Alerting them to "strong efforts being made on the House floor" by the environmental coalition to toughen the loophole-laden House bill, the NAM letter said: "You must wire or telephone today to urge your representative in Washington to *support* . . . the House bill . . . and *vote to defeat* any efforts to . . . revise the House bill." (emphasis in original) "Tomorrow is too late," Gullander exhorted his minions. "It is important that you contact your congressman today on the House water pollution control debate." (The letter closed with a postscript mentioning that NAM will "be calling on companies across the nation to speak up to their representatives in Washington" in the future because "the pressures on Congress to enact unrealistic legislation will continue.") Gullander's letter had its desired effect—setting off an avalanche of well-financed industrial opposition which buried the clean-water proposals. One congressman confided that he had been contacted by every single large industry and campaign contributor in his district. Congressman John Dingell of Michigan summed it up: "It feels like I was hit by a steamroller."

Organized special interests thrive on their ability to remain invisible and, hence, free of public scrutiny. Tightening the flimsy lobbying disclosure laws, which are even more primitive than the laws in the campaign finance area, must therefore be a first priority. To ensure that abusive underenforcement of the lobbying laws is ended, the citizen must have the right, as in the campaign finance area, to go to court and seek enforcement when the Justice Department looks the other way. Equally important are the ad hoc techniques for bringing the lobbies out into the open. TV documentaries, increased press coverage, congressional investigations, citizen-sponsored investigations, countervailing lobbies exposing one another—all these need both institutional and informal encouragement. Finally, the secrecy of Congress itself (discussed in chapter 3) must be ended to counteract the advantage of those who can secure special access.

But whatever is done to air the actions of the organized lobbies, a citizens' lobby must at the same time become a political counterweight, growing in numbers, resources, and sophistication. Public interest advocates can be created within the government itself, as is the projection for the newly designed Independent Consumer Agency. Or it can be encouraged by the government via tax credits for contributions to public interest lobby groups, or by at least putting these groups on an equal tax basis (regarding deductions) as the private lobbies. But ultimately, the backbone of any citizen lobby must be citizens—active, interested, and informed.

3

Who Rules Congress?

I could see I wasn't going to get anywhere. Nobody listens to what you have to say until you've been here ten to twelve years. These old men have got everything tied down so you can't do anything. There are only about 40 out of the 435 members who call the shots. They're all committee chairmen and the ranking members, and they're all around 70 or 80.

——Congressman Everett Burkhalter, upon announcing his retirement in 1964 after one term

We all recall the neat textbook diagrams outlining "how a bill becomes a law," that very logical process which is our legislative trademark. A congressman submitted a bill; it went to a committee which refined it and then reported it to the floor; if it passed, and if the other chamber had passed a similar measure, it went to a "conference committee" to iron out any differences; after repassage, the president signed it into law. Things were so simple.

Unfortunately, life does not imitate art. The diagrams don't show 535 local heroes and potential presidents jousting among themselves for power and prestige. They don't show who holds the levers of power, or how those who control the process control the law. They don't explain the *dynamics* of power, the shift and flow of forces that make our laws. To get a more realistic picture, we must look at the ruling forces of Congress: the committee system, which gives inordinate power to forty-odd men; the seniority system, which chooses the men who will exert the power; the rules of secrecy and

power-brokering, which seal the system off from the
people. The result is more autocratic than democratic.
"The parliament of the world's greatest democracy,"
concluded Congressman Morris Udall, "is not a democratic institution."

Committees—"Dim Dungeons of Silence"

"Congress, in its Committee rooms," Woodrow Wilson observed in his 1885 *Congressional Government*,
"is Congress at work." Permanent congressional committees are a necessary outgrowth of the heavy and
complex work of Congress. A division of specialized
labor became necessary as far back as the early 1800s
in order to handle proposed legislation. In the Third
Congress (1793–95), the House created 350 ad hoc
committees, one to handle each bill. This clearly would
not do, so by 1825 Congress had trimmed the system
to 43 standing (i.e., permanent) committees, each with
a designated area of authority. But, as often happens,
neither house could control its creations. Committees
began to proliferate, as each member wanted "his" committee to provide him with a platform. By 1913, at the
system's grandiose height, there were 61 standing committees in the House and 74 in the Senate. Reforms in
1946 cut the numbers to 19 and 15 respectively, but a
new form of committee growth emerged: subcommittees. By 1970, counting standing committees and subcommittees, there were a total of 305 in both houses.

Committees vary in size and importance, and there
is a distinct committee caste system. The House Internal
Security Committee has seven members and is mostly
a nuisance to the few radicals it denounces. On the
other hand, the House Ways and Means Committee
and the House Appropriations Committee, with 25
and 55 members respectively, determine our tax structure and federal budget, which touch the pocketbooks
of us all. These two, plus the Senate Finance Committee
and the Senate Appropriations Committee, are the big
four of Capitol Hill, the ones with the most power and,
by Washington's perfect logic, the most prestige. When

Professor Richard Fenno asked members of Ways and Means and Appropriations why they sought out their committee assignments, the overwhelming majority said they sought "power," "prestige," or "importance." "The Appropriations Committee is the most powerful committee in the House. It's the most powerful committee in the Congress," said one congressman. "This is where all the money starts rolling." Another said proudly of his Ways and Means assignment, "It's the top committee in the House of Representatives. The entire revenue system is locked into the committee."

The appointment of freshmen to these committees is a matter for great care. They rarely get on the best committees because, said one veteran, "It would be too risky to put on a person whose views and nature the leadership has no opportunity to assess." A careful screening ensures that nonconformists do not slip through. Sam Rayburn and LBJ never let anyone sit on House Ways and Means or Senate Finance without asking what they thought about the oil depletion allowance. When a Maryland congressman was being considered for membership on the House Interstate and Foreign Commerce Committee, he was asked by Kentucky's John Watts, "What's your position on tobacco?" The congressman replied, "I don't smoke"—and was not appointed to the committee.

The newcomers still want to get on the "best" committees possible and struggle as intensively as the old pols to get there. (Each party in each chamber has a Committee of the Committees to place congressmen on committees; the Democratic members of the Ways and Means Committee form this supercommittee for Democratic members of the House.) Freshman congressmen begin jockeying for choice posts immediately upon arrival, if not sooner. Republican freshman Don Riegle from Michigan, for example, on the night of his election called House Minority Leader Gerald Ford, also from Michigan, to lobby for a seat on the Education and Labor Committee. It is usually essential to convince your state delegation to back you up before you can get anywhere. Even with such backing, Congresswoman Bella Abzug failed in her persistent attempts to get on the Armed Services Committee. But the backing of the New York delegation helped freshmen Representatives Herman Badillo and Shirley Chisholm get their initial assignments changed. Badillo, from the Bronx, felt that service on the Agriculture Committee was not the best way to serve his city of skyscrapers and concrete; he told Speaker Carl Albert, "There isn't any crop in my district except marijuana." Nor did Ms. Chisholm believe that all her considerable energy on the same Agriculture Committee could possibly aid her urban and mostly black Brooklyn district; "Apparently all they know here in Washington about Brooklyn is that a tree grew there," she said.

The appointment process (the lawyers go to Judiciary, and the farmers to Agriculture, for example) and the environment in which many committees operate help guarantee that certain predetermined lines will be toed. Chapter 2 has already described the web of influencers who surround congressmen and their committees. Industry interests often possess a special access to committee action and reports. "The thing that really makes me mad is the dual standard," complained a key Senate committee staffer. "It's perfectly acceptable to turn over information about what's going on in committee to the auto industry, or the utilities, but not to the public."

Similar pressures convinced William Hungate to resign his chairmanship of the House District Judiciary subcommittee. He felt that intense undercover lobbying by collection agencies, small loan companies, and others were biasing legislation in his committee and he feared a major scandal. Committee closeness with outside interests is not limited to the business sector. One AFL-CIO official said about the House Education and Labor Committee in 1965 that "with one exception in the last few years, John McCormack and Andy Biemiller [AFL-CIO's lobbyist] have decided who gets on that committee. . . . A year ago in January, Adam Powell got up at our legislative conference and said, 'Here are the names of six new members of the Education and Labor Committee.' He then read the names from a slip of paper and said, 'I got this slip from Andy Biemiller, so they are all right.' "

Committees serve two crucial functions. First, of course, they are the workshops of lawmaking—the place where legislation is buried or where it matures to be reported to the full chamber. If a bill fails to get out of committee, it is invariably dead. If it is reported out unanimously, it nearly always passes. A study of the Eighty-fourth Congress by Donald Matthews found that if a proposal was supported by 80 percent or more of the committee members, it passed every time (35 of 35); if 60–79 percent of a committee supported a proposal, it would pass 90 percent of the time; but if only 50–60 percent supported it (i.e., almost half the committee opposed it), it would pass only 56 percent of the time. This is not because committees are a representative sample of the whole chamber's views, but because legislators tend to follow the committee's judgment unless there's an unusual reason to doubt it. "When internally unified and buttressed in parliamentary privilege by special rules," wrote Stephen Bailey, "[the committees] can almost at will dominate the business of the parent chamber." The committees are just that decisive, and that is why some refer to them as "little legislatures."

Aside from processing legislation, the committees have a second important function: holding hearings to get information and publicize issues. The success and effect of the hearings, in turn, depend on two things: how carefully prepared and tightly focused the hearings themselves are, and how heavily the press covers them. Neither element alone is usually enough for public impact. When Congressman Kenneth Roberts held a series of revealing hearings on auto safety in 1956, the press ignored them and Congress passed the issue by. Nine years later, Senator Abraham Ribicoff's, and later Senator Warren Magnuson's, auto hearings were front-page news; one of the results was the Automobile Traffic and Safety Act of 1966. "If the sound of congressional voices carried no further than the bare walls of the chambers," former Congressman Clem Miller wrote,

"Congress would disband. . . . To the congressman, publicity is his lifeblood." While the Senate has learned that television is the way to milk maximum publicity from its hearings, the House's taboos against television or radio hearings have thwarted adequate publicity. (The rule against it no longer exists, but the custom against it does.) In the view of Tom Morgan, chairman of the House Foreign Affairs Committee, it has made his committee a minor-league version of the much-televised Senate Foreign Relations Committee.

The Rules of Congress

The committee system guarantees that *someone* will dominate Congress. The elaborate set of congressional rules determines just who the barons will be and how they will work their will.

SENIORITY—Mississippian William Colmer was elected to the House Rules Committee before Herbert Hoover left office. John McClellan of Arkansas was elected thirty years ago and went on the House Appropriations Committee. F. Edward Hébert of Louisiana, who has been in the House since before Pearl Harbor, and John Stennis, who began as senator from Mississippi a quarter century ago, are the two generals of the House and Senate Armed Services committees. And upstart Wilbur Mills of Arkansas, not quite 30 when first sent to Congress in 1938, has since 1959 shaped and shorn all tax bills from the chair of the House Ways and Means Committee.

They are all products of the seniority system Congress uses to allocate its power. Parodying Darwin, the system works simply to ensure the survival of the survivors. Under the seniority custom—enshrined neither in law nor in written rules—committee chairmanships are automatically awarded to the members of the majority party with longest continuous service on the committee. Its result: while Congress mandates retirement for federal employees at 70, half the thirty-eight congressional committee chairman are 70 or over, including three House patriarchs in their eighties.

The system itself is less antiquated than the chairmen it perpetrates on the House. From 1910, when it took hold, until 1945, seniority determined only three of every four House chairmanships. But since World War II, it has ruled absolutely, guaranteeing chairmanships for all but a handful of ornery veterans who committed the unforgivable sin of crossing party lines—and for Adam Clayton Powell, whose misfortune it was to be both spendthrift and black. In the Senate, where seniority began in the 1840s, only five senior members in 125 years have been refused chairmanships, the last of them 50 years ago. And those who become chairmen stay chairmen. Only one member of Congress, Theodore F. Green, chairman of the Senate Foreign Relations Committee, who stepped down in 1955 at the age of 91, found a chairmanship of a full committee too wearing. Only after Senator Karl Mundt of South Dakota had lain in a hospital bed for two years, wholly incapacitated by a stroke, did Senate Republicans reassign his position as ranking minority member of the Foreign Relations Committee.

So what? Mere antiquity is certainly no crime. Though occasional relics gain chairs, in what Jack Anderson hyperbolizes as the "Senility System," infirmity is not the chief vice of the seniority system. Its faults are more serious. A legislative branch encumbered by the seniority custom belongs in neither a republic nor a democracy: it bequeaths inherited congressional power to unrepresentative lawmakers in an undemocratic way.

In a country whose population is young, urban, and geographically dispersed, the seniority system turns over most positions of power in Congress to "representatives" who are old, rural, and Southern. In 1970, thirteen of twenty-one House committee chairmen hailed from rural districts. As long ago as 1859, a Northern Democrat bewailed the seniority system for giving "senators from slaveholding states the chairmanship of every

single committee that controls the public business of
this government. There is not one exception." Southerners consistently held more than half of all committee
chairs in Democratic Congresses from 1921 to 1966.
Today, somewhat on the wane, they still chair nine of
seventeen committees in the Senate and eight of twenty-
one in the House. But they retain all the most important
committees: Appropriations, Armed Services, House
Ways and Means, and House Rules.

The political bias that results is not hard to guess at.
In an analysis of thirty key votes reflecting the "national
Democratic position" in the Ninetieth Congress, a liberal
group discovered that more than half of the seventeen
losses suffered by the party were caused by "Democratic" committee chairmen—the old, rural, Southern
sovereigns. In all, the forty-two Democratic committee
and subcommittee chairmen voted against national
party programs an astonishing 87 percent of the time.

The only political arrangement worse than an unrepresentative congressman is an unrepresentative congressman who is also unaccountable. There are no
better examples of this double threat than committee
chairmen. Eighty-eight percent of committee chairmen
from 1950 to 1970 came from virtually one-party districts. Chairman Bob Poage of House Agriculture is
typical: the last time a Republican dared to oppose him
was in the 1966 election, when he sauntered off with
81 percent of the vote. Thus, safe districts spawn
seniority; and seniority spawns safe districts. Seniority
discourages voters from surrendering an unresponsive
oldster who chairs a committee to a newer and better
man who would take thirty years to rise to the same
powerful position.

Seniority is not without its supporters, mostly older
congressmen. It assures, they argue, independent leaders
who strengthen Congress's position relative to the dominant executive branch. Wilbur Mills, for example, is
second only to the president in influence over federal
taxes, and sometimes first. But the price of using seniority as a way of insulating Congress from the president is

insulating certain congressmen from the president, the voters, and the rest of Congress.

It may also serve as a buffer, some say, against the coercion of powerful special interests. The same seniority system that produced a Mendel Rivers also produced Estes Kefauver and Wright Patman, men whose chairmanships would have been fiercely opposed by the big banks and corporations for their zealous efforts to protect the public and the consumer. Given the power of big money to intervene in elections *in* Congress just as they intervene in elections *to* Congress, the net result of "democratizing" the process of selecting committee chairmen might be to give even more sway to the captains of commerce. What could be worse than an old fool? A young fool of GM or Standard Oil. The danger is a serious one, given the present powerful role of money in politics, but the seniority system itself is to some extent subject to the same criticism, though for a different reason. One of the most serious problems with seniority is its utter predictability. It permits the lobbies to zero in with all their resources on chairmen and potential chairmen—wooing them, supporting them, or (in some instances) backing their opponents—with full confidence that most of their money will be well spent. Once a chairman is theirs, he's probably theirs for life.

Assertions are also often trumped up that seniority places men of experience in power, thereby assuring competence and continuity. But if age implies talent, why have cabinet officers under President Nixon averaged twelve years younger than congressional committee chairmen? President Johnson's seventeen years younger? President Kennedy's nineteen years younger? As the adage goes, thirty years' experience may be no more than one year's experience, relived thirty times.

Despite frequent challenges resulting in some minor modifications, the self-sustaining seniority system rolls on. Seniority did suffer a temporary setback before the 1972 elections. Lured by new, higher-than-ever pensions ranging up to $34,000 a year, scared by the

18-year-old vote and, in some cases, redistricting after the 1970 census, a number of the elder statesmen in Congress finally resigned. No fewer than nine ranking Republicans stepped down.

Yet the long-term prospects are bleak. The average committee chairman a hundred years ago was in his forties. In 1910, he was 50. Today he is over 67.

The wait to rise to the top is today staggering. Computer simulations predict that the average congressman newly elected in November, 1972, will have to wait forty-one years to chair the House Appropriations Committee. Or thirty-nine years to lead Armed Services, thirty-seven years for Banking and Currency, thirty-nine years for Public Works, or thirty-eight years for Ways and Means. He or she will be 78 when enthroned on Rules, 76 on Appropriations. If you elect a new congressman today and are patient enough to wait until the year 2013, you, too, can enjoy the benfits of the seniority system. Unless, of course, you aren't around by then.

SECRECY—Congressional secrecy, especially secrecy in committees, began at the beginning of Congress itself. Following the practice of the earlier Congress of the Confederation, the Senate in 1789 met and voted entirely in secret. By 1795, the Senate opened its doors for regular legislative sessions, but still held secret ("executive") sessions to consider all treaties and many nominations.

Voting and other floor activities are today open affairs, but committee activities are not. In the 1970 Legislative Reorganization Act, committees had to make public their roll-call votes. But because many chairmen dislike that requirement, they avoid it by simply not taking roll calls. Many committee sessions are closed altogether. In 1969, 36 percent of all committee sessions were held in secret; in 1970, it was 41 percent. Congress did include in the same 1970 Legislative Reorganization Act the requirement that committee sessions be open to the public, unless the majority of the committee ruled otherwise; but in 1971, the first full year of the new rule,

fully 36 percent were still secret. One can understand
why an occasional Armed Services Committee meeting,
discussing confidential military data, should be held in
"executive session." But why the Post Office and Commerce committees? And why, for example, are nearly
all Senate Appropriations hearings held in public, while
nearly all House Appropriations are conducted in secret?

Beyond usual meetings and hearings, committee
"markup" sessions and "conference committees" should
also be public. At the markups, the details of a proposed bill are reviewed; it is here that outside interests
can slip in a loophole with the help of a committee
staffer. To prevent this, the public should have access to
markups, but with rare exceptions committees forbid it.

The conference committee settles any differences
between Senate and House versions of a bill. Calling
them the "third house of Congress," Senator George
Norris lamented in 1934 that "the members of this
House arc not elected by the people. . . . There is no
record kept of the workings of the conference committee. Its work is performed, in the main, in secret.
. . . As a practical proposition we have legislation
then, not by the members of the House of Representatives, but we have legislation by the voice of five or
six members." It is no less true today. As he left the
Senate in 1970, Tennessee's Albert Gore blasted the
conference committees as "secret meetings often not
even announced until the last minute [where] a few
men can sit down and undo in one hour the most pains-
taking work of months of effort by several standing
committees and the full membership of both Houses."
At times the chosen conferees are hostile to the bill
being negotiated, or unrepresenative of the views of
their chamber. So in 1970, when the House voted $290
million for the SST and the Senate voted to *end* the
program, the conference committee (stacked with Senate SST supporters) agreed on a "compromise" $210
million funding.

Such secrecy hurts both the democratic process and
the legislative result. It is, in the extreme, an antidemo-
cratic system which operates in darkness. The public

cannot adequately judge a system they cannot see; those
with special peepholes can better exploit it.

Secrecy also twists the results. "You certainly get
some different attitudes in a conference than you would
anticipate by listening to speeches on the floor," one
member told the Brookings Institute's Charles Clapp.
"There is one senator, for example, who is known
primarily for a particular position on foreign aid. Yet in
conference I never saw anyone fight more ardently for
a different position." In a memo that got into Jack
Anderson's hands, a Ford dealer summarized a discussion an aide had on auto safety with Senator John
Pastore: "The senator . . . told Bob that when a consumer issue is before him and the cameras are on, he
is not about to be anything but supportive of the issue."
Possibly his flexibility increases when only the Ford
dealers are watching. In a secret meeting of the House
Agriculture Committee, the cameras were *not* rolling
when New York's Congressman John Dow gave an
eloquent appeal against giving South Africa a larger
sugar quota. He lost 19–3 on an unrecorded vote, with
"public" civil-righters like Congressmen John Zwach
and Clarence Miller voting against him.

When members have to be publicly accountable for
their actions, however, the result can sharply differ from
secret lawmaking. Before the advent of recorded "teller
voting" in 1970 (previously votes on amendments,
which make up the bulk of our laws, had never been
recorded), SST funding was easily approved, with only
188 members voting. But the very first year that members had to go on public record with their SST vote, it
was defeated 217 to 203. The *Congressional Quarterly*
found that attendance in 1971 on key issues doubled
because of its rules change. "[Teller voting] means that
the primary factor in your voting," said Congressman
Charles Whalen, "is not whether you'll please Boggs or
Albert or Gerry Ford; you've got to think about what
your constituency wants." In the House Interior Committee, a recent proposal by Congressman John Melcher
to make strip miners repair the damage they inflict was
shouted down by a voice vote; but when Melcher called

for a "division," which meant that each committee member would have to be recorded, this environment amendment *won* by a lopsided margin. "Sunlight," Justice Louis Brandeis once perceptively observed, "is said to be the best of disinfectants."

If, as official Washington assumes, information is power, committee meetings and conference committees must be opened up to public scrutiny, with transcripts and votes publicly available. To those who fear that congressmen would play to the public, one could answer that this is called democracy, the accountability of a public official to his constituency for his actions. Would public access disrupt markup sessions? The House Education and Labor Committee and the Interior Committee have encouraged public markup proceedings without any noticeable loss of efficiency. Anybody can walk into the room and observe the process. Would open procedures simply lead to secret gatherings before the scheduled meeting? If so, it would expose conspirators to the charge that they are breaking the law. Also, "the only people who would go to the secret meeting," said one well-placed Senate staffer, "would be those who didn't want the public to know what they were doing. Congressmen who wanted to fight for the public interest simply wouldn't *go* to the secret meetings and make deals."

THE RULES COMMITTEE—On paper the Rules Committee makes sense. Before any bill moves to the floor for debate, the committee sets the agenda for its debate, such as specifying how much time will be allowed and whether members can offer amendments. But in practice the Rules Committee has become a star chamber for bills which do not strike its members' fancy, for they have the power to block a proposal by simply not reporting it to the floor. As Congressman Udall wrote in a newsletter, "The Rules Committee has an almost complete power to determine on important issues *whether the rest of us can vote at all*." (emphasis his)

From the 1930s until the early sixties, the Rules Committee was dominated by a coalition of Southern

Democrats and conservative Republicans who frustrated much progressive legislation. A reform called the twenty-one-day rule was introduced in 1949. This allowed the committee which first considered a bill to force it out of the Rules Committee if it had lingered there for twenty-one days. Two years later, the rule was repealed. Its power restored, the Rules Committee later showed that it could thwart the will of *both* Houses. After President Eisenhower's proposal for federal aid for school construction had passed both the House and the Senate, the Rules Committee refused to send it on to a House-Senate conference, thereby killing it.

The new Kennedy administration had similar troubles and decided it could not tolerate this nest of obstructionist conservatives. With the cooperation of Speaker Sam Rayburn, the administration managed to increase the size of the committee from twelve to fifteen, and to stack it with enough liberals to give an 8–7 liberal majority. Subdued, the committee has flaunted its power less since then. But it lashes out occasionally: at the end of 1970, it killed two bills by refusing to report them for floor action. One was to create an independent consumer agency and another to strengthen the powers of the Equal Employment Opportunity Commission. Early in 1972, as the House prepared to pass bills to end the West Coast dock strike, the Rules Committee sat on the bill that had come the normal route, through the Education and Labor Committee, and reported out its own bill instead.

One thing the Rules Committee continues to do is report certain legislation to the floor under the so-called closed rule, which means that no amendments are permitted. Tax bills from Ways and Means are invariably reported out with a closed rule, which effectively tells the House either to take it or leave it. This converts the great majority of representatives into mere rubber stamps, dependent on the Ways and Means panel and especially its dominant chairman, Wilbur Mills. "The legislative process has been brought perilously close to parody," wrote the *New York Times* of the effect of the Rules Committee's closed rule on the 1971 tax bill. "It is not that all of Mr. Mills's judgments were wrong but that he is accountable to no one except the voters of his one-party rural district in Arkansas in making them." Even the *Wall Street Journal,* which views Mills with tenderness, thought the closed rule on tax measures unnecessarily restrictive: "But it is not an all-or-nothing choice. A limited-amendment rule could allow at least up-or-down votes on each major section of omnibus tax bills so that the members wouldn't have to consider the whole package on a take-it-or-leave-it basis."

THE FILIBUSTER—The Senate's tradition of allowing unlimited debate—known and ridiculed as the filibuster —is, like the seniority system, an unofficial custom which has acquired the durability of Divine Law.* To its supporters, the filibuster is the highest example of the right of free speech. "I think it is of greater importance to the public interest, in the long run and in the short run, that every bill on your calendar should fail than that any senator should be cut off from the right of expressing his opinion," said Senator George F. Edmunds, expressing the Senate's normal sense of proportion, in 1881. To cartoonists and comics, the filibuster is a gold mine, providing scenes of posturing politicians reading selections from the phone book, or favorite recipes. But the filibuster is more than a caricature of itself; it is an offense to the concept of majority rule, a device which allows a minority to obstruct what it does not like. It has been used in a variety

---

* Senators can talk on the Senate floor until hunger, sleep, illness, nature, or cloture stops them. Cloture, established by Rule 22 in 1917, is a two-thirds vote to stop debate. This has been attempted fifty-three times since 1917, but has succeeded in only eight of them. The record for consecutive talking in the Senate is Strom Thurmond's twenty-four hours and eighteen minutes in August, 1957, against the civil rights bill of that year. In second place, talking for twenty-two hours and twenty-six minutes on the tidelands oil bill of 1953, is Wayne Morse, who used to pin a rose to his lapel and threaten to hold forth until the petals wilted.

of situations, most commonly and notoriously during civil rights debates in recent years.

Proposals to be able to cut off debate by majority vote, rather than the two-thirds vote of the entire Senate now required by Rule 22, have been periodically made. In 1958 Vice President Richard Nixon, in his capacity as presiding officer of the Senate, ruled that a new Senate session was not bound by the rules of the past, but could decide for itself whether a majority or two-thirds vote would be necessary to invoke cloture. Given the recent influx of Democratic senators in the 1958 elections, chances for reform looked good—until Majority Leader Lyndon Johnson began trading choice committee assignments for a vote against the Nixon proposal. So Senator Thomas Dodd, for example, who had earlier vowed to do battle with Rule 22, now supinely went along with LBJ and got a choice seat on Appropriations for his obedience.

Vice President Hubert Humphrey tried the same parliamentary move at the start of the Ninetieth Congress, but at the moment of truth was also abandoned by some key liberals. Senator Mansfield saw any change in Rule 22 as "a path of destruction to the Senate as an institution"; while "majority rule is basic and vital to our society," he contended that if applied to the chamber's debate, "the Senate should be destroyed." It is hard to see why. The House prohibits unlimited debate, and is still standing. And determined minorities can already make life difficult for the majority by the composition of the committee system. At the least, reducing the number necessary to invoke cloture from 67 to 60 would better realign minority rights and majority will. But the Senate, to date, will have none of it.

Efforts to reform the right to filibuster have been frustrated by Southern conservatives, who have threatened civil disobedience—to go on talking whatever the chair ruled—if a majority tried to shut them off. At the same time, liberals like Senators Church, Cranston, and Mathias feel they, too, constitute a powerless minority on many key issues and need the filibuster threat, in Church's words, to "veto a proposal clearly against the public interest." But one man's public interest is another's threat to the Republic, and filibustering remains a double-edged weapon.

The Rulers of Congress

1. COMMITTEE CHAIRMEN—In the Sixty-seventh Congress, during the 1920s, Rules Committee Chairman Philip Campbell of Kansas at times refused to report to the House resolutions approved by a majority of his committee. When they protested, he said, "You can go to hell. It makes no difference what a majority of you decide. If it meets with my disapproval, it shall not be done. I am the committee."

Today's autocrats are less blunt but nearly as powerful. Congressional reforms in 1946 and 1970 checked some of the worst excesses—regular meetings were to be held, and a majority could force a meeting over a chairman's objection. But sly circumventions of the rules, as well as the retention of the bulk of their power, have rendered the reforms far from meaningful.

Morris Udall noted that "the committee member who has served twenty years is not just 5 percent more powerful than the member who has served nineteen years. If he is chairman he is 1000 percent more powerful." For the chairmen still are the committee. And since it is the committee system that effectively controls Congress, it is the chairmen who effectively run Congress.

Committee chairmen can exercise their power in an impressive variety of ways. First, they can set up subcommittees and choose selected cronies to head them. Here seniority is not rigidly observed, as when Chairman John McMillan of the House District Committee skipped over senior critics to appoint allies to head up four of his subcommittees. "I don't think any chairman in the Congress who has any sense would appoint subcommittee chairmen who wouldn't back him," he said. Once subcommittee rulers are properly picked, a chairman can then refer a bill to whichever subcommittee he thinks will treat it best. When some of House Government Operations Committee Chairman Chet Holifield's subcommittee heads began disagreeing with him on consumer issues, he simply erased their subcommittees; and Appropriations Chairman George Mahon just as simply transferred environment and consumer matters from one subcommittee to another dominated by his conservative allies. More impressive yet is the technique of Senator Long, who chairs Senate Finance, and Congressman Mills, who chairs House Ways and Means. By refusing to create any subcommittees at all, they keep the committee's whole jurisdiction right under their thumbs.

A second tactic is adroit use of committee staff. Chairmen hire and fire committee staff; if the staffers are at all shrewd, they learn to be loyal to the chairman rather than to the committee at large. Consequently, the chairman learns things the others don't, and the rest of the committee becomes even more dependent on him.

Third, the chairman can turn to the old ally, delay. In talented hands, premeditated procrastination can be more effective than votes or bargaining. Congressman John McMillan has long been a foe of home rule for the District of Columbia. To hold off home rule bills, he persuaded his allies on the committee to introduce as many bills as possible on a wide variety of subjects so his committee would not be able to get to a home rule bill.

Fourth, the big and powerful chairman can offer bargains that regular congressmen can neither match nor resist. To get his way, the chairman can offer to set up a subcommittee, to pass a bill with the representative's name on it, to allow liberal traveling expenses, to sponsor hearings where the representative can make his name. Warren Magnuson, head of the Senate Commerce Committee, lets Senator Pastore run his communications subcommittee with an entirely free hand and frequently hands out special-hearing assignments to other members. In exchange, Pastore supports Magnuson's consumer bills and the rest of the committee goes along with Magnuson.

Finally, the chairman controls a multitude of small

powers which further enhance his status as first among equals. He can usually decide when a committee will meet and what it will hold hearings on. He decides the agenda for meetings, chooses the floor manager of a bill, and helps the speaker or majority leader select delegates to the conference committee. With these and other powers at his disposal, there is little beyond his power. "If he wants to be a bastard," says one writer, "he can." Yet, chairmen are rarely challenged. "[It] is not done because it doesn't pay off," said a committee staff director. "There's no percentage in it. He could make the committee member's life miserable and futile for a long, long time."

Not all the chairmen exploit to the hilt what their position allows. Some, like George Mahon of Appropriations and John Blatnik of Public Works, use only a fraction of the tools at their disposal; others use them all and scheme to get more. Chairmen as a group are quite diverse in terms of personality, intelligence, stature, and drive. But they hold one thing in common: they are the rulers of Congress.

Wilbur Mills of Arkansas was bitten with the presidential bug in the fall of 1971, which puzzled many of his House colleagues. Congressman Sam Gibbons of Florida asked him, "Wilbur, why do you want to run for president and give up your grip on the country?"

Gibbons's question was a good one. As chairman of the House Ways and Means Committee since 1958, Mills is the true potentate of Congress, where he has spent the last thirty-three of his sixty-two years. His committee's jurisdiction spans Medicare, national health insurance, and welfare, as well as taxes, revenue-sharing, tariffs, and trade quotas. Negotiations with foreign governments is not on the list of constitutional powers granted to Congress, but that did not deter Mills in early 1971 from persuading Japanese textile manufacturers to voluntarily restrict their U.S. imports. When, in 1967, LBJ began to take Mills for granted, he quickly got put in his place. Mills's committee unceremoniously quashed Johnson's proposed tax increase at a closed committee session, leaving Treasury Secretary Fowler, who had come to make a presentation he never gave, spluttering in anger. Johnson then had to court Mills by White House and Texas ranch dinners and by the promise of reduced federal spending, to get back in his good graces.

If foreign governments and presidents have good reason to court Mills, so do American businessmen, for he holds the key to the special tax breaks and import restrictions that they cherish. Mills made the front pages in 1971 when an alert reporter spotted him getting off a private jet plane lent to him by Sears, Roebuck. Some Mills-for-President supporters made news when they came from Washington to help in the New Hampshire primary. The group included high-level lobbyists for interests like oil and banking. In addition to $6,000 in campaign money from ten breweries (who are subject to federal excise taxes on beer, set in Ways and Means), Mills got $45,000 from dairymen funds for the 1972 presidential primaries. One of the salaried members of Mills's campaign staff was the son of David Parr, main political operative for TAPE, the milk group that sent Mills the largest check.

Moneyed supporters like these have every reason to be grateful. Loopholes in the tax laws which Mills's committee administers, for example, permitted thirteen hundred Americans with incomes over $50,000 to escape paying any income tax in 1971. Big corporations like Gulf Oil, with only 1.2 percent tax on its $990 million, have also done well by Ways and Means. In 1971, Mills's committee quietly buried numerous tax reform proposals and instead had measures passed to redistribute income *to* corporations: the Revenue Act of 1971, which cut federal income taxes by $9 billion annually, with over $7.5 billion of that cut going to corporations, a $70-million tax cut for banks, sponsored by Chairman Mills himself, and numerous other, similarly inclined, bills.

The road to control over loopholes like these began for Mills back in tiny Kensett, Arkansas, and included an uncompleted law degree at Harvard. As a fledgling congressman, the brainy Mills learned his legislative tactics over bourbon and water from the grand master, Speaker Sam Rayburn, and then from Senate Majority Leader Lyndon Johnson. (When he and President Johnson clashed openly over tax matters in 1967, Mills said that he would not back down from his demand for spending cuts even "if it costs me a friendship of twenty-nine years.")

Mills has set himself apart from his House colleagues by his brilliant understanding of complicated tax codes and by his sheer endurance. He is often the only one at hearings on tax legislation, where he sits and nods politely to each witness—"like he has Novocain in his ass," says one veteran congressman. Beyond that, he has consolidated his clout by skilled Machiavellian maneuvering. When he became chairman in 1958, he abolished all subcommittees and concentrated all the power in his own hands. He keeps junior committee members starved for information. They sometimes learn about hearings —such as those on tax treatment of single and married people, for only one example—by reading about them in the morning newspapers; copies of the press release are not even sent to each office. Mills also prohibits committee members from bringing professional staff into secret sessions, although he occasionally lets dozens of Treasury Department staff sit in and participate. Mills's mastery of the tax laws over his thirty years on the committee gives him the last word on many issues just because his potential adversaries are unable to rebut his arguments. There is an extra bonus for obedient members. It is known as "Members' Day." As Tom Stanton has described it in the *New Republic:*

> Twenty-four gentlemen of Ways and Means (plus one lady, Martha Griffiths of Michigan) seat themselves around a large green felt-covered table, close the doors, and pass around tax bills that often are specially written bonanzas for favored constituents. Each member is given a chance to offer a bill for consideration. After it is accepted (possibly in modified form following staff com-

ment), the next member presents his bill—and so on around the table until everyone is satisfied. Depending on the appetites of the members, the process may stop after one round, but may go on for two or three. Sometimes members use the occasion to correct minor inequities in the past laws; or to "deliver" favors to other congressmen for reciprocal favors at a politically opportune time.

In theory, the rest of the House could repudiate Mills's creations on the floor. But because of the closed rule on any tax matter reported out of Ways and Means, the members must either accept it all or vote it all down, and the latter is hard to do. Mills avoids even potential controversy by judicious scheduling. The 1971 Revenue Act is a good example. It sheared corporate taxes by $7.5 billion—more than the combined 1972 budget amounts for the Environmental Protection Agency, HUD, the Department of State, and the whole federal court system. Mills had the bill shouted through by voice vote during lunch when only about thirty congressmen were present. He avoided a roll-call vote because, as Mills explains, "Where there is a questionable gain politically, I do not ask for one."

The biggest stick Mills wields over his fellow members is the nonlegislative assignment the Democrats on Ways and Means have. They also serve as the Democratic Committee on Committees, which determines committee assignments for all House Democrats. When a member considers challenging Wilbur Mills, he remembers that Mills's Committee on Committees can accelerate or blunt his career. One liberal Democrat has said that Mills plays "a sly devious game" to keep the important committees loaded with persons of his political persuasions, which Mills denies.

Mills has skillfully exploited the power vacuum in the House left by the weakness of its recent leadership—McCormack and Albert—to expand his own behind-the-scenes influence. Few dare to challenge him, including Democratic Majority Leader Hale Boggs. Recently Mills wanted to raise the interest rate on the national debt, a good deal for the big banks, who lend, but not such a good deal for the borrowers, who pay. Banking Committee Chairman Wright Patman asked Boggs to speak out against Mills's interest rate raise, and Boggs agreed. But Mills found out about it and said to Boggs, "Hale, I wouldn't make that speech if I were you. I made you leader and I can unmake you just as easily." Boggs decided not to make his speech after all.

Predicting what Wilbur Mills will do has become a favorite pastime of Washington columnists, requiring a skill not unlike that of the Kremlinologists or China-watchers. "Trying to pin him down philosophically," said one long Mills acquaintance to the *Wall Street Journal,* "is like trying to bite a balloon." His enigmatic zigs and zags from one course to another, say many who know Mills, simply reflect his one clear guiding principle: he likes to win. Often described as supercautious, Mills maintains his invincible image by remaining non-committal until a consensus has developed, and then going its way; sometimes being so strategically positioned he creates the consensus.

F. Edward Hébert of Louisiana, 71, became the chairman of the House Armed Services Committee in 1970 when South Carolina's Mendel Rivers died. To understand Hébert and his present position, it is necessary to understand his two predecessors. Carl Vinson, who served fifty years in the House, was chairman from 1947 to 1964. Affectionately called "Swamp Fox" and "Admiral," he once spiked a rumor that he was going to be named secretary of defense by saying, "Shucks, I'd rather run the Pentagon from up here." Vinson delighted in intimidating military titans when they appeared as committee witnesses by asking them, "What did you say your name was, Admiral?" Rivers succeeded him and quickly dominated the committee, filling his South Carolina district with more military installations than comfortably fit. He gloried in this fact, using as a campaign slogan "Rivers Delivers" and jocularly saying that the Yankees will think twice before they war with the South again. Rivers saw himself as a per-

sonification of the Pentagon and once said of his Armed
Services Committee, "This is the most important committee in Congress. It is the only official voice the
military has in the House of Representatives."

Hébert understood well the tradition handed down
to him, and paid it due homage. "I loved Mendel
Rivers," he said shortly after Rivers's death, "and my
goal is the same as his. The goal is that the United
States have an uncontestable military defense and overwhelming offensive power." He later told the *Congressional Quarterly* in an interview, "I intend to build the
strongest military we can get. Money is no question.
The yardstick should be necessity, not money."

First elected to Congress in 1940, Hébert had been
the city editor of the *New Orleans States*. On a tip in
1939, he sent a photographer to the home of Governor
Richard Leche, heir-apparent to Huey Long, to catch
state-owned trucks delivering building materials. The
resulting picture and story of illegal campaign contributions set off an investigation that landed Leche and
others in jail, and launched Hébert on a publicity wave
that carried him into Congress.

He has applied the same talent in military affairs. In
1951, he chaired the investigative subcommittee that
turned up evidence of waste in military contracts. Two
decades later, his inquiry into the My Lai massacre
concluded that military and State Department officials
tried to cover up the evidence. So it is with some justifi-
cation that he says, "Yes, I'm a friend of the military,
but I'll take them to the woodshed and spank them
anytime." In the absence of scandal, however, he goes
down the line with the Pentagon. Hébert fought off
attacks on the C5-A and F-111 airplane projects and
the ABM and MIRV missile systems. He has opposed
all efforts to end the draft, reduce the military budget,
or set a date to end the Vietnam War.

Hébert is a staunch Southern Democratic conservative and segregationist. During student demonstrations
in the late 1960s, he said, "Let's forget the First Amendment." He vetoed his own Junior ROTC program in

Louisiana after "a couple of liberal congressmen insisted it be fully integrated. We couldn't have that." And of the Vietnam War, Hébert has said, "We should move and destroy everything—everything that is in the hands of the enemy."

His sentiments cross the line between opinion and government policy when they touch items his committee controls. There are two theories about Hébert's use of the chairman's power. Many see him as more amicable and less doctrinaire than Rivers, even to the extent of his tolerating debate and dissent on the committee. "I doubt there are very many things that Hébert and I agree on," says liberal Massachusetts Representative Michael Harrington, "but I must say he's been more than fair to me. I think he gets a kick out of being indulgent." But others see him using the power he himself calls "awesome" in as high-handed a way as his predecessors. Representative Don Riegle of Michigan bluntly expressed his view in his book *O Congress* after Hébert refused to permit any end-the-war date from his committee:

> Who the hell is he to block the setting of a date? Nearly 80 percent of the American people, the polls say, want a date for our troops to leave Vietnam. So do 191 members of this House. Why should more young men have to die because Hébert says so?
>
> Suddenly I felt an urge to smash Hébert in the face.

William Robert Poage, 72, has been the representative from the eleventh district in Texas for thirty-six years, which puts him sixth in seniority in the House. His views are ultra-conservative ("I am in favor of establishing a university of thugs, mugs, and other hippies in the southwest corner of the walls of Huntsville"—which is the Texas state prison). But to his constituents, judging by his election successes, he seems just right.

One reason for his local popularity is that he is chairman of the House Agriculture Committee, a power which makes the local folks proud. The committee does much to control the $7-billion farm budget, which covers everything from food stamps for the poor to price supports for the rich. As the number of farmers, and hence "farm districts," has declined, so has the power of the Agriculture Committee. But it still can bargain with members from the cities because it controls food stamps and pesticides. For example, when Poage and other conservatives agreed not to pass an amendment that would prevent strikers from getting food stamps, liberals repaid the favor by opposing Congressman Silvio Conte's effort to lower the ceiling for farm subsidies from $50,000 to $20,000.

Poage is a cotton grower himself, running the 1,900-acre W. A. Poage Estates in his home district. Is this a conflict of interest with his chairmanship of Agriculture? "There's a theoretical conflict of interest in any business," he says with a grin. He runs his committee with an equivalent insensitivity. Harry Graham, a former lobbyist for the National Farmers Organization, complained in an interview that the House Agriculture Committee met every Monday night for twenty-seven weeks with Agriculture Department representatives in secret session on the 1970 farm bill. "There were no records, no hearings, and no one knew officially what they were doing," he said. "There was no opportunity to suggest revisions and no bill was submitted to us. . . . [Poage] tries to keep liberals from getting any power by holding committee hearings instead of subcommittee hearings."

When it comes to his views and activities on food, hunger, and the poor, Poage's red-neckism flares. He is opposed to setting a minimum wage for migrant workers, calling it "illegal, impractical, and immoral." When a team of nutritionists issued a report, *Hunger, USA,* charging that many Southern counties were "hunger" counties, Poage fired off a letter to the county health officers in each of these counties. "From my limited knowledge of nutrition, I would assume that it was true that many Americans suffer from improper diet, but that the problem there is one of education or personal decisions."

After widely covered Senate investigations of hunger in 1967, Senator Stennis of Mississippi sponsored a bill which ultimately required the Agriculture Department and the Public Health Service to spend $75 million in two years for emergency hunger and medical needs. At a private meeting on October 5, 1967, with officials from HEW, Agriculture, and the Bureau of the Budget, Poage pounced: "This program is so loosely drawn I can get food from it when my wife is out of town," he shouted. The well-fed Poage got his committee to kill the proposal and it never even got to the House floor. This is power at its crudest—the power to keep thousands of people hungry. During a hearing later that month on food stamp reforms, Poage slipped into a virulence, which congressmen, even if they feel it, usually conceal: he asked an Urban Coalition witness why he was "so concerned in maintaining a bunch of drones. You know what happens in the beehive? They kill those drones. That is what happens in most primitive societies. Maybe we have just gotten too far away from the situation of primitive man."

Jamie Whitten, to the American consumer, environmentalist, and farmer is the most powerful subcommittee chairman in Congress. A courtly Southern Democrat from the hill country of northern Mississippi, Whitten has parlayed his thirty-two-year seniority in the House into an astonishing array of key committee posts on the House Appropriations Committee. He is also the second ranking member of the House Appropriations Committee, and, most significantly, chairman of the Appropriations subcommittee which has financial control over the $7-billion farm budget, the Environmental Protection Agency, the Food and Drug Administration, the Council on Environmental Quality, and the consumer protection programs of the Federal

Trade Commission. "Everyone is terrified of Whitten," reports one leader of a conservation group. "He controls the purse strings for so many programs he can twist arms throughout government."

Whitten earned his reputation through years of stewardship of farm appropriations in the House. A strong philosophical conservative with a passion for work and an affection for detail, Whitten exercises more intimate control over the 100,000-man Department of Agriculture (USDA) than perhaps any subcommittee chairman in history. His annual hearings on USDA programs are considered models of the genre. His knowledge of the intricacies of farm legislation—which Arthur Schlesinger has called "a modern form of alchemy" and "a conspiracy against public understanding"—is legendary.

But while Whitten takes pride in the achievements of conservation, rural development, and agricultural research, he has been severely criticized by liberals and black leaders for neglect of the poor and hungry. A consistent opponent of civil rights legislation, Whitten has been credited by former Secretary of Agriculture Orville Freeman, among others, as the major obstacle to food relief for hungry people in the late sixties. Whitten's record does consistently show an insensitivity to the human casualties of technological change in rural America. In the late 1940s, he helped destroy a USDA agency which had the temerity to inquire into the social conditions of black sharecroppers in Mississippi, and in 1969 he forced HEW to delete Mississippi from the states to be covered by the National Nutrition Survey, the first official effort to measure the magnitude of malnutrition in the United States. In the view of *Washington Post* reporter Nick Kotz, Whitten has "anesthetized his soul to human misery and indignity."

Whitten has also been regarded as hostile to environmentalists. "His" book, *That We May Live,* was designed, and later underwritten, by the pesticide industry as a rebuttal to Rachel Carson and her *Silent Spring.*

In 1971, the League of Conservation Voters rated

Whitten a low 6 and ranked him 382nd out of 435 congressmen for his votes on environmental issues.

Whitten considers the attack by the hunger lobby and environmentalists as unfair. He points out that he has gone along with increased food stamp appropriations for the last two years ("My name is on all these bills"). He also claims to be an advocate of environmental protection—he considers his work in soil conservation his greatest achievement—but claims that he takes a harder look at the risks as well as the benefits of environmental programs than do his critics. On his stands generally, Whitten says, "I do what I think is right. I don't owe anybody anything and if it develops I was wrong, I can change. . . . Whatever I do is for the United States. I have a national committee. I've never had a platform except to do the best I could. Who's to say I haven't done it?"

Nevertheless, environmentalists and consumerists wish they had a man more sensitive to their point of view in Whitten's seat. When EPA chief William Ruckelshaus came before Whitten's subcommittee last year, the congressman observed, "Mr. Ruckelshaus, I feel sorry for you. Congress has given you far more power than a good man would want or a bad man should have or that any ten men could handle." Ruckelshaus could have said the same of Mr. Whitten, but didn't.

Russell Long of Louisiana was selected to the Senate in 1948 at the constitutionally minimal age of 30, and hasn't had a serious campaign challenge since. With his braggadocio style and blend of populism and conservatism, he wears the mantle of his famous father, the "Kingfish," Huey Long, whom Russell reveres as "a political Messiah . . . the greatest thing the good Lord ever put on this planet."

It was not until 1964 that Long began to build himself into a Senate power. At that time he was assigned the task of being the floor manager for President Johnson's $18-billion tax reduction bill. During a week-long debate, he repulsed 150 attempted amendments. His

performance was so skillful and persuasive that Senator
William Proxmire of Wisconsin, an opponent of the
bill, remarked:

> If a man murdered a crippled, enfeebled orphan
> at high noon on the public square in plain view of
> a thousand people, I am convinced after today's
> performance that, if the senator from Louisiana
> represented the guilty murderer, the jury would not
> only find the murderer innocent, they would award
> the defendant a million dollars on the ground that
> the victim had provoked him.

In 1965, Long became majority whip, based on performances like this one. It led Tom Wicker to project
that Long might succeed Kerr as "the uncrowned king
of the Senate." Power-accumulation continued the next
year when he took over the chairmanship of the Senate
Finance Committee.

But since Long's ascent in the mid-sixties, his power,
although still substantial, has somewhat declined. Trying
to repeat his success at floor advocacy, he achieved the
opposite result in his defenses of a public campaign-
funding law and Senator Thomas Dodd. His oratory
became intimidation, and persuasiveness was replaced
by stalling tactics, which outraged allies and opponents
alike. The Louisiana politician came through, except
that the place was the Senate of the United States, not
Placquemines Parish. In 1969, when Ted Kennedy
challenged him for the whip position, Long went down
to a decisive defeat. But his musings afterward revealed
as much about senatorial logrolling generally as it did of
Long himself: Long anticipated Eugene McCarthy's
vote because "I helped every time I could honorably do
so. I fought alongside him when he was accused of
having some association with special interests," and
"it is more to his advantage to work with me—his
committee chairman—than with Kennedy." Long expected Senator Gaylord Nelson's vote because he had
helped the Wisconsin senator with legislation giving a
$22-million tax break to Detroit's American Motors

and he had given Nelson the chairmanship of a small-business subcommittee on monopolies. He knew that Senator Joseph Montoya's "ambition is to serve on the Appropriations Committee"—and had he not, said Long, helped Senator Gale McGee get a seat on the Foreign Relations Committee?

Long has retained his place as Senate Finance Committee chairman, and it is here that he plays the powerful "Princefish," as some have called him. His committee must pass on matters concerning taxation, Social Security, Medicare, foreign trade, welfare, and revenue-sharing. Ending the oil depletion allowance or the oil import quota must get Russell Long's approval. But as he is a wealthy oilman himself and the self-proclaimed "darling of the oil industry," repealing the Constitution stands as likely a chance.

His power to control the committee is vast. At the end of the 1970 session, he attempted to maneuver some of his pet ideas through the Senate in the form of a giant conglomerate of a bill. This legislative dinosaur included an extremely protectionist trade bill, a health insurance section, a novel welfare plan, a pact to increase veterans' benefits, and another section to fund day care centers. The "bill" collapsed of its own weight. But his control of the committee continues. "Like the House Ways and Means Committee," writes V. O. French, a former assistant to Senator Fred Harris, "Senate Finance has no subcommittees, no staff for majority party members except for the chairman, no record of individual votes on amendments and bills, no public access to the markup sessions, and almost no rules." This doesn't seem to bother Long. "We just make ourselves up as we go along."

2. THE LEADERSHIP—The "leadership" usually means the speaker of the House, the House majority and minority leaders, and the Senate's majority and minority leaders. The word is misleading, as the real power lies with the committees and their chairmen. Jack Anderson wrote of John McCormack's speakership, "Under 'Old Jawn,' the office of speaker, formerly the second most

powerful post in the country, has become Buckingham Palace—honored and respected, but more ceremonial than functional." And under Speaker Carl Albert, as well as Senate Majority Leader Mike Mansfield, this trend continues. Leaders have become more buffers than bosses, elevated more because of inoffensiveness and general popularity than because of leadership abilities. One representative accurately said of congressional leadership, "They want someone who will do them favors and speak at their fundraisers and not make too many demands of them."

The speaker of the House is the only one of these leadership positions specifically mentioned in the Constitution. Henry Clay, a brilliant thinker and powerful orator, entered the House in 1811, at age 34, and was promptly selected speaker. His power and charm were so abundant that soon he and his "War Hawks" had actively seized control of their chamber and were pressuring the hesitant President James Madison into declaring war on the British. One leading student of the speakership, Mary P. Follet, has concluded that Clay was "the most powerful man in the nation from 1811 to 1825." Clay deposited some of his own power and prestige in the office. Few of his successors have equaled his eminence, but others have exploited the job's potential power. James Blaine, chosen in 1869, "Czar" Thomas Reed in 1890 ("The only way to do business inside the rules is to suspend the rules"), and Joe Cannon in 1903 were some of the strongest. Cannon, for example, decided whether a congressman could speak after first finding out what he intended to say. Eventually this was too much for the rest of the House, and rebellious members stripped Cannon of many of his powers in 1910. The main blow was removing the decisive power of appointing committee chairmen. Since then, speakers have had a harder time dominating, but one managed: Sam Rayburn. His central ability was that of forming coalitions by dint of his personal persuasiveness—a talent equaled in modern times only by his Texas protégé, Senate Majority Leader Lyndon Johnson.

In the Senate, strong leaders have been even rarer than in the House. Woodrow Wilson observed in the late 1880s that a senator, "however eminent, is never more than *a* senator. No one is *the* senator. No one may speak for his party as well as for himself; no one exercises the special trust of acknowledged leadership. The Senate is merely a body of individual critics." Even after the Senate created floor leaders in the 1920s, Wilson's observation remained largely true.

A number of key prerogatives have been retained by the top leadership positions in each House. The speaker presides over his chamber and has the right of recognition, decides points of order, refers bills to appropriate committees, and selects members of the conference committee. When he is not presiding, the majority leader can be recognized by the chair before all other senators, participates in handing out committee assignments, and can help determine which senators will get money (and how much) from the Senate Democratic campaign committees. As chairman of the Democratic Policy Committee and the Democratic Steering Committee, the majority leader is well placed to shape his party's and the Senate's legislative program.

Institutional arrangements, however, often have less to say about the power of these offices than does the personality of the man in the office. Sam Rayburn and John McCormack held the same job, with the same strings to pull and hurdles to overcome. But Rayburn used it as base for single-minded domination of the House, while McCormack listlessly observed events. A look at the present congressional leaders shows their strengths and weaknesses:

Mike Mansfield of Montana has legendary patience, a detached, scholarly mien, and the ability to meet an interviewer's trick question with a simple "yup" or "nope." In a chamber of politicians he is the professor. It surprises many that he has become majority leader of the Senate, hardly a place lacking intrigue and ambition. It surprises Mansfield also, who is at best a reluctant leader. He didn't want to be LBJ's majority whip, but in 1957 Johnson convinced him. And when Johnson departed, Mansfield refused to take the leadership until President Kennedy, in 1961, personally asked him to.

What has made powerhouses persuade this singularly uncolorful, undynamic man to take on tasks others yearn for? The answer seems to be Mansfield's immense popularity and modesty, which in combination are unmatched in recent Senate history. Republican Minority Leader Hugh Scott expressed a common view in calling Mansfield "the most decent man I've ever met in public life. He's fair. His word rates in fairness above the gold at Fort Knox." Of himself Mansfield has said, "I'm just a lucky man who's had all the breaks, lots of good friends, and who hopes that in small part he has been able to repay the people who sent him here."

The first son of Irish immigrant parents, Mansfield ran away from home three times as a youth. Twice he was arrested and returned, but the third time he managed to join the Navy in 1918 at the age of 14. After stints in the Marines and the Army, mostly stationed in China, he returned to Montana, where he spent eight years working in the Butte copper mines. Unwilling to spend his life deep in Montana mine shafts, Mansfield pulled himself out. By 1930, he had obtained, nearly simultaneously, a high school and a college degree; by 1934 he was a professor of Latin American and Far Eastern history, which he taught for ten years. Mansfield served in the House from 1943 to 1952, during which time he went to China on a confidential mission for Franklin Roosevelt. In 1952 he won a close race for the Senate, where he has since remained.

Mansfield today maintains the same modest competence which characterized his climb. Instead of Johnson's ranch-size suite of majority leader offices, Mansfield took a more modest set; he is equally unusual in hiring no permanent press secretary. His style as majority leader is similarly low-key. "One reason I'm leader is maybe I can keep the party together and prevent us from breaking up into argumentative fragments," he says. In his view, the function of majority leader is to preside more than to lead, to cement factions together rather than to mold them. He has abandoned the practices of counting heads before votes—a pressure tactic at which Lyndon Johnson and aide Bobby Baker used to excel. Should he twist more arms? "In the first place I could not do it," Mansfield answered in an interview. "In the second, if I were to do it and I got away with it the result would be temporary. Sooner or later they'd just tell you to go to hell and do what they wanted to anyway." When comparison is made with Majority Leader Johnson, Mansfield modestly demurs. "It's not a fair comparison. . . . Johnson was the greatest majority leader the Senate ever had," he told the *National Journal*. Former Senator John Williams, Republican of Delaware, caught the difference between the two. "When Lyndon was the leader he liked to play tricks on you. The game was always trying to outfox Lyndon. But I would never try to pull anything like that on Mike. Why, he'd just turn around and say, 'The senator, of course, is perfectly within his rights. . . .'"

If he does not fully tap the powers and prerogatives of his office, Mansfield still has considerable influence in the Senate and the government. He worked with Senator Ted Kennedy to pass the Senate bill giving the vote to 18-year-olds. Mansfield considers this his most significant legislative achievement. He persuaded Senate Democrats to adopt, by a 3–1 margin, a resolution calling for the total withdrawal of all U.S. forces from Vietnam by the end of 1972. On his third attempt, Mansfield managed to get the proposal passed. His sudden move in May, 1972, for a 50 percent reduction in U.S. forces stationed in Europe sent the Nixon administration into a frenzy. They considered Mansfield's proposal serious enough that they launched a massive rebuttal campaign to defeat it—and did.

Yet ultimately, Mansfield has more prestige than power, both because of his own nature and the nature of his office. There is already serious speculation that he will retire as majority leader in the next four years —he has served in that post longer than anyone else— in order to concentrate on his first love, foreign affairs, especially the Far East. But then, he never really wanted to be majority leader anyway.

Carl Albert is the speaker of the House of Representatives, and third in line to the presidency. But the first time he appeared on the House floor back in 1947, the 5' 4", 120-pound legislator was mistaken for a page. (A Republican representative gave him a batch of papers to deliver—which he obligingly did.) Today everybody in the House knows who Carl Albert is.

Like many other politicians, Albert's rise to power and eminence has overtones of Horatio Alger. The son of a poor miner, he studied and wrestled (literally) his way out of Oklahoma and into a Rhodes Scholarship at Oxford. Once elected to the House, "I made it a point to be on the floor all the time I could," says Albert. "I learned the rules of the House, who the members were, how they voted, what they talked about, their problems." His diligence earned him the attention of Speaker Sam Rayburn, from neighboring Texas, to whom he was something between a protégé and a son. This status, when combined with his unflagging integrity (he refuses campaign contributions if they are too big) and his amiable disposition (there is hardly a representative who doesn't like Albert), kept him moving up the ladder. He became majority whip in 1954, majority leader in 1962, and speaker in 1970, all with little or no opposition. Said one congressman in 1970, "The leaders of the House are chosen by the dead hand of the past. Carl will be speaker because Sam Rayburn picked him to be whip in 1954. No one can beat someone who is on the ladder."

While Albert's personal popularity is clear, his effectiveness is open to question. He has at times performed actively and aggressively: shortly after becoming speaker, he held a series of press conferences at which committee chairmen publicized the alternative Congress offered to President Nixon's programs; he worked hard for two proposals that eventually failed: a strong equal-employment bill and a reform that would cut the Rules Committee's arbitrary power. When Congressman

Harley Staggers launched his imprudent campaign to punish CBS television for its program, "The Selling of the Pentagon," Albert engineered Staggers's defeat. But Albert has also occasionally taken positions contrary to the House Democratic majority on important issues such as SST spending, the release of D.C. subway funds, and the "Mansfield Amendment" on Vietnam troop withdrawal. This weakens his influence, as does his reluctance to fully exploit the powers of his station. When, for example, members of the liberal House Democratic Study Group complained to him in 1971 that Wilbur Mills's tax package would not do enough for certain states, Albert implicitly deferred to Mills, saying, "Well, Wilbur assured me it was a lot better than the one last year." ("We just went away muttering," said one of those at the meeting.) Similarly, in 1971 Albert declined to take an official position on a controversy over two versions of the Independent Consumer Agency Bill, for fear of antagonizing Commerce Chairman Chet Holifield who was pushing a weak version. In fact, Albert is careful not to upset the chairmen. "The legislative leadership is in the committees," Albert has modestly said. "You can't even tell a member how he ought to vote, let alone push a chairman."

While Albert doesn't want to push his luck as speaker, he is refreshingly uninhibited in using his influence on behalf of his district. In July, 1972, two Indian tribal leaders came into his office seeking a law to let native American tribes sue each other in court. Impressed, Albert immediately called the first and second ranking members of the House Interior Committee, asked for prompt legislative action, and is getting it. Recently Albert found out that the Naval Ammunitions Depot, the largest employer in his district, was about to be closed by the Defense Department. An officer at the depot tells what Albert did: "He contacted the secretary of the Navy and was informed by the secretary that recommendations had been made to close the depot and that the letter was on his desk at that time. I don't exactly know how Carl did it, but about three or four weeks later, [the depot] was taken off the list of base closures. . . . I understand he went to the president, who gave the order to delete us from the list of base closures."

But history will judge Carl Albert as a speaker more than as a representative. He came to the speakership a full generation younger than John McCormack was when he left it. Young House liberals expected important reforms or at least more dynamic leadership, but so far they have gotten little of either. Like McCormack, he is liked but not too much respected. "Carl Albert's misfortune is that he has no enemies," said a Western representative. "To be a leader who exercises power you have to make enemies. He has pleased everybody and will be elected by everybody and will be indebted to everybody."

Ralph Waldo Emerson's description of Congress as a "standing insurrection" is hardy apt today, if it ever was. Instead of an open system with people and ideas in a state of creative flux, Congress is quite set in its ways. Its rules and rulers encourage secrecy, procrastination, and baronies of power—which in turn entrench the rulers more firmly. Recently there has been some change—recorded votes on amendments, some younger members winding up on important committees —but the change is glacial. The seniority system endures, the right to filibuster remains, and committee chairmen are still grand seigneurs.

The effect is not evenly divided among Republicans and Democrats, liberals and conservatives. Real power in Congress now resides in a Southern Democrat–conservative Republican coalition, both because of their disproportionate control of committee chairmanships and because of rules which allow a determined minority to stymie a majority. The four giants of the Senate in the past fifteen years have been Lyndon Johnson of Texas, Bob Kerr of Oklahoma, Richard Russell of Georgia, and Everett Dirksen of Illinois. The liberal, Democratic East is a vocal but ineffectual guest in both houses. When it comes to dividing the spoils of a federal welfare plan or a federal revenue-sharing plan, why does New York always give more than it gets, and South Carolina get a surplus? It's because New York senators lack the raw power that Southern veterans have stored up. Liberal "success"—like cutting off the SST, or rejecting Carswell—show not that progressives have power, but that they are not entirely impotent.

These wounds are partly self-inflicted. "The liberals are always ten years late in figuring out where the power is," said a Senate staffer. "The liberals scrambled for years for seats on committees dealing with issues that seemed more glamorous, such as foreign policy, or of more concern to their constituents, such as education and labor and housing," writes Elizabeth Drew. "They were loath . . . to move to committees where the work is complex and sometimes heavy going, where they would be outnumbered and outmaneuvered by the conservatives, and where there might be less opportunity for publicity. Many a liberal prefers a press release to power." Nor do liberals take easily to nitty-gritty procedural and parliamentary details which can mean the difference between legislative success and failure. Procedural experts, writes Bella Abzug, "are old-timers, not liberals. The average liberal thinks up what he wants to do and then runs off to somebody else to ask, 'Now what procedural step do I take in order to do this?' Consequently, liberals rarely get anything significant accomplished."

Recent liberal congressmen have tried to alter these patterns. Les Aspin and Wright Patman, for example, challenged Mills's private process of "members' bills," and with some initial success. Representatives Aspin and Michael Harrington got assigned to Armed Services, and Badillo and Chisholm fought their original misassignments. Jerome Waldie of California courageously attempted to get the Democratic Party Caucus to vote no-confidence on Speaker John McCormack; he failed, and earned the leadership's enmity. Morris Udall went so far as to run against McCormack in 1968, even while realizing that his gesture was at best symbolic. When Udall did seriously attempt to become majority leader in 1971, some of the bitter residue from his earlier campaigns hurt his candidacy. Of his defeat by House Democratic whip Hale Boggs of Louisiana, Udall reflected, "The leadership ladder bit—tradition, promotion, seniority—was stronger medicine than I originally thought." But at least Udall made the attempt. Such efforts do represent novel rumblings of change in the Congress, which in turn reflect vibrations of unrest and awareness from outside Congress. It will take accelerating outside awareness, as well as the Waldie- or Udall-type forays, before the closed circle of rules and rulers which control Congress is penetrated.

4

The Broken Branch:
Congress vs. the Executive

I want to be President.
—Senators George McGovern, Edmund Muskie,
Hubert Humphrey, Fred Harris, Henry Jackson,
Richard Nixon, Lyndon Johnson, Eugene Mc-
Carthy, Robert Kennedy, John Kennedy; Repre-
sentatives Wilbur Mills, Pete McCloskey, John
Ashbrook, John Schmitz . . . . *et al.*

During its springtime sessions in 1972, the Senate at
times had difficulty gathering a quorum, because so
many of its members were out campaigning for the
presidency. It now seems logical that a member of
Congress should want to rise to be president, but it was
not always this way. More than a hundred years ago,
in the decades leading to the Civil War, those who remained in Congress—men like Daniel Webster, Henry
Clay, John C. Calhoun—had more to do with directing
the nation's policies than did presidents like Millard
Fillmore or Franklin Pierce. John Quincy Adams ran
for a seat in the House after retiring from the presidency
in 1829; one can hardly imagine Lyndon Johnson or
Richard Nixon doing the same today.

This change in the president's relation to Congress—
the transformation of the presidency into the summit of
prestige and power—happened so long ago that it is no
longer newsworthy. What the newspapers do cover
when they compare Capitol Hill with the White House
are the legislative skirmishes which mark each congressional session. Regularly come reports of showdowns
over bills the president wants and Congress obstructs or

items that Congress has passed and the president
threatens to veto. More recently, the popular image of
the president and Congress has come from Congress's
attempts to limit the president's apparent right to conduct a war for as long as he wants, in the way he
chooses.

The danger of these incidents is their suggestion that
a true struggle is on between two strong sides, and that
whichever side is stronger on an issue will win. This
impression becomes even firmer whenever Congress
seems to dominate the president—as the House Rules
Committee did when it stifled many of President Kennedy's proposals, or as the Senate did in rejecting two
of President Nixon's Supreme Court nominees.

A battle does go on, but the field has been moved
miles within one side's lines. No matter how hard the
Congress may struggle on one issue, it is overwhelmed
by the vastly greater forces of the presidency. Whether
Congress wins or loses, the president ends up on top.
The clearest example of this change is in proposing new
laws—the most basic of Congress's jobs. In the years
before 1900, the heavy majority of laws passed each
year originated within Congress; senators or representatives drafted them, pushed them, saw them passed.
During this century, however, the source has shifted.
The greatest change came at the beginning of the New
Deal, when the president was so firmly in control of
lawmaking that the speaker of the House could address
freshman representatives like a pack of Marine re-
cruits and say, "We *will* put over Mr. Roosevelt's
program." Since then, according to political scientist
James Robinson, Congress has "yielded to virtually ex-
clusive initiation by the executive." Putting it more
plainly, a Republican congressman told a witness from
President Kennedy's administration, "We're not supposed to draw up these bills—that's your job, and
then you bring them to us."

In the last two decades, roughly 80 percent of the
major laws passed have started in the executive branch.
So, even when the president is stymied in one area—as
President Nixon has been, when Congress refused to

pass his six "key proposals"—most of the laws that *do* pass will be his.*

This change is important to all of us, not just the academics or congressmen. For all its flaws, Congress is still the most responsive and open branch of the government. As the executive has grown more powerful, it has also become more isolated. Power has flown to an isolated staff of White House advisers, accountable only to themselves and liable to strong temptations from private interests. These members of the president's staff, along with more traditional parts of the executive bureaucracy, have matched their grip on legislative initiative with control of Congress's other jobs: getting laws passed, apportioning money for them, and reviewing the way they are carried out. These incursions are less newsworthy than antiwar resolutions or nomination fights, but they say far more about what's gone wrong with our government.

Logrolling and Arm-twisting

To persuade Congress to pass the laws he sends them, the president can use the old trick of logrolling. This is a game of trading favors. Usually the president gives away bonbons and pastries, while Congress gives away steak and potatoes. Eager to buy a vote for a bill, the president can do it at little cost by showing up alongside the congressman at a local school dedication, or giving him a pen used at the ceremonial signing of a bill announcing mammoth outlays for his district. It is more than vanity which lets congressmen succumb to these blandishments. For many of them, especially those who have moldered away in the House for years, a presidential pat on the back can be a big boost. Even

---

* Of course, there are exceptions. In consumer and environmental legislation, recent Congresses have been far more creative than presidents. The Joint Committee on Atomic Energy has been the main force behind nuclear energy development, and Senator McGovern's Select Committee on Nutrition and Human Needs forced a reluctant administration to expand food stamp programs.

if he's from the other party, the impact is to let the
voters know that their man circulates with the biggies
in Washington.

If his daily schedule prevents traveling to the sticks,
the president can give a congressman the feeling of
power even more easily. In the last few years—as
congressional unhappiness about a war it knows little
about has risen—this has become a more necessary
tactic, and one at which recent presidents have become
adept. It has the masterful simplicity of any great plan:
the president or one of his confessors (recently, Henry
Kissinger) takes the congressman aside and whispers a
few words in his ear. The congressman, obscure and
ill-informed only seconds before, suddenly becomes an
insider. He understands the burdens that the president
faces—the ideas which those trivial men still carping
back in Congress cannot fathom. As Thomas Rees of
California described one of these briefings:

> Last week [February, 1971] President Nixon held
> a briefing for a hundred or so Democratic mem-
> bers of Congress on Vietnam, revenue-sharing, and
> government reorganization. . . . I was looking
> forward to comparing the styles of President Nixon
> and ex-President Johnson. The leadoff was the
> Vietnam briefing.
>   Nothing had changed. There were the same star-
> studded, medal-bedecked uniforms, but on differ-
> ent generals. The same top-secret charts and the
> same self-assured masculine tones explaining ex-
> actly how we were winning the war to save the
> fighting little democracy of South Vietnam. . . .
>   White House briefings make you feel so good.
> Instant solutions pop up, and problems recede
> back into their holes.

It is a comment on how starved for glamour Congress
is that even scraps of information can buy their loyalty.

The more usual type of presidential patronage is dis-
tribution of government favors. Chet Holifield, 69-year-
old congressman from California, learned some of the

nicer refinements of the technique in 1971. Holifield represents the city of Whittier, one of many areas the president holds dear, but he is important to the White House because he is chairman of the House Government Operations Committee. In 1971, the president announced a proposal for reforming the government: an executive reorganization plan, announced in a special address, which would have lumped seven existing departments into four giant agencies. To no one's surprise, Congress hated the proposal; since each congressional committee takes as much interest in the executive department it oversees as an Italian prince did in the security of his small domains, Congress naturally resists any change. Holifield leapt to the front of the opposition, denouncing "the whole grandiose plan" as "political grandstanding for the purpose of putting Congress on the defensive for the political use of the president in the 1972 campaign." His opposition mattered, because his committee would consider the plan.

But Holifield had other interests besides the minutiae of executive organization: main among these was nuclear power plants. Like other early boosters of the nuclear-plant program, Holifield hoped that the final stages of the system—breeder-reactors—would be finished before he was. By coincidence, many of Holifield's constituents also worked for one of the main contractors, North American Rockwell.

Inconveniently, the Nixon administration did not share Holifield's passion for breeder-reactors. Not, that is, until March 26, 1971, when Nixon invited Holifield to take a ride on the presidential jet, *Air Force One*. There is no way to know what was said on the flight, but afterwards Nixon pushed the breeder-reactors, and Holifield found new virtues in the reorganization plan. Never a great bargainer, Holifield made another flight five months later in the plane, with similar results. Nixon again pushed breeder-reactors and Holifield supported an administration version of a consumer-protection law.

Since the many offices on the president's side of government determine when and where much money will be spent, the president can offer other favors. For John Stennis of Mississippi and Margaret Chase Smith of Maine, the president's Defense Department has arranged contracts for local shipyards. Even if the decisions are already made, the president can use them as bargaining tools by making them appear to be the product of a diligent congressman. And so, when President Nixon was fighting for Senate confirmation of his Supreme Court nominee G. Clement Haynsworth, he channeled an announcement of a $3-million urban renewal grant through the office of West Virginia Senator Jennings Randolph (instead of the usual route, through Congressman Ken Hechler, who represented the district). *You scratch my back:* Randolph looked to the voters as if he'd fought for extra money. *I'll scratch yours:* Haynsworth got Randolph's vote.*

Similar favors can come almost spontaneously from the depths of the executive bureaucracy. In 1960, the Agriculture Department was alarmed by the results of congressional redistricting. Its long-time champion— chairman of the Agriculture Appropriations subcommittee, Congressman Jamie Whitten of Mississippi— had been redistricted to run against another incumbent, Cong. Frank Smith. According to Cong. Richard Bolling, "Certain employees of the Agriculture Department fed Whitten politically advantageous announcements of department plans for new projects to be built in the new congressional district. These actions gave the clear impression to the voters of that district that Whitten was in a position to do more for them, if elected, than was Smith."

The president's role as leader of his political party opens up whole new crates of favors to hand to congressmen. These include promotion of the loyal: in return for unquestioningly promoting administration

---

* Although the Haynsworth and Carswell nominations gave senators a taste of their rights and powers, they should not be taken as signs that the president's appointment power is seriously curbed. During Nixon's first year in office, Congress had to approve 72,635 appointments—most of them with only a few seconds' "deliberation."

measures in Congress, Senator Robert Dole of Kansas has become chairman of the Republican National Committee. When dealing with congressmen from the opposite party, the president may also give the political blessing of "benign neglect." President Nixon applied this tactic during the confirmation debate over Supreme Court nominee Harold Carswell. Trying to get the vote of Democratic Senator Howard Cannon of Nevada, according to Richard Harris in *Decision,* "an administration spokesman called and promised that if he voted for the nomination, he would get a 'free ride' in the fall—that is, a weak Republican opponent." Mainly because of its crudeness, this free-ride offer failed. Then the administration rolled its machinery of vengeance into view, to demonstrate the other half of the presidential influence equation: what the president gives, the president can take away. When the post-Carswell election came in Nevada, Cannon found himself facing not a patsy, but an opponent, reportedly selected by Spiro Agnew, who got the full rhetorical and financial backing of the national party. ("You can win a Senate seat cheaper in Nevada than anywhere else," one executive aide explained.)

Like party favors, the benefits of government programs can also be snatched from the lawmakers, to manipulate them into position. This use of powers which are governmental, not presidential, is alarming, but the practice is so common that almost any case of lawmaking provides examples. In the debate over the SST, several senators got the message that public works funds—supposed to build hospitals or schools in their states but which had been temporarily suspended for "budgetary reasons"—might remain forever in limbo if the senators voted wrong. When Haynsworth was being inspected, one Midwestern senator—who, as Richard Harris has put it, was "ready to back Shirley Temple if the president named her to the Court"—got a call from the U.S. Department of Agriculture. He was told that the fertile mulch of agricultural subsidies, which USDA had applied to the state for years, might be applied no more unless the senator voted for Haynsworth. In this case, the pressurers had broken the cardinal rule in dealing with the Senate: they had made the senator's subservience all too clear and left him no room to save face. He responded with an explosion of rage and a No vote.

If the carrot and stick technique fails, the executive moves into the massive-retaliation stage of persuasion, trying to drub the irritating legislator out of Congress. Charles Goodell could tell many tales about this process. Long an unexciting representative from upstate New York, Goodell landed in the Senate to fill Robert Kennedy's seat. In the more invigorating air of the Senate, he expanded and became quickly a major irritant for the Republican administration. After failing administration tests on Haynsworth, Vietnam, missile systems, and other issues, Goodell had to run against both the Republicans and the Democrats in the 1970 election. Although he was running on the Republican ticket, Goodell endured regular haranguings from Vice President Agnew, and knew that the administration backed Conservative party candidate James Buckley, the eventual winner. After the 1970 election, President Nixon foreswore any further fratricidal ventures, but liberal Republicans like Senator Charles Mathias still glance nervously behind them when they vote against the party line.

The president's stranglehold on recalcitrant congressmen tightens an extra bit when he takes advantage of his enormous propaganda power. Only partly out of envy, congressmen bitterly resent the slavish attention which television and newspapers give the slightest utterance from the Executive Oracle. Compared with the difficulty a representative has getting his proposals into any printed page besides the *Congressional Record,* the president has not only free advertising for himself and his program, but also a guaranteed pulpit from which to blast his enemies. When faint-hearts had been making trouble about the war policy, presidential aide H. R. Haldeman appeared on the "Today" show to suggest they were traitors. In the same vein, the elusive Henry Kissinger told a group of prisoner-of-war families that the people delaying their sons' and husbands' releases were the doves of the Congress. Stating the problem none too harshly, Senator Stuart Symington replied that Kissinger's speech "appears to be an attempt to brand in the public's mind those of us who oppose some aspects of foreign aid as something less than good Americans."

When even ideological name-calling does not succeed, the executive can dig right down to the bottom of its "Pressure Tactics" barrel for a final few surprises. In the 1970 senatorial elections, for example, presidential aides Charles Colson and Harry Dent, according to the *Washington Post,* helped create a series of smear ads against Democratic candidates in eight states, charging that men like Maryland Senator Joseph Tydings were doing their best to bring legalized drugs and unpunished murders to the land. Following the White House example, the Internal Revenue Service also turned to personal pressure when political argument failed. In 1971, while the IRS was dreaming of a grand new office building, Representatives Ken Gray and Jack McDonald were delaying the plans in the Public Works subcommittee. As if by magic, Gray and McDonald found out that their personal tax returns were being audited by the IRS. The timing, the IRS said, was coincidental.

Thought Control

Like the private interests which prefer to avoid the bother of lobbying by getting the "right kind of men" elected in the first place, the executive would just as soon pass up all the arm-twisting and character assassination. The way to do this is to make sure the congressmen never get to know anything that would put wrong ideas in their head. With a thoroughness that would have done credit to the old antipornography crusaders, the presidents and their staffs have done their best to control what gets into the congressmen's minds. Congress, too, has played its part by failing to open new sources of information.

The formal name for this is "congressional liaison,"

but the best metaphor for it is an Oriental court in which the sultan, sealed off from the world by high walls, knows only what his courtiers and mandarins whisper in his ear. In time, he becomes their tool, since his world is bounded by what they choose to tell him.

To a surprising degree, Congress knows little more than what the president tells it. When it gets ready to pass a new law for missiles or highways, it turns to the Defense Department and the Federal Highway Administration. While a stray outside witness—from a public interest group, or a wandering refugee from academia—turns up at congressional hearings, the bulk of what congressmen find out about new laws comes from the president's departments. Congress itself is largely to blame, since committees can choose their own witness list.

Explanations for this range from sloth to inability; a major practical barrier is a shortage of staff. Another important reason is that Congress has not figured out that "Information Is Power." Executive departments started to get the message shortly after World War II, and jumped into action. Led by the ever-vigilant Defense Department, they set up the congressional liaison system—which is another phrase for congressional lobbying by the executive. Starting with one lone assistant secretary of defense for congressional liaison, the network has grown to include at least 531 agents from twelve departments.* They have charmed their way into not only the congressional heart but its buildings as well; the alleged space shortage on Capitol Hill does not keep the Army from spreading its offices over a huge suite in the Rayburn Office Building.

The points of stashing these agents within the halls of Congress is to make sure Congress knows the right

---

* In 1970, the Center for Political Research reported the following liaison staffs: Defense, 312 (with 177 for the Air Force); Army, 95; Navy, 67; Treasury, 28; Post Office, 33; Securities and Exchange Commission, 35; Office of Economic Opportunity, 10; Veterans Administration, 43; Transportation, 28; State, 26. The CIA has a liaison office, but refuses to say how many people work in it.

facts about each department. In theory, the liaison agents are not supposed to "influence" the congressman, especially by appealing to the public to put pressure on Congress. A 1913 law, the Executive Anti-Lobbying Act, says "no funds may be used . . . to influence in any manner a member of Congress to favor or oppose, by vote or otherwise, any legislation or appropriation by Congress." The only exception is that executive agents may "communicate with Members of Congress on request, through proper channels"—a clause that has been opened up to let the whole liaison troop roll through. No one has ever been prosecuted under the law, although it is routinely violated—as with the administration's efforts for the SST. Ready to answer any congressional request with an illustrated brochure about, say, New Steps in Defense or Advances in Securities Regulation, ready even to anticipate requests and shove possibly interesting documents into open hands, the liaison offices steadily mold congressmen's minds. Assuming that politicians, like mountains, can be worn away by light but steady pressure, they see constant evidence of their success when Congress rubber-stamps executive bills.

Many congressmen are unhappy about the hazards of relying on the executive, but their moans are often muffled as they sink deeper and deeper into the executive lap. Congressman John Rooney, for example, uses FBI agents to help his committee evaluate the performances of the Justice Department, of which the FBI is a part. The House Ways and Means Committee relies on experts loaned from the Treasury to help draw up committee reports. When it convenes in closed session to vote on tax bills, the doors stay shut to all outsiders except dozens of Treasury Department officials who comes to advise. When the House Public Works Committee wants to evaluate new transportation plans, it turns to the Transportation Department. What's wrong with this cooperation? Not just danger that the departments will deceive—as a former liaison for the Equal Employment Opportunity Commission said, "We don't lie to them. We just tell them what will be the most persuasive, and don't volunteer all the facts." The real issue is that Congress might as well not even bother studying or approving the executive's plans when all it has to go on is the executive's information.

The final problem is that Congress often can't even get the information it specifically asks for. More and more, the real policy decisions are made, not by the secretary of state, or the Department of Health, Education, and Welfare, but by the president's personal staff—the Henry Kissingers and John Ehrlichmans and Peter Flanigans. These men don't have to talk unless they want to. The Senate Foreign Relations Committee can always get commonplace figures like the secretary of state to testify, for what it is worth; one week before the Cambodian invasion of 1970, Secretary of State William Rogers calmly said that nothing big was about to happen. Henry Kissinger, on the other hand, is recognized as the most important foreign policy adviser in the government—but he has never publicly appeared before Congress. Senator William Fulbright considered it a great coup when Kissinger deigned to eat lunch with him, in lieu of showing up before the Foreign Relations Committee. The domestic policy advisers—John Ehrlichman and Peter Flanigan—similarly turn down invitations to testify. In fact, the only senior White House aide to testify before Congress during the Nixon administration has been Flanigan—who gave in to public pressure and testified about the ITT affair, but only after giving a specific list of questions he would and would not answer.*

As the presidential staff grows strong from sustenance gained at the expense of its satellite departments, Congress might well contemplate two further threats to its power. One is the president's blunt intrusion into the mechanics of legislating. Like the "liaison officers,"

---

* This simultaneous oozing of power from Congress to the executive, and from the executive department's to the president's own staff, has led to strange alliances. As part of his committee's assault of the president, for example, Fulbright has sponsored bills that would strengthen the State Department; it, unlike Kissinger, is subject to congressional scrutiny.

the presidential staff is not supposed to lobby Congress. But, as columnist Jack Anderson has reported, "Lobbyists for the Nixon administration swarm over Capitol Hill in flagrant disregard of the law. Before an important Senate vote, they often operate right out of Vice President Agnew's office, a few steps from the Senate floor." Another example of this backstage lobbying came in August, 1972, when the Senate was voting on the president's arms-limitation agreement with the Russians. As reported in the *Congressional Record:*

> *Sen. Church:* Some could be misled as a result of what is going on right now out in the Vice President's office. I was taken in there a few minutes ago and shown two models. One model is of the [Russian] SS-9. It stands . . . fully 2 feet off the table. It is a very menacing looking weapon. One is especially struck by the size of the scale model of the SS-9 when it is compared with the model, also to scale, of the [U.S.] Minuteman missile which sits next to it. . . .
>
> *Sen. Fulbright:* May I ask the senator, since I have not been invited into the Vice President's room, whether the Vice President is now a substation of the National Security Council? Is it used for the purpose of influencing the votes of the senators? . . . I thought it was a ceremonial hall for the Vice President. However, it is now an exhibit hall for the National Security Council. Is that what it is now?
>
> *Sen. Church:* Apparently so.
>
> *Sen. Fulbright:* Mr. President, this is rather peculiar in view of the fact that officials of the National Security Council, including Mr. Kissinger, refuse to come to the Hill for committee hearings. Now instead of coming to the Hill to testify, they have the exhibits here and ask senators into the Vice President's room so they can see these models.

Unlikely as it sounds, the other danger of increased presidential power is the *even greater* amount of pandering to private interests it encourages. After even a brief look at Congress's many cozy ties to private lobbies, it is hard to imagine that any other part of the government could be as thoroughly influenced. Recent presidents, however, have not just responded to the secret desires of private industries, but have actually spurred them on. The Clean Water Bill of 1971 illustrates the story.

Trying to please both sides, President Nixon had talked himself into a corner on this bill. Early in 1971, he had nagged Congress for not passing his environmental bills, concluding with a rhetorical outburst:

> The fundamental fact is that of choice. We can choose to debase the physical environment in which we live, and with it the human society that depends on that environment, or we can choose to come to terms with nature, to make amends for the past, and build the basis for a balanced and responsible future.

Congress responded more eagerly than Nixon had expected, and by November the Senate had passed a strict water-quality bill that meant high pollution-control outlay for many industries. The law's sponsors, notably Edmund Muskie, had packed in a series of tough clauses, including one which let the federal government veto state water standards if they seemed too lenient.

In public, the president's staff opposed the bill because it infringed on "states' rights." But four days before that, in an extraordinary display of concern for the struggling corporations of America, the president's staff had held a pep rally to encourage private interests to fight the bill. "The notion that somehow industry 'got to' the administration and pushed them into [opposing the bill] is really the reverse of what happened," said Douglas Trussel, vice-president of the National Association of Manufacturers. "The administration took the initiative, and many executives were ignorant of what was going on." At the November 4 meeting—

when seven trade representatives came to the White House to see presidential aides John Whitaker and Richard Fairbanks—Fairbanks made what one trade agent called "an incredible speech":

> His pitch was, "We fought a lonely battle over here on this bill. Where the hell were you guys when we needed you? We could have gotten some of the worst provisions changed if you'd gotten into this in a big way."

This view of the president as promotion man is hardly cheering to those who dream of a separation of Business and State. But it cannot come as a surprise, since Congress is so weak—when so many administration officials are on brief sabbatical from corporate work. President Nixon's former congressional liaison, Bryce Harlow, had to leave his job as congressional liaison for Procter and Gamble to come to the White House. When he left the administration, he returned to P&G where he teamed up with Mike Manatos—former special assistant for Lyndon Johnson. John Connally, man-of-all-work for Nixon, has been a private-interest lobbyist; Peter Flanigan, before coming to the White House in 1969, was an investment banker and president of the Barracuda Tanker Corporation of Liberia. Lyndon Johnson's former aides, Clark Clifford and Myer Feldman, now work as lawyer-lobbyists in Washington law firms. All in all, they make the presidential lobby into what Lambert Miller, senior vice-president of the National Association of Manufacturers, called in 1971 "the most pervasive, influential, and costly of any such in the whole country."

Power of the Purse

Money can't buy happiness, but it should buy power. If Congress gets ignored, or lied to, or lobbied, or manipulated in passing legislation—why should it care? It still holds the purse strings. Let the president send up missile plans or domestic programs: since Congress determines where the money goes, it should be able to reorder the priorities to suit its taste. War getting costly? Trim down the funds. People starving in the city? Send in a little more aid. President bowling congressmen over? Just use the Power of the Purse to put him in his place.

In practice, Congress has not been able to find salvation through appropriation. Even more miserably than in passing laws, Congress has failed to manage the budget. It retains the right to control the budget, but not the ability to do so. In the few cases where it does not dutifully rubber-stamp the president's programs (usually with a few modifications to salve its conscience), it finds that the president can do what he wants anyway—and often keeps Congress totally unaware of what he is doing.

As in information-gathering techniques, Congress has simply been passed by time in the budgeting system. Forty years ago, economists figured out that if countries wanted to avoid the boom-and-bust cycles which had led to the Great Depression, then *someone* had to keep track of how much money was coming into the government (through taxes) compared with amount flowing out. The president was set to take on this job, since the Budget and Accounting Act of 1921 had given him the power to draw up a "national budget" for the whole federal government. Congress might have tried to share the power—and, for a few brave years in the forties, it did prepare a "legislative budget"—but it gave up. In this simple abdication we have the full story of why the president appropriates money now, not Congress. He who makes the budget sends the money on its way. Those who "approve" the budget are spectators.

The trouble Congress has dealing with the budget is a much exaggerated version of its troubles passing laws: it arrives too late and knows too little. By the time the congressional appropriations committees sit down to examine budget requests, the president's staff has already invested more than a year of research and scheming in them. Through rounds of haggling and calculation, the Office of Management and Budget

(OMB) and the various executive departments have worked out compromise estimates for the next year's programs. When they send the figures to Congress, they're not in the mood to make many more changes. However much HEW may have protested (in the secret counsel of the executive) when OMB decided to end a special education program or shift funds elsewhere, few bureaucrats want to bring the complaint into the open before Congress.

Congress, too, is in a hurry. It gets the budget estimates at the start of each calendar year—and must pass new budgets before the next fiscal year starts in June. Even if the Appropriations committees had staffs as large as the OMB, that would leave them only half as much time as the budgeters had. With Congress's diminished resources, five months is barely time to insert the pork barrel items each legislator loves. The Senate, which waits for the House to act, has even less time.

The Appropriations committees still make an attempt to review the budget. When they do, they find the familiar roster of information problems facing them. Whom do they interview to find out more about the programs and estimates? Why the same officials who drew up the program—whose testimony must be approved by the OMB. Congressmen often do a creditable job of asking about successes and failures, but the instances of surprising revelations are few. At times, the agencies may even dissemble in front of their congressional superiors. Usually this takes the form of telling less than one knows. Each agency, for example, prepares a program memo—an evaluation of its different projects—to send to the OMB at budget time. Congressmen do not get to see the memoranda. More overt cases of deception usually involve the Pentagon—whose customs of waste, conflict of interest, secrecy, and classification may confuse the line between truth and fiction. In the mid-sixties, congressional committees were reduced to speechlessness by Defense Secretary Robert McNamara's virtuoso budget presentations. Now, they have become more suspicious. Recently, for example, Defense experts rolled out a chart showing the relative strengths of Soviet and American fleets. A suspicious congressional investigator later discovered that the figures had been doctored to exaggerate the Pentagon claim that the Navy needed more ships. While the American fleet total had been reduced to take account of ships idle in port, the Russian total was not.

Even this distorted testimony is better than nothing at all, which is sometimes the alternative. When Wisconsin's Senator William Proxmire began to press Budget Director Robert Mayo, asking questions about items in the Defense request, Mayo loftily replied that "the president's flexibility is better served by not getting into a debate on what is and what is not in the Defense budget."

If relatively true information, and more time for study, are two reasons why the OMB can make a budget and Congress cannot, the third is that Congress works in a fashion so fragmented that no overall planning is possible. There are parts of the legislative process where that doesn't matter: those who authorize agricultural subsidies don't need to know a thing about new airplane projects. But when dividing a set amount of money among many competing needs, there must be one giant funnel through which all the decisions pass. OMB and the White House provide that; Congress is a funnel turned upside down. Budget power is split between the House and the Senate; between the dozen fiefdoms which each Appropriations subcommittee creates; between taxing committees and spending committees; between committees that pass new programs and committees that allot the money. As long as there is someone else to take an overview, then Congress's anarchy is not disastrous; it simply means that the president will make the budget and Congress can make only minor, tinkering repairs. A country can run this way (as ours has for the past twenty years)—but it faces the prospect of one-man or one-agency rule from the White House (as ours has for the past twenty years). The solution is not to hobble the executive, bringing it down to Congress's level, but rather to make Congress move into the modern budgetary world. As the *Journal of Commerce* put it: "What Congress needs—'as we and many others have said before'—is a prestigious joint committee on the budget. It needs a committee to perform for the legislature the function performed by the [OMB] for the executive department."

Despite these obstacles—information, staffing, fragmentation—when Congress applies its pressure to one small point in the budget, it can, like a spike heel, make a dent. In August, 1972, Congress brazenly took $1.7 billion from the Defense budget and added the same amount to the appropriations for the Departments of Labor and HEW. The change, said Senate Majority Leader Mansfield, "demonstrated Congress's sense of priorities—a will to spend more for health, schools, and manpower programs, and less for providing arms for allies." President Nixon then vetoed the HEW bill, and Congress conceded.

More often, Congress's changes reflect a motive less subtle than "sense of priorities": the ancient rite of carving up the pork. Such gothic figures as South Carolina's Mendel Rivers or Mississippi's John Stennis provide easy illustrations of how closely committee chairmanship may be tied to government benefits. This is not to suggest that only foxy Southern politicians reach into the greasy barrels up to the elbows. In fact, New England patricians and Iowa farmboys succumb to the same temptation. Senator Warren Magnuson, the farthest cry from a Southerner in the Senate, has used his chairmanship of the Commerce Committee and his high rank on Appropriations to funnel outlandish amounts of public works money to Washington state. As numerous reference works show (the best of them are the *Almanac of American Politics,* by Michael Barone and others, and the Nader Congress Project profiles), the simplest way to tell whether a district is rich or poor in government projects is to see how long its representative has been in Congress.

The success of pork-barreling proves, in its perverse way, that Congress has not entirely faded out of the appropriations picture. Throughout the executive bureaucracy, administrators cater to the whims of powerful legislators. Often, in the desire to please a powerful and fussy chairman, the executive will bow to his demands, no matter how bizarre they may be. For example, when Assistant Secretary of the Navy Graeme Campbell Bannerman came to the House Armed Services Committee to ask that the outmoded midshipmen's dairy at Annapolis be closed, committee chairman Mendel Rivers made it clear that he would defend the middies' right to home-made ice cream:

> *Congressman Rivers:* I just want to tell you if you have any notion of closing it I would advise you to get it out of your head because if you have any notion of closing it, it will be written into that law and I would rather hear you say you have abandoned that idea. . . .
>
> *Secretary Bannerman:* The plan to close it has not been abandoned. . . . Mr. Chairman, if I had my "druthers" at this moment, I would close it.
>
> *Rivers:* I'm glad to hear it. You don't have your "druthers."
>
> *Bannerman:* That is entirely possible.
>
> *Rivers:* That is a fact of life. . . . Those boys over there . . . want to get that milk, and you can't get it. I lived through Parris Island. . . . They were cutting out the ice cream at Parris Island.
>
> Now they don't get any ice cream, period, unless they happen to get a little old thing at lunch. Before . . . they had all these machines making ice cream. . . . Everybody was happy. . . .
>
> *Bannerman:* I think the original . . . creation of the dairy . . . was undoubtedly a very wise thing. This happened about sixty years ago. I guess at that time there was no assured source of healthful milk.
>
> I think for this reason the dairy was created. . . .
>
> There isn't any question now, however, in anybody's mind, that you can't get good healthy milk commercially. We are all drinking it.

Rivers: You can't get it in abundance.

Bannerman: We are doing it, Mr. Chairman, all over the country.

Rivers: I don't think we can get the milk in abundance. We own it; we operate it; why get rid of it?

Such small-scale congressional tyranny is about as reassuring a sign of Congress's power as are its piqued delays and obstructions of selected administration bills. If Congress's contribution to the budget is silly or venal, should even these powers be taken away? A better solution would be to restore some significant budgetary power to Congress. To do this will require a legislative budget, a congressional OMB, or some similar dramatic change.

The Executive Shell Game

Even if Congress passes a law on its own initiative and funds it according to its own ideas, the executive can still get its way. In the civics textbooks, there is not a hint that the president can run programs that Congress has outlawed, or delay forever laws the Congress thinks have gone into effect. But a set of innocuous-sounding practices—"impoundment," "reprogramming," "transfers"—gives the president surprising and almost unbounded control over the government's financial affairs.

The catfish farmers of Tupelo, Mississippi, know what impoundment can mean. In 1965, Congress had voted $32,500 to build an experimental catfish hatchery in Tupelo. The Interior Department, however, had scheduled the national catfish project for extinction. Congressmen knew that, but they decided Tupelo's farm was worth preserving. If the president was sufficiently annoyed, they reasoned, he could veto the bill. Johnson signed the bill, but the money never got to Tupelo. It lay "impounded" in the federal treasury.

How could this happen? The legal answer is a clause in the 1950 Budget Act. "In apportioning any appropriation," it says, "reserves may be established to provide for contingencies or to effect savings whenever savings are made possible by or through changes in requirements, greater efficiency of operations, or other developments." In other words, the president need not spend all the money Congress gives him, if the reasons are good. This sounds acceptable in theory. In practice, the president has repeatedly withheld funds, often for blatantly political reasons. In these cases, the Congress might as well never have bothered to propose bills, pass them, and appropriate money. By impounding funds, the president can ignore the Congress:

• In 1971, Congress appropriated $8 million extra for the Veterans Administration hospital system—intending that the VA use it to hire 8,600 more workers, including 800 more doctors. Meanwhile, the OMB refused to release $71 million of VA funds, which prevented the hiring of 11,000 people.

• The administration asked for $2 billion for the food stamp program in 1972; Congress added $200 million more. Instead of vetoing the bill, the president just told the OMB to set the "allowable spending" level at $2 billion.

• As thirty-six senators complained in a letter to Nixon, mass transit funds totaling $900 million have been frozen by the OMB.

• The Farmers Home Administration lends money to rural families to improve their farms; but it lends $75 million less than Congress intended, because of an OMB freeze.

• According to Congressman Paul Rogers, chairman of the Public Health subcommittee, the administration has spent only half the money Congress voted for anticancer research.

• While the Environmental Protection Administration complains that tight funds hamper it, the administration requests less money than authorized by the Clean Air Act of 1970, and spends less than is appropriated.

• In water pollution control, the administration spent only $262 million of the $800 million appropriated in

1970, and $475 million of a $1-billion appropriation for 1971. Together with freezes in urban renewal, highway construction, and dozens of other programs, the impoundments totaled $12 billion in 1971, when Congress finally got the first complete list of them.

The impounded funds may be used as political bargaining pieces. In the fall of 1970, California Democrat B. F. Sisk found that some $10 million was being withheld from the Wetlands Water Project in his district. Since his district had an extremely high unemployment rate, Sisk complained. There was no action until October 31, only a few days before the election in which Republican Senator George Murphy would try to hold his seat against John Tunney. Murphy appeared on a telethon that day with Ronald Reagan and Richard Nixon. Reagan announced that, due to Murphy's dogged efforts, the water project money had been released. A week later, Murphy had lost. Since then, Sisk has not been able to get the promised funds from the OMB. But, late in 1972, the funds suddenly began to flow more quickly than the project could absorb them. Election time had come again.

Unlike the executive branch's lead in the appropriations process, this is not simply one branch getting a superior grasp on a power the other could share if it tried. The impoundments represent an arrogation of power which Congress is unable to fight, unless it amends the Budget Act. Presidents have always had some discretion over the timing of federal spending, but as political scientist Louis Fisher points out, "An entirely different situation has developed under the Nixon administration, where funds have been withheld from domestic programs because the president considers those programs incompatible with his own set of budget priorities. . . . To impound funds in this prospective sense—holding onto money in anticipation that Congress will enact an administration bill—is a new departure. . . . Impoundment is not being used to avoid deficiencies, or to effect savings, or even to fight inflation, but rather to shift the scale of priorities from one administration to the next, prior to congressional action." By spending money only where he pleases, the president writes his own laws.

Its resentment smoldering, Congress began to challenge the use of impoundment. In 1971, North Carolina Senator Sam Ervin, quick to notice branches of constitutional balance, held special hearings on impoundment. "What concerns me," Ervin said, "is the use of impounding practice to void or nullify congressional intent." At the hearings, Ervin accomplished what many believed impossible: he managed to get a list of all impounded funds from the OMB. The list, the most recent version of which appears on pages S 3847–3849 of the *Congressional Record* for March 31, 1972, is the best available guide to the comparative priorities of Congress and the president.

The OMB submitted another list in 1972, this one showing an apparent total of "only" $1.7 billion impounded, not the $12 billion which OMB had admitted the year before. Ervin quickly detected the crude accounting trick the OMB had tried. The $1.7 billion was only the impoundments for which the executive branch could find no other excuse; they were purely political decisions which, in Ervin's words, "fly in the face of the constitutional duty of the Congress to set the priorities of our government." Another $10.5 billion more had been withheld for "routine" or "administrative" reasons. Together, they total $12.2 billion—an increase from 1971.

Until 1971, and Senator Ervin's hearings, congressmen fought impoundment on an item-by-item level. Since impoundment's greatest advantage is its secrecy—there are troublesome news stories when the president vetoes a clean-water bill, but no one knows if he freezes the funds—Congressmen have tried to focus attention on the cases they have discovered. Shortly before the 1970 elections, for example, criticism from Democrats led to the release of impounded education funds. More recently, Ervin has proposed a bill which would require the president to tell Congress whenever he impounded money. If Congress did not ratify the impoundment within sixty days, the president would have to spend the money. The obvious intention of the bill is to restore the constitutional balances—to eliminate the possibility of a secret veto on an item he doesn't like. Because of opposition from Holifield and others, the bill will probably not pass in this session.

Impoundment is only half the picture. If the president could *spend* money with the same abandon with which he withholds it, his bypass of Congress would be complete. He's not there yet; but, like impoundment, "reprogramming" and "transfers" have vastly expanded the president's ability to run the country the way he wants.

Defense Secretary Melvin Laird learned about these tactics in 1971, when he was worried that Congress would cut off $52 million he wanted to send as military aid to Cambodia. In August, 1971, the Joint Chiefs of Staff told Laird not to fret; he could get the money (1) by transferring the $52 million from economic aid programs to military aid, (2) by applying $52 million from some other program with both military and civilian uses, which could then be sent to Cambodia, (3) by jacking up the Army's request by $52 million, and then "loaning" the money to Cambodia, or (4) by declaring some of the Army's equipment obsolete, and then selling it at bargain rates to Cambodia.

In an article in the *Washington Monthly,* journalist Timothy Ingram pointed out the full range of devices the executive branch can use to write its own appropriations. His list includes:

• Transfer authority: The secretary of defense is allowed to shift up to $600 million from the program Congress authorized to some other use. He may also send funds from civilian to military programs if "security" demands it. A provision of the Foreign Assistance Act says that 10 percent of the money earmarked to any one country may be rechanneled to another. President Nixon took advantage of all these loopholes when financing the Cambodian invasion of 1970. By the time he asked Congress for $255 million to pay for the project, he had already spent $100 million of it.

• "Obsolete" excess stocks: At a time when Congress kept reducing money for aid to Taiwan, the Defense Department kept a flow of military goods running from its piles of extra weapons.

• Secret funds: Louis Fisher estimates that $15–20 billion of appropriations, mainly for defense, is never even explained to Congress. While some congressmen denounce this—but cannot, of course, find many details to support their argument—the late Senator Allen Ellender took a milder view. "What can you do?" he asked. "I believe in having one strong commander in chief. Once war matériel is ordered, no member of Congress—no one—is supposed to follow through to see how it's used. It's to be used by the commander in chief as he sees best."

• The pipeline: Some appropriations have to be used up during the fiscal year or returned to the Treasury. Others have "full-funding" clauses, which means that the money stays in the department's hands if not spent. Ingram estimates that the Pentagon has $50 billion waiting in the pipeline—enough to run the war with no congressional appropriations, and enough so that for the last several fiscal years the Pentagon has spent more than Congress voted it.

• Cost overruns: A Defense Department statute allows the Pentagon to pay for cost overruns whenever the "national defense" is at stake. Liberally defined, this has excused many billions of dollars in overpayments. The Pentagon can go even further to accommodate erring contractors, by changing the terms of the deal along the way. When, in 1968, the Pentagon discovered that its C5-A was going to cost roughly $2 billion more than estimated—$5.3 billion instead of $3.4—its accountants obligingly changed the contract from a fixed-price one to "cost-plus," an open ticket for whatever the company wanted to spend.

Congress can now and then rebuke the executive for the worst of these abuses. But, as Timothy Ingram says,

It can threaten fund cutoffs, mandate the use of funds as directed, and exercise its oversight function. But as the executive detours proliferate,

Congress discovers that its problems go beyond relative weakness. Increasingly, Congress is less the underdog and more the old fighter who is no longer even invited into the ring.

Congress's "Oversight"

Congress is, or ought to be, the watchdog of the public purse. Even if it no longer initiates legislation, even if it abdicated much of the budget-making process, even if the president can play a shell game with the funds Congress has appropriated, Congress should vigorously and constantly yap at the executive's heels to make sure that funds are not squandered, that incompetent administrators don't fritter taxpayer dollars away on worthless or marginal projects, that the executive is obeying the laws and enforcing the laws. Congress is the only representative of the people—whose money, after all, is being spent—that has the power to see that the executive is doing its work.

With felicity rare for congressional jargon, this area is called "legislative *oversight*." The double meaning is a perfect guide to the topic. For just as Congress tries to oversee its laws once they are passed, much of its weakness here is due to oversights. The reason for oversight—or "review"—is that laws don't always live up to their ambitions. Everyday experience provides examples of legislation that has not accomplished its purpose—such as the "War on Poverty." A series of lesser-known illustrations shows how pervasive the problem is:

• In 1967, after a series of nauseating articles about meat packinghouses, Congress passed the Wholesome Meat Act. By 1969, all state slaughterhouses were supposed to meet federal standards or be taken over by the U.S. (except for a special one-year grace period in some cases). The deadline came and went, and federal inspectors moved into only one state. The others were approved—not, in most cases, because they had improved their standards, but because the federal standards had dipped to meet them.

• The Civil Rights Act of 1964 said that no federal funds could be spent to support projects practicing racial discrimination. Five years later, the Agriculture Department was running an extension service which, in many states, was overtly segregated.

In addition, Congress is responsible for the "quasi-legislative" agencies. These regulatory bodies, such as the Interstate Commerce Commission and the Federal Trade Commission, officially function with powers delegated by Congress. Because Congress cannot deal with each railroad rate claim or advertiser's complaint, it passes the powers to regulatory agencies. Congress is still responsible to see that the powers it has delegated to the agencies are used well.

• Finally, there are the problems which affect any bureaucracy—waste, inefficiency, corruption. Someone has to guard against possible abuses, and in theory Congress is the one.

The procedures for congressional oversight range from special hearings, or investigations of an agency, to informal queries, or questions at appropriations time. The important fact about all of them is that they have proved increasingly inadequate. As Jerry Cohen and Morton Mintz say in *America, Inc.,*

> In theory the deficiencies of the independent regulatory agencies and of units of the executive branch with regulatory powers would be alleviated and on occasion maybe even corrected if Congress reliably and seriously exercised its responsibility to oversee their performance. The unhappy truth is that reliable, serious, and sustained oversight is the exception rather than the rule on Capitol Hill. Not even in remote degrees have the oversight mechanisms of Congress kept pace with the enormous growth of the executive.

The reasons behind the failures of oversight are displayed clearly in one of the few *successful* instances of oversight. The House Government Operations Committee is, in the main, a useless appendage. Under the gerontocracy of, first, Representative William Dawson of Illinois, and recently Chet Holifield, its investigations into government performance have led to more trivial reports than substantive ones. But its Subcommittee on Intergovernmental Operations is another story. The subcommittee's chairman, L. H. Fountain of North Carolina, shows few of the traits of an agitator. In the midsixties, however, he became obsessed with the Food and Drug Administration and the ways in which it was not fulfilling its responsibilities. For the last six years, Fountain's subcommittee has grilled a succession of FDA commissioners on an impressive range of topics. The agency has had to defend its policies on the sale of birth control pills, on control of pesticides, on recalls of poisonous foods, on removal of cyclamates from the market, and, most recently, on its approval of the cattle-fattening but cancer-causing hormone DES. Aided by two committee staffers, one of whom once worked for the FDA, Fountain's committee has come closer than any other to exercising good oversight.

That is fine as far as it goes—but consider what has been left out in the process. One of the committee's Republican members, Guy Vander Jagt of Michigan, complained in a letter to Fountain that the committee's single-minded inquisition into the FDA was forcing it to ignore many other areas. The committee was simultaneously responsible for at least a dozen other agencies, many of them as big and important as the FDA. Even with best intent, Congress cannot supervise the ever-expanding, ever-more-complex activities of the federal government. After a while, the frustration may make congressmen give up: as a member said, "You wait two hours so you can get a shot at the secretary of defense, and then it lasts only five minutes. The only thing you know is that you're getting bullshit from him, and there's nothing you can do about it."

Many congressmen show a decided distaste for oversight, because it seems pointless and because it does not interest the electorate. Bills sponsored and projects obtained can be used in the constant quest for reelection, but oversight usually wins little public attention.

There are exceptions—as Fountain shows at the best end of the scale, and Joseph McCarthy at the worst—but not frequently enough to give legislators an incentive to spend their time in oversight hearings. It is significant that during the last few years, the more effective oversight has come in "glamour" areas: consumer protection (Fountain and others), Defense spending (led by Senator William Proxmire), foreign policy and the war (Senator Fulbright's Foreign Relations Committee has taken a notable step by hiring its own investigators to make on-the-spot studies in Laos, Greece, and elsewhere). At times, Appropriations committees also conduct effective oversight. Jamie Whitten's House Agricultural Appropriations subcommittee, while promoting some of its chairman's pet plans, also reviews agriculture programs in detail. Other areas, equally important but less newsworthy, are for the most part neglected.

Congressmen may at times even go out of their way to avoid oversight. Thus, Wright Patman of Texas, usually an effective overseer, accused Nixon of unfair price and profit guidelines. If the administration didn't shape up, Patman warned, he might hold oversight hearings. But he also made clear this was only as a last resort: "It should be emphasized that we prefer to avoid oversight hearings," he said. And when, in 1967, a few rash congressmen suggested that revelations about the CIA's role in funding the John Hay Whitney Trust Fund might merit an investigation, Everett Dirksen quashed the idea, saying, "I can't imagine the British Parliament investigating the British intelligence system."

The New Czars

If Congress has abandoned its oversight responsibilities, two outcomes are possible. The agencies and departments might roll along, unsupervised, or someone else might pick up the reins Congress has dropped. The second has happened, with the presidential staff in the driver's seat.

To see how the White House has succeeded, we need

only review why Congress failed. To do a good job of oversight, Congress would need, first, a much larger staff of investigators. It would need some system for regular reviews of the agencies, instead of relying on haphazard coverage. It would need to know when policies or performance changed. Most of all, it would need to know that what the administrators told it was true.

Rolled together and placed on the White House staff, these reasons describe the Office of Management and Budget. As part of the reorganization which changed its name from the Bureau of the Budget, the OMB was given greater responsibility for reviewing the impact and worth of programs, as well as their budgets. This, of course, is another way of phrasing "oversight." The OMB has gone at its task with a vigor the Congress might well imitate.

Because of its privileged position within the executive, the OMB can exercise both before- and after-the-fact review. Before any programs get under way, OMB analysts have screened budget requests and program proposals. While the projects are running, the OMB parcels out the money, or withholds it. And when agencies propose new rules or decisions, the OMB can often screen them before Congress has its chance.

This has led to a situation in which an appointed agency, entirely shielded from public scrutiny, has more impact on administrative policy than any elected congressman, or group of them. A few illustrations show the danger. While the president should have the right to coordinate the policies of the Labor Department or HEW, he has no place setting the policy or priorities of the independent agencies, which are not part of the executive branch. But in February, 1972, the chairman of the Federal Power Commission, John P. Nassikas, came to Congress to complain that the president was doing just that. Nassikas told a Senate subcommittee that his agency was disappearing into the White House. Because he must send his budget requests through the OMB—not directly to Congress—his agency is subject to the same policy coordination as the executive departments. This OMB screening, Nassikas said, "results in some control of the policies, programs, and priorities of the independent regulatory agencies."

More than "some control" was evident in the OMB's treatment of the Federal Communications Commission. As its most ambitious project ever, the FCC undertook a mammoth audit of American Telephone and Telegraph. In 1972, however, the FCC dropped the study, saying it was short of funds. Senator John Pastore pointed out that the OMB had withheld $1.8 million from the FCC—enough to pay for the project. Only after another wing of the executive—one section of the Pentagon, one of AT&T's largest customers—complained that AT&T was being let off the hook, and offered to supply spare auditors if needed, did the FCC resume the study. (Shortly afterwards, Defense Secretary Laird withdrew the offer.) Drawing on this example and Nassikas's testimony, Senator Lee Metcalf has proposed a bill which would let the independent agencies send their budgets directly to Congress, avoiding the OMB filter.

The OMB can interfere even more directly in the agencies' policy process. A famous memorandum, issued on October 5, 1971, requires *all* federal departments and agencies to send the OMB copies of new regulations "which could be expected to . . . impose significant costs on, or negative benefits to, non-Federal sectors" (that is, private industry) before they are publicly announced in the *Federal Register*. Congress has no such chance for a preview screening of regulations; the public certainly does not. And OMB has even altered the regulations. In 1971, the Environmental Protection Agency drew up a new set of guidelines for state air pollution control boards. They were tough— so tough that OMB diluted them before they were published. Peter Bernstein of Newhouse News Service described the process:

> OMB intervened at the request of Commerce Secretary Maurice Stans, Federal Power Commissioner John Nassikas, and several other federal

officials who share big industry's viewpoint. Government sources say [EPA Administrator William] Ruckelshaus defended the original draft at subsequent meetings, but finally lost out when two key White House aides intervened on the side of big industry. They were presidential assistants John D. Ehrlichman and Peter M. Flanigan.

A year later, in 1972, the OMB struck again. The EPA prepared a report on a plan to clean the Great Lakes. It was ready for Nixon's February 8 message on the environment, but along the way it disappeared into OMB's maw. Congressman Abner Mikva of Illinois then found out about the plan; with twelve other congressmen, he appealed to OMB to reconsider its decision. The plan would have cost $141 million in its first year—less than just the research costs for the space shuttle.

While exercising this tight supervision over executive departments and "independent" agencies, OMB can also interfere with whatever attempts Congress may make to assert its own supervisory power. The most important technique for doing so is OMB's screening of testimony administration witnesses plan to give Congress. Combined with the witnesses' usual ellipsis, this means that congressmen are often frustrated when they try to oversee the executive. On July 26, 1972, a Pentagon witness demonstrated an extreme degree of his noncooperation. Appearing before a Senate subcommittee investigating "environmental war" (rainmaking) in Vietnam, Benjamin Foreman, assistant general counsel at the Defense Department, refused to answer Claiborne Pell's questions:

> *Pell:* Are you under instructions not to discuss weather modification in Southeast Asia?
> *Foreman:* Yes, sir.

The expanded OMB is just one part of the extreme suction of executive power toward the White House, which began years ago but has accelerated under Nixon.

Perturbed by the growth of what he called "palace guard government," Congressman Morris Udall commissioned a study in 1972 to see just how many people were working directly for the president. After considerable difficulty, Udall found that the presidential staff had grown 25 percent in Nixon's first three years, from 1,766 members to 2,206. The annual growth rate had quadrupled from its level under Johnson. The OMB had grown by 60 percent, the National Security Council by 50 percent, and nine new satellite agencies had joined them under the presidential aegis, including the Domestic Council, the Office of Telecommunications Policy, special assistants to the president, the Council on Environmental Quality, the Office of Intergovernmental Relations, and several more. The total payroll for the executive office of the president had risen from Johnson's $32 million to $41 million in fiscal year 1973.

Udall's study rose from a sense of congressional unease about presidential government; another manifestation of unease came from Congressman J. J. Pickle, in June, 1972. Offering an amendment to cut appropriations for the OMB by $4 million, Pickle said:

> The Office of Management and Budget is the unseen government of today. It is an invisible force that has more to do sometimes with your own district than you do. . . . This is not a severe cut . . . just to try to get the office to tighten its belt a little and let them know Congress should be running the government and not the Office of Management and Budget.

Aside from its denunciations, what more does Congress have to throw against the OMB? Not too much. For supervision of the executive, congressmen must mainly rely on committee staff members.

In all, the congressional committees have 1,600 staff members, and half of them are secretaries or clerks. For the range of jobs to be covered—from appropriating money to passing laws to overseeing the executive—this is too few. Congress's other potential ally is the General Accounting Office, the legislature's staff of investigators. The GAO is a relatively bright spot in Congress's general prospect, and any reassertion of congressional power will probably begin there. But its manifold problems and weaknesses once more emphasize how Congress has lost control.

The GAO is an arm of Congress; its job is to help congressmen study the government. Before 1950, it spent most of its time doing purely accounting work. After the Korean War, however, Comptroller General Joseph Campbell led GAO into more adventuresome areas. Campbell began a series of studies of war industries and produced, during the fifties, reports on profiteering and wasteful construction. Campbell, who had been treasurer of Columbia University before coming to the GAO in 1954, favored a candid style rare in government reports. His audits were studded with phrases like "excessive cost" and "congressional intent as to cost limitations circumvented," shockers in a society accustomed to squishy government prose.

Campbell soon ran afoul of the Defense Department and the defense contractors; by 1965, they had conveyed their unhappiness to Chet Holifield. In his response to the Pentagon complaints, Holifield illustrates one of the most potent executive tactics for controlling the legislature: by setting up one congressman with favors and patronage, the executive can count on him to beat down other critics. Holifield's Committee on Government Operations held hearings on the GAO in 1965, which Holifield began by mentioning "the great concern that has been shown in industry circles, and, recently, in the Department of Defense over the difficult and sometimes awkward situations created by the GAO audit reports." By the end of the hearings, the GAO had been tamed. It agreed to a list of conditions, including an agreement to stop using company names in the reports and an effort to be more "constructive."

With that behind it, and with cautious bureaucrat Elmer Staats now as comptroller general, the GAO walks a fine line between toadyism and giving offense, but it still is the most important investigative tool Congress has. It showed its split personality well in a recent study of, once again, defense contractors. While the audit itself was factual and critical—revealing that seventy-seven weapons systems would cost $28.7 billion more than estimated—and that the average profit rate was a fantastic 56 percent—the GAO sent the report to the industry before publishing it, and then incorporated many industry alibis into the text and toned down its own changes.

Despite its occasional disappointments, the GAO offers congressmen their main defense against the analysts of the White House and the OMB. Whenever congressmen ask, the GAO will make studies of specific problems. And in 1970, it was authorized to make cost-benefit studies of programs. Unfortunately, few members of Congress take advantage of the service. An average of 300 requests per year come from Congress—nearly all of them from a few enthusiasts. Between July, 1969, and April, 1972, for example, of the 160 Senate requests, 37 came from Proxmire; of the 200 House requests, 11 came from H. R. Gross of Iowa, 6 each from two other congressmen, and the rest in ones and twos from others.

If, as we have argued, information is the key to the executive's power, Congress will have to do more than ask for an occasional GAO study. What is needed is a major overhaul of Congress's information sources, so that it can deal on a more equal basis with the executive. As former White House special assistant Joseph Califano wrote recently in the *Washington Post:*

> The Congress is presently the separate but unequal branch of the federal government. . . .
> The basic reason for the decline in congressional effectiveness and status, however, lies not with the executive branch or some federal bureaucrats.
> . . . Responsibility for its separate but unequal status rests largely with the Congress itself. . . .
> The Congress is dependent upon the executive

branch for most of its information, with an occasional and too often superficial assist from outside experts. . . .

Congress has ignored the revolution in analytical technology. . . . The Congress has only three or four computers, and those computers operate in large measure on payrolls and housekeeping matters. . . . Contrast the executive branch, which now has some 4,000 computers working almost entirely on substantive policy issues. . . .

The stark fact is that neither the Congress nor any of its committees has the consistent capability —without almost total reliance on the informational and analytical resources of the executive branch—of developing coherent, large-scale federal programs.

Incapable of creation, with authority but little power, Congress has become a broken branch. If it becomes upset with the executive branch, it expresses itself in the only way it can—by obstruction or delay. The country needs more.

As a secret government replaces the one elected by the voters—as Congress placidly hands its remaining powers over, one by one, to the president and his advisers—the president's thirst for power seems actually to increase. Along with assuming Congress's normal powers of lawmaking, appropriating, and overseeing, the president in the last few years has increasingly extended the powers inherent in his office:

• He has made law by "regulation," as with the "Accelerated Depreciation Range." As part of President Nixon's economic measures in 1971, this gave corporations tax breaks worth some $3.9 billion. When Congress began to complain about the enactment of this tax charge through "alterations in Treasury regulations," Nixon agreed to submit it to Congress. On short notice, it was rammed through by Congressman Wilbur Mills, whom presidential aides had courted by flying to his Arkansas home.

• In foreign affairs, the president has obviously had

just as free a hand. Whenever Congress prepares to
curb the presidential war—by repealing the 1965 Gulf
of Tonkin resolution, by voting a series of end-the-war
amendments in the seventies—it finds either that (as
Nicholas Katzenbach told a hearing in 1967) the president didn't need the Tonkin resolution in the first place,
or that (as Nixon said after an antiwar resolution was
passed in 1971) the president can simply ignore antiwar
clauses.

• With a slightly more plausible pretense of legality,
the president has used Executive Orders to write laws
Congress won't give him. In 1971, after Congress had
turned down President Nixon's request to revive the
literally useless Subversive Activities Control Board
(which had so little to do that its members would not
come to the office for long stretches), Nixon evaded
Congress by issuing an executive order to keep the
board in operation.

• The foreign-policy equivalent of executive orders
are executive agreements. Although these secret deals,
signed by the president and a foreign country, bind the
nation with the force of treaties, Congress knows
nothing about them. According to Senator Clifford Case,
some four thousand of the agreements are now in effect.
In an attempt to limit them Case has proposed a bill
which would make the president report the agreements
to Congress and have them approved.

If this is not tyranny, autarchy, abuse of power, then
the Constitution writers had nothing to fear. Congress
has its problems, but the only way to restore balance to
the government is for it to stand up for the rights it
retains—and to fight for the return of those that have
been taken from it.

5

Lawmakers as Lawbreakers

It could probably be shown by facts and figures that there is no distinctly American criminal class except Congress.

—Mark Twain

"What this country needs is a little law and order." The cry comes from many quarters, but there is little agreement about who the violators of law and order really are: wise-guy protesters, troublesome blacks, street criminals, executives whose firms exploit and pollute, governmental agents who trample over the law in an attempt to enforce it. Yet a good place to start would be the American Congress. The most obvious reason is symbolic: if chosen men have the power to make the law, then they should respect the law. If they do not, they can scarcely expect that others will.

Corruption involving criminal conduct has shaken Congress at least since 1873, when the House censured two members for their roles in the Crédit Mobilier stock scandal. While Congress and the country have passed through fundamental metamorphoses since then, one constant theme has been the public's suspicion of the people it sends to Washington. This was not the constitutional mistrust that had plagued the Founding Fathers—the gnawing fear that men in power would become tyrants. Instead, it was the suspicion of personal venality, that the men in government were somehow turning a profit. In 1965, Gallup pollsters found that four times as many people thought that "political favoritism and corruption in Washington" were rising as thought them falling. Two years later, as Congress washed its hands of Adam Clayton Powell, Gallup asked whether the revelations about Powell had surprised the public. Sixty percent thought that Powell's offenses—which the questionnaire called "misuse of government funds"—were fairly common. (Twenty-one percent disagreed.) Powell had protested, in victimized anguish, that he was only one public scapegoat among many quiet offenders. "There is no one here," he said to his accusers, "who does not have a skeleton in his closet."

The skeletons vary in size. The smallest are the personal peccadilloes—which are the stuff of public amusement, scorn, and regular exposure by Washington columnists. Outweighing these in importance are the systematic violations of Congress's own rules and laws, offenses which are not quite crimes, but which are not quite cricket, either. Conflicts of interest are the next biggest skeletons in congressional closets. Finally, there is the *summum malum* of congressional crime, instances of bribery, perjury, and influence-peddling. Taken together, the pervasiveness of lawbreaking amounts to a grim commentary on those who govern us.

Not Quite a Crime: Peccadilloes, Rules, and Laws

Congressmen are people, and subject to the same temptations and flaws as other people. At times, their visibility makes them suffer more for their failings than they otherwise would. An omission or mistake which would pass unnoticed in a plumber may become big news when attached to a politically important name. This does not excuse congressional misconduct. Just as the public expects higher standards of personal morality from those who instruct its children than from those who fix its drains and pipes, so it expects high standards from those who make its laws.

In order to assure them freedom to exercise their duties free from harassment, congressmen are granted immunity from arrest for statements made, or actions taken, in Congress, or while coming from or going to Congress. This desirable privilege, however, has frequently been abused by congressmen caught in unsavory escapades. In his prepresidential days, for example, Senator Warren Harding was surprised by two New York policemen while visiting friend Nan Britton in a hotel room. As the police prepared to arrest him on charges of fornication, carnal knowledge, and drunken driving, Harding successfully argued that as a senator he could not be arrested. It was hardly what the Constitution intended for congressional immunity, but it worked well here.

Several years ago, Texas Congressman Joe Pool rammed his car into the back of another car stopped at a red light. Pool refused to accept a traffic ticket from a policeman and, later, from his sergeant. Instead, he repeated over and over, "I am a congressman and I cannot be arrested." Unimpressed, the police held him for six hours before releasing him. "He kept saying he was a congressman," said the policeman, "but he didn't look like one or sound like one." Later, Pool confided to a friend, "I thought they couldn't arrest a congressman unless he'd committed a felony. But it turns out they *can* unless he's en route to or returning from a session of Congress."

They *can,* but they *don't.* On the way to a party in the summer of 1972, Mississippi Congressman Jamie Whitten—who normally conducts himself with decorum —ran a stop sign in Georgetown and struck a car, an iron fence, two trees, a brick wall, and another car on the other side of the wall. Whittten said his accelerator stuck, but an investigating officer said at the scene, "The guy's been drinking; there's alcohol on his breath. I don't think he's drunk. But he's shook up." No arrest was made and no charges were filed. "The first thing [Whitten] did," said the owner of the wall, "was to get out of the car and begin shaking everyone's hand."

The same scene is played out in endless variations. Imagine the discomfiture of the Washington cop who, in August, 1970, watched a large car cruise through a red light and gave chase, lights flashing and siren screaming. More than a mile later, the fleeing car lost its spirit, pulled to the side of the road, and disgorged

Senator Strom Thurmond. Thurmond claimed he hadn't run the light, and was immune even if he had. The policeman and his chief went along. Their embarrassment, however, could not compare with that of another D.C. policeman who, in May, 1969, had the bad luck to be in Congressman Charles Chamberlain's way. Chamberlain's car hit the policeman and then drove on. Onlookers caught up with him within four blocks, but Chamberlain successfully claimed immunity from ticketing or arrest. So did Congressman Peter Kyros, who had trouble like Whitten's on the same Georgetown streets. He careened from side to side down one road, hit two parked cars, drifted around a corner, and hit another car. He then left the scene. To the casual observer, this has elements of being a hit-and-run. To the police, it was a pointless and nonenforceable case: Kyros was "immune from arrest when going to and from the halls of Congress"—even though he had actually been going to and from a dinner party.

Annoying as these cases might be, they are small potatoes. They involve single, unplanned romps, not deliberate self-enrichment or serious affairs of state. If this were the extent of congressional lawlessness, we could all sleep a little easier at night.

But it's not. Worse is the hypocrisy of congressmen violating their own rules. A classic illustration is junketing. Congressmen who legislate about foreign affairs or military bases may do a better job if they've seen some of the areas for themselves. That's the theory. In practice, however, many trips are personal vacations (with family) rather than public fact-findings. In 1971, 51 percent of Congress, or 53 senators and 221 representatives, took foreign trips at public expense; the total cost to taxpayers was $1,114,386. Hong Kong and the Caribbean turned out to be favorite destinations for those supposedly seeking self-education. "Scratch hard in December," one congressman joked, "and you'll come up with a quorum in Hong Kong." There may even be motives beyond the chance of a vacation. "Those who do get away," Jerry Landauer has written in the *Wall Street Journal,* "will enjoy little-known opportunities [double-billings, for example] for lining their own pockets—opportunities that some have exploited in the past."

A second hoary example of bending the rules for private benefit is abuse of the franking privilege—the congressman's right to free postage. Every time you receive mail with his signature where the stamp usually goes, you are receiving franked mail. In theory, the frank can only be used for official business and never for political mail. The line is fine, and the effort it would take to inspect the hundreds of bins full of mail which roll down congressional office corridors every day would hardly be worthwhile. The cost of abuse can still be serious. In 1968, Senator Everett Dirksen was found to have given some of his franked envelopes to an overtly political organization—a Republican voter registration group. There was no estimate of the cost involved, but there was in an earlier case involving Senator Robert Griffin. After looking through some of the newsletters Griffin had sent out during the 1966 campaign, the Post Office decided that some were political campaign material. In a typical, doomed display of strength, the Post Office demanded $25,000 from Griffin to pay for the postage. Griffin, astonished, said that his mail was no more political than anyone else's. This gives scant consolation to the Post Office or the taxpayers, but it removed the heat from Griffin. The Post Office conceded the struggle with the droll statement that use of the frank is "a matter strictly between the member of Congress and his conscience."

Large-scale juggling of committee rules and committee staff is also widespread. Committee chairmen, as chapter 3 noted, can be tyrants. When it serves their purposes, they can simply ignore the rules, or, when it serves their purposes, they can become maniacal defenders of every conceivable rule and technicality. "It's my game, baby," Chairman Adam Clayton Powell once explained to the grumbling members of his House Labor and Public Welfare Committee.

But one rule is almost universally violated: committee chairmen use staff members who are assigned to the committee as if they were their own personal employees. It is almost impossible, for example, to separate men who work for Senator Warren Magnuson from those who are supposed to serve the Commerce Committee, which Magnuson chairs. This springs less from any special avarice in the chairmen's souls than from the committee and seniority systems themselves. The fond references that a chairman will make to "my" committee shows how deep the confusion runs. When a chairman lifts a researcher from "his" committee and puts him to work on some other task, more than the committee suffers. The system of fortresslike power bases, built around the mighty chairmen, grows stronger as well. Before his downfall, Senator Tom Dodd reportedly had thirteen of the twenty-one staff members of the Juvenile Delinquency subcommittee working for Dodd's office. Occasionally, voices rise in complaint—as a *New York Times* editorial did against a similar abuse by former Congressman Charles Buckley, who chaired the House Public Works Committee—but toleration is the rule.

Congressmen suffer equally mild twinges of conscience about using their own staff members for political campaigns. The element of abuse is clear: staff men are paid by the government, not by the senator or representative; they are paid to serve *the office,* not to help the man who happens to be in office to stay there. In 1968, the two Senators Kennedy admitted that twenty of their staffers were working on Robert Kennedy's presidential campaign. If other senators do not reveal how many of their staffers serve reelection drives, it is probably because no one realizes it's wrong. When interviewers from the Nader Congress Project asked about this practice, few congressmen realized it was illegal. But it *is* illegal: Public Law 89-90 says an assistant can't be paid "if such does not perform the services for which he receives such compensation, in the offices of such Member . . ." Because the law is so widely violated, violation becomes custom, and custom replaces law. There are many instances of this phenomenon. Nearly all congressmen violated the archaic 1925

Federal Corrupt Practices Act (replaced in 1972), which aimed to limit campaign funding and to require some disclosure of campaign finances, yet no one has ever been prosecuted for it. An 1872 law directs House and Senate officials to deduct from a member's salary a day's pay for each day's absence, except for illness; in the last hundred years this has been done exactly twice, although there are absentees daily.

Nor is Congress always attentive to even international or constitutional law. Congressman John Rooney, for example, has managed to obstruct American funding of the International Labor Organization because he fears its leftist leanings. In so doing, he violates our UN obligation to support the ILO. Similarly, the whole Congress defied UN agreements with one clause of the 1972 Military Procurement Act. In one of its shoddiest exhibitions—since, according to many witnesses, alcohol affected some members in the late-night debate—the Senate on September 30, 1971, passed a provision requiring the president to break the international embargo against Rhodesia by buying Rhodesian chrome. In April, 1971, a federal district court judge said that the 117 senators and representatives who were officers in the Army, Air Force, or Naval Reserve violated "the principle of separation of powers." No congressman, according to the Constitution, may hold any other position in the government. As of this writing no congressional reservist has voluntarily resigned his commission.

In feudal societies, man and job were identical. The king and the shepherd lived their roles every hour of the day. When 5:30 rolled around, they did not put down their work and retire to identical houses in the suburbs. The king had his courtiers and courtesans to remind him of his rank; the shepherd slept with his sheep. Though things have changed since Louis XIV said *"L'état, c'est moi,"* the pull of old ways is strong— especially to those on top. Like their feudal predecessors, the men who make our laws begin to see themselves as part of the law itself. They are only temporary potentates, brief occupiers of office—but in their few moments of power they feel themselves as durable and as permanent as law. They know that they will decide the rules that the rest of us must live by. If they can shape and manipulate the laws that are to come, can they not manipulate the laws which already exist? "Men tinged with sovereignty," Senator Paul Douglas once said, "can easily feel that the king can do no wrong." The privileges of the office—the staff, the prestige— inevitably start to seem like natural rights. In most cases, congressmen do not think they are doing wrong. For such small stakes—avoiding a traffic ticket, junketing to Hong Kong—few would consciously hazard the glories of office. If money were their only goal, they could earn $30,000–$40,000 by giving speeches, or they could follow George Smathers's route from the Senate to the wealthier fields of Washington lobbying. The lawlessness we see is simply the result of guidelines gone rotten from neglect.

Conflicts of Interest

Congress correctly demands a high standard of impartiality from those it confirms for executive and judicial appointments. In 1969, when President Nixon tried and failed to get Judge Clement Haynsworth onto the Supreme Court, the most compelling reason against the nomination was that Haynsworth had tried cases involving businesses in which he held small bits of stock. When industrialist David Packard was nominated as assistant secretary of defense, Congress required that he put $300 million of his personal fortune in a "blind trust," one which manages the money entirely out of Packard's sight. The ex-president of GM, Charles Wilson, and the ex-president of Ford, Robert McNamara, had to unload $2.7 million and $7.1 million respectively of their companies' stock before being confirmed as secretary of defense. The rationale behind these requirements is biblical and clear: since no man can serve two masters, Congress insists that federal officials put their private interests aside before assuming public duties.

Unfortunately, this diligence stops when it comes to the congressmen themselves. No one scrutinizes their stock holdings to check for potential conflicts; no one insists that members sell sensitive shares. The only group with the power to screen the members—their voting constituency—is usually too ill-informed to make any serious judgment. And such conflicts are not considered a crime. In many states they violate the law, but not in Congress, simply because Congress, which writes the laws, chooses not to call what it does illegal.

With so few barriers against it, potential conflict of interest becomes commonplace in Congress. "If everyone abstained on grounds of personal interest," former Senator Robert Kerr claimed, "I doubt if you could get a quorum in the United States Senate on any subject." Kerr's own position neatly illustrated the problem. As a millionaire oilman from Oklahoma, Kerr stood to lose or gain huge sums, depending on the government's tax rules for oil. As a powerful member of the Senate Finance Committee, Kerr was one of the men who decided what the tax laws would be. It does not take long to see the conflict. "Hell," Kerr bragged, "I'm in everything."

Conflicts of interest in Congress take two main forms: business dealings and legal practice. Banks are the most obvious illustration of the first. In 1971, according to the National Committee for an Effective Congress, one hundred representatives held stock in or were officials of some financial institution. A dozen also served on the House Banking Committee. Nine of them had at some time accepted loans at special reduced rates from the National Bank of Washington.

Indeed, favors from banks to congressmen are frequent. In 1962, the first new national bank to receive a District of Columbia charter since 1931 let Senator John Sparkman—then heir-apparent to the chairmanship of the Senate Banking Committee—buy $10,500 of its shares at preferred terms. Congressman Seymour

Halpern got even more personal attention. While struggling to pay off loans outstanding, Halpern in 1969 managed to get another $100,000 from banks in unsecured loans. His committee was considering banking legislation at the time. The First National City Bank of New York, for one example, loaned $40,000 to Halpern while its lobbyists were pushing for a mild version of the bill Halpern was considering.

The same pattern extends to other business holdings. From evidence turned up in 1969 financial disclosure forms, *Congressional Quarterly* estimated that 183 congressmen had interests in companies which either did business with the federal government or were subject to federal legislation. Eleven had interests in airlines, for example, 59 in firms with substantial defense contracts, 54 in oil and gas, 25 in power and light, 20 in radio and television, 19 in farms and timberland, and 16 in real estate. In the late 1960s, Clarence Brown of Ohio, for specific example, held the majority stock in a broadcasting station—and sat on the House subcommittee regulating broadcasting. Brown might have been wise enough to keep his personal affairs out of public decisions. But whenever he took a stand—such as his opposition to public television—his financial stake in the outcome gave at least the appearance of impropriety. He was not alone. The late Robert Watkins, a former Republican congressman from Pennsylvania, was the chairman of an interstate trucking firm whose profits depended on rules passed by Watkins's House Commerce Committee. James Eastland, the Mississippi Democrat who is president pro tempore of the Senate, and his wife received $159,000 in 1971 in agricultural subsidies; at the same time, he sits on the Agriculture Committee and votes against ceilings on farm subsidies.

One of the few congressmen who have bothered to defend such self-serving behavior openly is Senator Russell Long of Louisiana. Like Kerr, Long is an oilman. In the five years before 1969, his income from oil was $1,196,915. Of that, $329,151 was tax-free, thanks to the curious oil depletion allowance. Long is also chairman of the Senate Finance Committee, which recommends tax plans, including oil depletion clauses, to the Senate. A conflict of interest? Not to Long. "If you have financial interests completely parallel to [those of] your state," he explained, "then you have no problem." Even if it were true that the interests of a state and all its people can be lumped with that of one giant industry —which it is not—the haughty premise that lies behind this reasoning is alarming. What Long is saying is that each senator is alone the sufficient judge of his own propriety. Once he convinces himself that his companies are really in the best interest of his folks back home, "then you have no problem." It must ease Long's conscience to know that he is helping others when he helps himself.

Occasionally there are men for whom even these lush fringe benefits of political office are not enough. They count the moments wasted which they must spend on the tedium of bills and votes. Such a man was George Smathers. Even while serving as Florida's senator, Smathers was melancholy. "A person with my background can make more money in thirty days [as a lobbyist]," he said, "than he can in fifteen years as a senator."

In preparation for the easy days ahead, Smathers spent the closing days of his Senate career collecting IOUs from private interests. According to *Newsday,* Smathers led a posse of Florida congressmen in a secret attempt to salvage a floundering Florida company, Aerodex. Because of what the Air Force called "poor quality work which was endangering the Air Force pilots and aircraft," the Defense Department wanted to cancel a multimillion-dollar contract with Aerodex. After Smathers's effort, the contract stood.

In 1969, when Smathers retired, he claimed his reward. He became a director of Aerodex and got an attractive deal on stock: $435,000 worth of it for $20,000. The company also put Smathers's Washington law firm on a $25,000-a-year retainer. Smathers is now comfortably installed as a lobbyist, fulfilling his earlier exuberant prediction that "I'm going to be a Clark Clifford. That's the life for me."

The second important type of conflict of interest comes from congressmen who maintain legal practices. The moral problem here is subtler than that of the oilmen or bankers. A lawyer's business, like a doctor's or writer's, is built on reputation and skill. But when a lawyer also holds government office, his clients might conclude that he can do more for them than another person of similar talent. A widely circulated, widely respected study by the New York City Bar Association strongly condemns the lawyering congressmen. They are the fiduciaries of the public—administrators of public functions, the Bar study says. Accordingly, they must administer this public trust for the public's benefit, not their own. Instead, "law practices have played a disproportionate role in the history of congressional scandals."

More than a century ago, New Hampshire's Daniel Webster kept in practice for his Senate orations by appearing as a private lawyer for the Bank of the United States. He argued the private bank's case some forty-one times before the Supreme Court. There was no Committee on Ethics then, and Webster did not have to conceal the relation. When, in his senatorial role, he was considering legislation to extend the bank's charter, he wrote his clients to remind them that "my retainer has not been received and refreshed as usual." While the standards change, certain practices do not. The irrepressible Thomas Dodd, writing to his Hartford law firm for more money, stated the problem candidly. "I'm sure you know that there's a considerable amount of business that goes into the office because of me. Many men in public life receive a steady income from their law practices because of the value of their association [and] my name and association is a realistic fact which definitely has value."

Dodd is gone, but (according to Common Cause) there were still fifty-seven congressmen affiliated to law firms in May, 1972. One was Sam Gibbons of Florida. He sits on the House Ways and Means Committee; there he judges tax bills whose clauses can mean profit or loss for corporations. Gibbons's local law firm in

Florida has among its clients six of the country's largest insurance firms; the second biggest car rental firm; and the biggest grocery chain in the South. Congressman Joshua Eilberg also has a law firm. One of its clients is the National Liberty Corporation, a mail-order health insurance firm. Eilberg lauded National Liberty in the pages of the *Congressional Record*. Customers trying to choose an insurance plan could thereafter read advertisements claiming "National Liberty commended in the *Congressional Record* of the United States Congress." (Eilberg later repudiated this insertion, saying National Liberty had misused it.)

If a congressman can endure the Bar Association's frowns, there is little to stop him from keeping up his law practice. There is a point, however, when the law imposes a limit. An 1863 statute forbids congressmen-lawyers from representing clients who have claims before the federal government. To avoid embarrassing problems while keeping the business thriving, congressmen have therefore devised an ingenious "two-door" system. On the front door of the law firm is the congressman's name; through this door come the many clients who value his help. Another door is just the same, except the congressman's name is missing. Here enter those proscribed clients with claims before the government. The ruse is within the letter of the law, but it still irritates purists. Journalist Robert Sherrill, for example, has said that Congressman Emanuel Celler's double doors are "one of the longest-standing and most notorious embarrassments to Congress." To this, Celler has had a standard reply. "Your constituents are the final arbiter of any conflicts, and I'm always reelected."

In 1972, after fifty years in the House, Emanuel Celler lost in his Brooklyn Democratic primary.

Crime and Punishment

It takes no special knowledge of franking laws or staff rules to understand the overt crimes, the calculated offenses against law and morality, committed by congressmen. Motives are easy to find: when the potential payoff is millions of dollars, risks for some people become worthwhile. The numbers are grimly impressive. In the last five years, five congressmen or their aides have gone or are about to go to jail for bribery, influence-peddling, or perjury; three more were convicted but given suspended sentences; another awaits trial; another was censured; and another was excluded from Congress. In this century, twenty-four senators and representatives have been indicted for crimes; fifteen were convicted, and two cases are still pending. Some of their stories, and their falls from grace, follow:

BOBBY BAKER. In 1942, with sixty dollars in his back pocket, 14-year-old Bobby Baker left Pickens, South Carolina, and never looked back. Like a lamprey searching for a host, he made his way to Washington, found the Senate, and attached himself for a twenty-year ride. First as page, then as clerk, he moved up the ladder. His break came when he made a friend, Lyndon Johnson. His friend became majority leader of the Senate and did not forget the small people he had met along the way. From 1955 until 1963, even after Johnson had left the post, Baker was secretary to the majority leader. "You're like a son to me," Johnson purred as he helped Bobby up. To Baker, Johnson was, if not a father, at least "my best friend around the capital." By 1960, Baker was being introduced to freshman page boys as "a powerful demonstrator of just how far intelligence combined with a gracious personality can take a man."

The tragedies of 1963 were a bad omen for Bobby. His old friend had become president—but had risen too high to keep in touch with Bobby. Critics began to grow suspicious about Baker's wealth. From a net worth of $11,000 in 1955, he had become a multimillionaire—an annual rate of increase of $200,000–$300,000—all while earning a salary of $19,600 per year. One explanation for the gap came when a civil lawsuit claimed that Baker had used his influence to help a firm win a government contract. With that, the Senate Rules and Administration Committee took a closer look at him. By 1965, the Democratic majority had issued a report citing "many gross improprieties" in his behavior—but no legal violations. To many senators, both Republicans and Democrats, this looked like a crude whitewash. Over the next few months, Senator John Williams of Delaware earned himself the title "conscience of the Senate" by hounding Baker and his apologists.

The legal ax fell in 1966, when Baker was finally indicted for fraud, larceny, and tax evasion. The major charge was that he had collected $100,000 from a group of California savings and loans executives for campaign contributions, and then kept $80,000 of it himself. Even as he protested his innocence, Baker realized that his exposure was straining some of his former cronies. "My friends in Congress," he said with slight bitterness, "have had no choice but to think of me as a bad dream or something." No one had less choice about the matter than Baker's best friend, the president of the United States. He retained public composure—even indifference—over the matter.

The callousness of politics was old news to Baker; he had seen friendships bloom and die in the seasons of convenience. He knew that "the American people would have destroyed and defeated President Johnson had he attempted in any way to do anything on my behalf." Still, Baker must have clung to some strand of hope. If a man had risen with a patron who was now president—could he be left entirely alone with his troubles? As far as Johnson was concerned he could. Baker went to trial, was convicted, and was sentenced to one to three years. By 1971, when he was released, the bad memories may have lingered, but the punishment was over and he was still rich.

ADAM CLAYTON POWELL. It was not his romances that drove the white folks mad—his colleagues had tolerated that in others—nor was it his laziness, nor his endless vacation trips. It was not even the way he turned every power of his office toward his boundless hedonism. Congress had seen it all before, and had forgiven. Adam Clayton Powell's sin was flagrance—

his refusal to hide what he was doing. Others might filch dollars from the cash box at night: Powell skimmed off his profit in full public view. While Congress was in session and the committee he chaired slogged away at its work, Powell posed for photographers with Miss Ohio at his island haven in the Caribbean.

For a while, Powell tapped a special mood of the times. The same panache which enraged other congressmen made Powell a hero to his Harlem constituents: he was winning at the white man's game. In the two decades of his prime—at the time when he was being ridiculed in the House cloakroom as "the congressman from Bimini" or "the Harlem Globetrotter"—Powell sailed through elections as if anointed. He won his first term in 1944. By 1961, enough other congressmen had died or lost so that Powell became chairman of the Education and Labor Committee—the second black chairman in congressional history.

Toward the mid-1960s, after an earlier vigor and productivity, Powell began to spend large chunks of the terms vacationing—sometimes with false names, usually with lady friends, always at government expense. He kept up his family ties by putting his wife on his office payroll at $20,000 per year, a gracious gesture to a woman then living in Puerto Rico. A first brush with the law left Powell unscarred: in 1958, he was indicted for income tax evasion, but escaped the charge after paying $28,000 in back taxes and penalties. If he had stopped then, curbing the excesses and cutting down on the publicity, Powell might have spent another ten terms as pleasantly as the first ten.

He could not, or did not, stop, and in the late sixties Congress caught up with him. Already, he had become an exile in his own district. After being convicted of libel—for calling a black woman the "bag lady" for a graft operation—Powell could not return to the district he represented for fear of being arrested. In 1966, the disgruntled members of his committee began to hack away at his powers. Other congressmen sharpened their knives, too.

Their grievance was that Powell was bringing them

all down. When one congressman is a clown, how seriously could the rest take themselves? Their own self-respect was only part of it. The constituents were also angry. "Nobody blames me for Howard Smith or H. R. Gross," one congressman said, mentioning two of the chamber's troglodytes, "but whites all over America blame their congressman for Adam." Morris Udall produced a letter from a constituent, addressed "in care of Adam Clayton Powell's Playboy Club (formerly U.S. House of Representatives), Stinksville Station (formerly House Post Office), Washington, D.C."

In 1967, the Democratic caucus voted to remove him as chairman. By a thumping 365–65 vote, the full House then voted to deny him his seat pending further investigations. Soon afterwards the Justice Department compiled a fifty-page draft indictment telling of falsified expense vouchers worth $20,000 and of Powell's secret destruction of incriminating papers from his committee; but no formal indictment was ever issued by Attorney General Ramsey Clark. Finally, the House declared his seat vacant and ordered a special election for April.

Powell won the election, and then won a more important victory when the Supreme Court ruled that his exclusion had been unconstitutional. The only formal losses were his seniority and a $25,000 fine for penance. Powell had survived, but in the process something had gone sour between him and his district. In 1970, he lost in the primary to Charles Rangel. Two years later, unrepentant, he died, at age 63.

In a Congress of untainted men, the harassment Powell underwent might have been understandable. Amid the mixed morals of both houses, however, Powell often seemed more a scapegoat than a culpable villain. As Richard Harwood put it in the *Washington Post:*

> Like former Representative James Roosevelt of California, he has acquired three wives and a reputation for his romantic goings-on. Like Rep. Wayne Hays of Ohio, he has journeyed first-class to Europe at public expense accompanied by female assistants. . . . Like Rep. Joe Pool of

Texas, he has ostentatiously defied the orders of an American court. Like Rep. Richard Bolling of Missouri and others, he has placed a wife on the congressional payroll. . . . Like the late Speaker Sam Rayburn of Texas, he dispenses whiskey in his Capitol office.

"You are looking at the first black man who was ever lynched by Congress," Powell had said.

THOMAS DODD. "I believe in God and Senator Dodd and keepin' ol' Castro down," Phil Ochs sang. And Dodd fit the billing. When the young Tom Dodd faced one of life's forking paths, he grappled with the question of whether he should become a priest. Instead, he plowed his energies into politics. If he was not combating sin in the individual soul, he could attack its manifestations in the national spirit; perversion, pornography, Communism—all must be defeated.

Although Dodd's targets were the classic ones, attacking them in the Senate won him few friends. In a body which is almost as tradition-conscious as the Church, the Connecticut senator stepped roughly on others' dignity. He overlooked the minor niceties; he called names; he impugned motives.

Thomas Dodd would not be a household word today if impoliteness had been his only error. Dodd's talent—his malign genius—was invested in another cause, his financial frauds. His staff was the first to notice. They had gathered evidence of a stunning range of dishonesty. Dodd had pocketed, for private use, at least $160,083 raised at campaign dinners, supposedly for campaign expenses; he had double-billed the government and other groups for other expenses, keeping the surplus; he had taken repeated private vacations and charged the government; he had used his office to promote the career of a retired major general who was a propagandist for German right-wingers; he had taken money from private firms, and then pressured government agencies for special treatment.

Doubts and difficulties afflicted the staffers. James

Boyd had been Dodd's closest aide for the previous twelve years; Marjorie Carpenter had been his secretary. For half a year, the two wavered. "We shifted from day to day," Boyd says. "We kept wondering 'who are we to take him on?' "

A further problem was what to do with the data. "To whom do you go to get a U.S. senator investigated?" Boyd asked. The Senate Ethics Committee was likely to forgive an erring brother; the Justice Department was part of Johnson's administration, and Johnson was one of Dodd's friends; even the FBI was suspect, since Dodd had once been an agent. Their minds set, Boyd and Carpenter eventually took seven thousand documents from Dodd's files and gave them to the trustees of frustrated exposés, Drew Pearson and Jack Anderson.

Pearson and Anderson unloaded the charges in twenty-three columns, but for a while Dodd felt safe in ignoring them. He spread the false story that his staff was getting back at him because he had caught two of them making love in the office. Other senators closed ranks against their threatened fellow; according to Taylor Branch of the *Washington Monthly,* Birch Bayh wrote, "We're all with you on this yellow attack by Pearson," while Russell Long said, "I'll support you all the way on this, Tom, even if you're guilty." Dodd had his own explanation for the trouble: "The Communists have always regarded me as a prime enemy."

But Dodd made a crucial mistake. He demanded a Senate inquiry. It was a dramatic ploy, but one which proved his undoing. "Never ask for an investigation," one of his cohorts had said. "You might get one." The Senate Ethics Committee thus began its first investigation. Its report was less than Boyd might have hoped, but did unanimously recommend that Dodd be censured on two counts: for diverting the campaign money, and for the double-billing. On June 23, 1967, Dodd was officially censured by the Senate for the first count. His defense was an inspired peroration on the Senate floor, which concluded, "I am telling you the truth and I am concealing nothing. May the vengeance of God strike me if I am doing otherwise!" The plea moved many but convinced none. By a vote of 92–5 (Dodd, Ribicoff, Tower, Thurmond, and Long against) the Senate censured Dodd for his personal use of the campaign funds. Having done this much, the Senate pulled back and refused, by a 51–45 vote, to censure Dodd for double-billing.

Dodd's formal punishment was light. He served three more years in the Senate, gamely ran as an independent for reelection in 1970, and succeeded only in siphoning off enough votes to ensure that Republican Lowell Weicker won. The Democratic Campaign Committee—whose thirteen members had voted to censure Dodd three years before—contributed $10,000 to his 1970 campaign, even though he was running against a Democrat.

But the scandal left Dodd broken. He died of a heart attack in 1971, a bundle of contradictions. Exhorting law and order, he placed himself above the law; demanding staff loyalty, he was loyal to none but himself. In the mid-sixties, after Bobby Baker's fall but before his own, Dodd had angled to get the great glass chandelier that had hung in Baker's office. He never got it, and shared with Baker only his acquisitive ways.

JOHN DOWDY. A ten-term congressman from rural east Texas, John Dowdy is known mostly for his chairmanship of a House District subcommittee (where he has continually criticized the D.C. government for its "permissiveness"), for his campaign against homosexuals (or "perverts" as he calls them), and for his crusades against obscenity and pornography (a bill he introduced would have declared "obscene" any books, movies, and magazines that dealt with "lewd and lascivious scandals, intrigues between men and women, and the immoral conduct of persons"). But in January, 1972, despite earlier election successes and popularity back home, John Dowdy announced he would not run for reelection. He cited health problems. But something else was undoubtedly bothering him. For on December 30, 1971, John Dowdy was convicted of conspiracy, perjury, and bribery. The jury found that businessman

Myrvin Clark had delivered $25,000 in cash to Dowdy in the Atlanta airport on September 22, 1965, in order to get Dowdy to thwart a federal investigation of the Monarch Construction Corporation, a firm which had swindled hundreds of Washingtonians on home improvement jobs between 1963 and 1965.

At the announcement of his indictment Dowdy had stoutly maintained, "I am absolutely not guilty of any wrongdoing or violating any laws of the United States." A staunch segregationist and conservative, Dowdy was portrayed as a martyr by the Liberty Lobby, a "victim of an attempted frame-up by leftists." But the stress of the case took its toll on Dowdy. His weight fell from 210 to 160 in the next year; he looked years older and his voice, never loud, grew weak. The trial had to be delayed six times because of his infirmities. However pathetic Dowdy's decline, he outdid himself after one cancellation, when the Bethesda Naval Hospital had found him physically and mentally unable to stand trial and "unable to consult rationally with counsel in his own defense." Dowdy then repaired to Congress, presumably a less taxing environment, where he resumed his seat and presided over a D.C. Education subcommittee hearing.

His conviction was met with indignation by his admirers. A supporter back home in Texas said that "folks down here believe a white man can't get a fair trial in Maryland." Another explained that "if he took the money, I'm sure he hasn't pocketed it." "There is no one who is more honest and honorable," wrote one ardent constituent to the *New York Times*, "or who has given more of himself to his good work. . . . We want him to be our representative in Congress forever." In the elevator after the verdict, which Dowdy had received red-faced and solemn, his wife bitterly said, "It's because you've always hated the government, John." (Three months later, Mrs. Dowdy, who had been on her husband's office payroll, announced she would run for her husband's seat.) Dowdy himself was no more gracious to his prosecutors. He claimed to the end that he was the "innocent victim of homosexuals, urban renewal interests, and other members of the Eastern liberal establishment."

Two other members of Congress, one retired and the other serving out his last term, have been accused of serious crimes by a grand jury. But unlike the case studies above, they have not yet been tried and have, in fact, claimed their innocence.

One of them is former Senator Daniel Brewster, who loved the races, whether the contestants were horses or politicians. In 1945, Brewster returned from the war to Baltimore County, Maryland, a hero with seven wounds and a bronze star. A millionaire's son, he turned first to horseracing, and became a moderately successful steeplechase rider on the East Coast Hunt racing circuit. But he was also interested in politics, and got elected to the Maryland House of Delegates in 1950. Although money was no problem, Brewster shortly thereafter joined a law firm. Success followed success. He was elected to Congress in 1958 and 1960, and, when a Senate seat became vacant in 1962, he ran and won it.

For Brewster success became ruin by late 1968. He lost his reelection bid that November, in a three-way race. While in June of 1968 he had been a trim, youthful, and vigorous campaigner, seven months later, after defeat by Charles Mathias, he was noticeably heavier, with red-lined cheeks and a slow step. He turned up in Annapolis in early 1969 to ask Governor Marvin Mandel for a Democratic party job, but he left empty-handed. Then on December 1, 1969, Brewster, whose fortune was more than $2.4 million, was indicted for allegedly accepting $24,500 in bribes from a mail-order house to influence his votes on postal rate laws.

The trial was delayed several times because of Brewster's ill health. "Former Senator Daniel Brewster of Maryland . . . suffered a severe mental lapse and is not competent to stand trial," said an Associated Press dispatch of February 24, 1970. "The report said that the chronic effect of alcohol was a contributing cause." He recuperated at his wife's Ireland estate. Brewster did appear at a hearing in May—in rumpled suit, his hands trembling slightly, stubbles of white whiskers on his face—to plead innocent. District Court Judge George Hart, Jr., dismissed all charges under the theory that congressional immunity encompassed any alleged bribery connected with a senator's vote. But the Supreme Court disagreed and ordered a new trial. It is scheduled for October, 1972.

Since Brewster's indictment, he has been investigated by another grand jury in the Rayburn garage case. The grand jury charged a Baltimore contractor named Victor Frenkil with trying to get an extra $5 million, over his $11.7-million contract, for building two parking garages in the Rayburn Office Building. It also asserted that Frenkil got help from several Capitol Hill figures, including Brewster. Since any indictment would mention such public figures, Attorney General John Mitchell refused to approve the grand jury's recommendation for Frenkil's indictment. In yet another incident, the FBI is investigating allegations that Brewster received substantial contributions from Seafarers International Union while he was giving his support for legislation to remove the Maritime Administration from the Commerce Department. And in July, 1972, Brewster was fined $220 for drunk driving.

Congressman Cornelius Gallagher from Bayonne, New Jersey, is the other member with a pending criminal trial. A handsome, (once) popular congressman, a World War II hero, mentioned as possible vice presidential or gubernatorial material in 1964, Gallagher largely succeeded in offsetting the stereotype of the representative from Bayonne. Until, that is, August 9, 1968, when *Life* magazine published a story that shocked even a usually jaded Washington. *Life* charged Gallagher with being a collaborator of the Mafia, using his office to help promote the business interests of one Joe Zicarelli. "Beyond the facade of prestige and respectability lives another Neil Gallagher," said *Life,* "a man who time and time again has served as the tool . . . of a Cosa Nostra gang lord." Other, more macabre, allegations were made by *Life*, but its credibility was undermined when one of *Life*'s supposed sources, a Harold Konigsberg, denied the assertions attributed to him.

Gallagher roared back, calling the whole thing "preposterous," threatening a libel suit, and demanding a full grand jury investigation of the charges. This last tactic proved not to be wise, for Gallagher was indicted on seven counts of perjury and income tax evasion by a grand jury on April 11, 1972. The government claimed that he had purchased $500,000 in bonds under fictitious names and helped two convicted Jersey City politicians buy $300,000 more. The bonds allegedly were part of a contract kickback scheme; in addition, they supposedly enabled Gallagher to short-change the IRS by $102,000.

Gallagher now unloosed a crescendo of denials and countercharges. He claimed that he was a mere conduit of the bonds. He protested that he was the victim of the "new Caesars" of an American police state retaliating for his outspokenness against government wiretapping and computer banks. ("I have been standing up for political issues in this country. Those people who find that I have been trodding [sic] on their ground a little bit have been doing everything they can to silence me.") Finally, Gallagher explained how he refused to allow his House subcommittee, investigating invasions of privacy, to be used by the FBI in their battles against Robert Kennedy. As a result, Gallagher charged, the FBI tried to blackmail him: unless he quit Congress, they would spread slanderous stories about himself and his wife.

Gallagher has maintained his innocence throughout. He refused to quit his seat while under indictment, since he had not been convicted of anything. (The electorate made the problem moot, rejecting him in the 1972 Democratic primary.) Would he resign if convicted and jailed? No, said Gallagher, explaining that "a lot of people were convicted in Bangladesh. But that didn't make them guilty of any criminal activity, and when justice surfaced those people did go back to public office."

These cases portray some of the ways Capitol Hillers can run afoul of the law. At the same time they show similarities about the discovery, the explanation, and the sanction for being caught with one's hand in the cookie jar.

Most congressional corruption is discovered and publicized either by staff whistle blowers or by outside muckrakers like Jack Anderson and *Life* magazine. Tom Dodd's staff ultimately decided its highest loyalty was to the public, not its employer. Boyd and Carpenter then went to Pearson and Anderson, whose revelations have discomfited many officials. One can be quite certain that many politicians in Washington immediately scan the Anderson column in the *Washington Post* to check whether the bribe/lady-from-Duluth/slush-fund has been publicly exposed. When they are—as James Boyd describes the scene—

> The Senator's strength drains out in a puddle. He slumps in a flaccid heap and stares glassily at the accusing phone; the knowing place in the pit of the stomach sinks into infinity. . . . It is the moment of maximum hazard to a political career; a too-defiant denial, a telltale dodge, an injudicious admission can . . . undo 30 years of patient conniving. The Senator's glazed eyes conjure up newspaper headlines, the dock, the recall of Congressional credit cards, the cell door clanking shut.

This moment of "maximum hazard" can be met in various ways—whether the accused is culpable or not, since false but spectacular charges are an occupational risk for politicians. Some of the following categories were developed by Boyd himself, not unfamiliar with what he calls "the ritual of wiggle." *

---

* *Washington Monthly,* September, 1970, p. 28.

• Ignore it—Some disconnect their phones, leave for a trip, or simply say "no comment." The idea is that the thing will blow over. It can work if the accused or the event is inconsequential enough (a condition Abe Fortas did not appreciate) or if the reply is sufficiently disparaging (e.g., Dirksen said he could not "make heads or tails" of charges over abuse of his congressional frank, and the issue disappeared).

• Blame invisible enemies—This is especially handy for crusaders, who can always blame their problems on their historic targets. Of course, such targets may never have been prosecutors or accusers, but when one seeks scapegoats this does not matter. Thus we had Dodd's "Communists," Dowdy's "homosexuals," and Gallagher's "new Caesars."

• Deny the obvious—If repeated often and honestly enough, it can sometimes work. After Congressman Seymour Halpern, already in debt, got his $100,000 in unsecured loans while ruminating over banking legislation, he announced that there wasn't any conflict of interest. He suffered some bad publicity but was easily reelected. Robert Carson, former aide to Senator Hiram Fong, claimed that his $100,000 offer to Richard Kleindienst to help out an indicted friend was just a campaign contribution. The jury, however, called it a bribe and gave him eighteen months in jail.

• Say you'd do it for anyone—Congressman Robert Giaimo arranged a Caribbean cruise at government expense for a man who happened to be a racketeer. Giaimo explained that he would, of course, be glad to arrange a similar cruise for any of his half-million constituents. In 1971, lobbyist Nathan Voloshen and Martin Sweig, a close associate and aide, respectively, of Speaker McCormack, were convicted of influence-peddling and perjury; specifically, they defrauded government agencies by using the speaker's office and prestige on behalf of private clients. At their trial, Congressman Robert Leggett testified that it was not odd to give a lobbyist the run of one's office. He considered the whole country as his constituency and would certainly be willing to allow anyone to use his office for commercial clients.

This performance led one juror to tell the *New York Times* that "after hearing him, it is my opinion they should investigate *all* the members of Congress."

• Announce for reelection—This because the best defense is a good offense. Dodd declared for his third term the day he was censured. McCormack did so on the day he held a press conference to deny participation in Voloshen and Sweig's schemes.

• Plead for mercy on national television—The Nixon-Checkers and Kennedy-Chappaquiddick speeches are too well known to belabor, but look where each is now.

• Say you'll give it back—In the early sixties Representative John Byrnes, then, as now, a ranking member of the House Ways and Means Committee, helped get a favorable tax ruling for the Mortgage Guaranty Insurance Corporation out of the IRS. He then purchased $2,300 of their stock on terms not generally available, and within two years it was worth $25,000. In an emotional, weeping floor speech denying any wrongdoing, Byrnes announced that he would give any profits made to a scholarship fund for needy youth. His colleagues cheered. Seymour Halpern, when his bank loans were questioned, said he would pay them back, if necessary, by selling off his prize collection of famous signatures, which he had spent a lifetime collecting. It was, to many, a touching and convincing gesture.

• Threaten suit—This hardly ever works, but it makes good copy. The difficulty is that it is nearly impossible to prove libel under existing law when the person at issue is a "public figure." Still, Gallagher threatened it and Dodd actually filed a $5-million libel suit against Pearson and Anderson, losing every count.

• Get an OK from a Senate leader—Although all that may be involved is some classic backscratching, it is helpful to get exonerated by An Important Person. Former Senator George Murphy began to worry shortly before his 1970 race about his arrangement with Pat Frawley of Technicolor. Frawley gave the senator $20,000 annually, gave him free use of a credit card, and paid half of his $520 monthly rent. Murphy first asked

Dirksen if the arrangement was unseemly, and Dirksen gave his blessing (as he had given it to himself many times). Then Stennis, chairman of the Senate Ethics Committee, performed the laying on of hands. Senator Edward Long also got Senator Stennis to whitewash his "referral fees" from teamster lawyer M. A. Shenker, with hardly a glance at what really went on. But the voters sent both Murphy and Long looking for a new line of work.

• Claim immunity—Failing other ploys, many exploit the procedural. Congressional immunity is one way to finesse a tense situation, at least temporarily. Former Congressman Thomas Johnson was convicted in 1963 of pocketing $17,500 in exchange for helping a savings and loan office escape federal prosecution. But the Supreme Court reversed the conviction because part of his offense involved a floor speech for which, the Court said, he was immune. (He was reconvicted in 1968 and went to jail for six months in 1970.) Daniel Brewster also was able to convince a lower federal court that congressional immunity somehow exonerated an alleged bribery, although the Supreme Court reversed this decision and directed that Brewster be retried.

What, finally, were the sanctions meted out after discovery and explanation? Five of our figures went to jail (Johnson, Baker, Dowdy, Sweig, and Carson). Two were severely sanctioned by their respective chambers (Dodd and Powell). Seven were dis-elected or retired (Long, Murphy, Gallagher, Dowdy, Dodd, Brewster, and Powell). And five have either died or suffered deteriorating health (Dodd, Powell, Voloshen, Dowdy, and Brewster) after their exposure and punishment. Yet, occasionally scandal did not stand in the way of some later success. Jim Curley in the forties, Tom Lane in the fifties, and Adam Clayton Powell in the sixties all won a reelection despite the fact that the first two were in jail at the time and the last had been forbidden to participate in House activities. Articles by *Life* and Jack Anderson, respectively, alleging the underworld connections of Congressman Cornelius Gallagher and

Robert Giaimo, did not keep either from being reelected in their next campaigns, and remember how Dowdy was lionized by his followers. Such responses are more than mere quirks in a nation where Gallup polls show much of the population sympathetic to soldiers who massacre civilians or who fire guns into students. While some of the corrupt are punished, some are not. Congress, then, at times resembles Gambetta's description of the French Chamber of Deputies—"a broken mirror in which the nation cannot recognize its own image."

The Congressional Response

Timeless customs, inherited from the night-long vigils of tribal societies, bind members of a group together. The doctor's unwritten code discourages one from testifying against another. Lawyers in court are forbidden to criticize each other. Congress, too, watches out for its own. For nearly two centuries after its founding, Congress rested on the comforting assumption that the best supervisor of each member's behavior was the member himself. Only under pressure from "outside"— that is, from the public, upset by the Powell and Baker stories—did Congress take more formal steps toward self-regulation. In both houses, the response was a two-part system: financial disclosures and an ethics committee.

Unfortunately, neither of these steps has gone far enough to calm public anxiety over congressional crime and ethics. The financial statements which the Senate requires from its members, for example, are not made public. When the Senate was debating disclosure rules in 1968, Senator Clifford Case from New Jersey argued that publication of the statements was essential: "The knowledge that one's financial activities and interests will become known is the best stop-and-think principle." But the opposition, led by Everett Dirksen, said that the rules would be "impertinent" and would make senators into "second-class citizens." After all, Dirksen said, in typical obfuscation, "all life is a conflict of interest." His reasoning prevailed, and the publication clause lost 44–40.

The disclosure rules that finally emerged do require that the senator list his income sources, his tax returns, his clients who pay fees over $1,000, his corporate and professional attachments, his debts, and his other financial interests. But all this useful information is as private as the senator's own thoughts. With inspection from no one else, the senator folds his papers, stuffs them into an envelope, seals it, and delivers it to the comptroller general. Under normal circumstances, it will never be opened. Only if the Senate Ethics Committee formally requests it will the information be revealed. The only data which the senator must report to the public every year is any honoraria over $300 he has received, and any campaign contributions he has obtained.

Is it reasonable to ask for more? The reasoning behind Dirksen's second-class citizen rhetoric was that few other people have to file their tax returns with the press. The difference, obvious as it may seem, is that few other people are in the senator's position of public trust. Even the most scrupulous senator knows, when he is considering a bill, that it may affect his personal fortune for better or worse. That does not necessarily determine his action—but the public should know what his stake is.

The House disclosure rules are tougher by comparison—but only by comparison. Representatives must make public any commercial activities from which they earn more than $1,000 annually or in which they hold stock worth over $5,000. Another clause makes congressmen name any unsecured loans of $10,000 or more that they have held for more than ninety days. On its surface, this is a promising system. The flaw is that the members do not have to say *how much* above $1,000 or $5,000 their interest is: the owner of a million-dollar company and the holder of scattered shares worth $5,500 would look the same on the disclosure forms.

Again, the public has a right to ask for more. Some members do not disappoint them. For the congressional roll call is not solely the Dodds, Powells, and Dowdys.

There are also men like Douglas, Morse, Percy, Udall, Hechler, Cook—politicians who have set encouraging examples.

In the Senate, Charles Percy, Wayne Morse, and Douglas all voluntarily disclosed their financial holdings. The richest of them, Percy, has put his $6-million fortune in the hands of a blind trust. Douglas, Percy's predecessor from Illinois, used to refuse all contributions for personal expenses or from people with a financial interest in matters before the Senate. He turned down any gift worth more than five dollars. (For less, he jokingly said, he just couldn't be bought.) Marlow Cook, upon entering the Senate, revealed his interest in the Bank of Louisville, and asked not to be appointed to the Banking and Currency Committee. In the House, Morris Udall of Arizona relinquished his lucrative law practice back home and voluntarily makes public his financial statement. Ken Hechler of West Virginia gave up his commission as an Army Reserve colonel—one year short of a guaranteed $220 per month pension—when the House considered a military pay bill which would have boosted his pension about 10 percent. When some men take such care over $220 per month, the indelicacy of those who vote for their agricultural subsidies or bank regulations becomes especially glaring.

The second weapon in the woefully understocked congressional arsenal against corruption is the Ethics Committee. If the name is encouraging, its creation was not. The Senate Ethics Committee was almost an accidental conception. Its parent was the special Senate investigating committee which dug into Bobby Baker's past. The committee's chairman, Everett Jordan, made it clear to his colleagues that the group might be questioning senators' employees, but was "not investigating senators." That satisfying setup might have lasted indefinitely, save for the Senate's absentmindedness. At a routine session in 1964, a motion came up to establish a committee to investigate senators themselves. An aide to Clifford Case recalls what happened:

John Sherman Cooper offered the motion to set up the select committee and, to his and everybody else's amazement, it passed. I remember because I was on the floor talking with Senator Case. . . . As he talked with me he was listening to the tally and suddenly he broke off and said, "It's going to pass," and he went over to congratulate Cooper, and Cooper was looking stunned. Mansfield, who was nonplussed and didn't know what to do next, said "We'll have to consult the lawyers," and they recessed. It was one of the funniest things I've ever seen.

The Senate took to its new offspring with all the glee of a father who has found an illegitimate child dumped on his doorstep. For two years, no senators were assigned to seats on the committee. Few were eager to take seats as judges of their peers. Even reformer Douglas turned down an offer, his aide said, because "he didn't have the stomach for it." John Stennis of Mississippi finally stood where others had faltered; with Stennis as its first chairman, the Select Committee on Standards and Conduct (its formal name) was ready for action in 1966. Its nominal powers were impressive: it was to take complaints, investigate alleged misconduct, and recommend disciplinary action.

If this watchdog had any teeth, however, it quickly broke them on its initial subject. Tom Dodd's case was the first to come before the committee. To the surprise of many, it took the difficult step of recommending that Dodd be censured. Even while doing so, however, the committee shied away from some of the most serious complaints against Dodd. "How will Americans ever learn about patterns of privilege and conflict of interest," complained one of those who had exposed Dodd, "if only 10 percent of his unethical activities—and those the least important—is made public?"

Perhaps exhausted from its struggle with Dodd, the committee was far more docile in its investigation of Senator Edward Long. Like Dodd, Long was accused from the outside. In 1967, *Life* magazine published an article by William Lambert describing in detail how Long had taken more than $48,000 in legal fees from teamster lawyer M. A. Shenker in return for Long's efforts to help teamster boss Jimmy Hoffa four years earlier. The committee appeared to take the charges seriously: it met fourteen times in 1967 to investigate them. But when it was finished, the committee dismissed the incident with a four-page blessing of Long. The legal fees, it said, were really from five clients that Long "shared" with Shenker, and not for the jailed Jimmy Hoffa at all.

While his colleagues patted Long on the back, Lambert called the report a "whitewash" and added extra evidence in a later article. The fees involved, he said, were $160,000—not $48,000; Shenker, Long's associate, was a lawyer "who spent most of his career representing gangsters and gamblers in St. Louis and Las Vegas"; the five clients who had rewarded Long were all linked to organized crime. Lambert added that Long's behavior had been less than straightforward. At first, he had denied getting any money at all; then, as the facts came out, he called the money "referral fees" and, later, fees for "shared clients." Just what share of the services he performed to earn his money was never too clear—partly because the Ethics Committee never bothered to ask.

Lambert's reply stung the Senate Ethics Committee into promising to reopen its investigation. (The plans were called off when Long lost his Senate seat in 1968 to a rising Missouri politician named Thomas Eagleton.) It also pointed toward serious shortcomings in the committee's performance. "What on earth was the Ethics panel doing all this time?" the *Washington Evening Star* asked. "With access to information denied the public, how could it conclude so solemnly that it 'found no facts' when outsiders, not blessed with such investigative powers, managed to change the panel's mind?"

The House Ethics Committee, established in 1967 after a 400–0 vote ("Who can vote against ethics?" a California congressman asked), has had an equally hard time getting started. In its first three years of operation,

it conducted just two preliminary investigations—one of
Congressman Gallagher and another of "ghost voting"
(the trick by which members have their votes recorded
at times when they are actually away from the Capitol).
"If my acknowledging only two preliminary investigations makes it sound like we don't do any work," said
a member of the committee's staff, "then it will just have
to sound that way."

Since that time, the committee has completed one
major investigation. After Congressman John Dowdy
was indicted for bribery, the committee voted to forbid
anyone in Dowdy's situation to sit on committees or
vote on the floor. Their proposed resolution never made
it to the full House for a vote; William Colmer, whose
chairmanship of the Rules Committee gave him a tem-
p·rary stronghold over House business, refused to send
the proposal to the floor. Dowdy graciously broke the
impasse himself. In a letter to House Speaker Carl Albert, he promised that he would not vote in committees
or on the floor. His resolve lasted until mid-1972, when
it was revealed that Dowdy had been secretly voting by
proxy on close issues in the House District Committee.

Few, if any, people run for public office with the
secret intent to profit by illegal means. Rather, there is
something in the congressional environment which raises
this temptation and then pushes some over the brink.
That "something" may well inhere in the legislative
process itself: laws can seriously affect important people; politicians need money to stay in office; politicians
can be influenced to pass laws or sit tight; important
people can give money to politicians in order to influence
them. Thus, there are two sides to the coin of congressional power: there is the potential to improve the lot
of all Americans and there is the potential of corruption.
There is no panacea which can eradicate the latter without impairing the former.

But at the same time, there are a series of measures
which could reduce the built-in temptations and, hence,
the resulting lawlessness. Members with a financial interest could disqualify themselves from voting on re-

lated issues; as Thomas Jefferson, then vice president, wrote in his manual in 1801, "Where the private interests of a member are concerned in a bill of question, he is to withdraw." In the modern British Parliament one member can challenge another to "state his interest" in a question. Some state legislatures similarly require that a legislator not vote on an issue in which he has a private stake (although such laws are more often violated than observed). Congress might also take a lesson from the French National Assembly, whose members must declare any business activities they hold when they are elected or that they may acquire later. A complete package to insulate the legislation from personal interests would include public funding of most campaign costs, omplete financial disclosure, and the prohibition of outside legal practice. Such measures can reduce the need for outside monies and can create a more open environment in which green thumbs do not flourish.

It would be polite to end a discussion of congressional lawlessness by stressing that, while there are a few rotten apples, the overwhelming majority of congressmen are honest. This may be true, but how would we know? Their public financial disclosures do not tell us enough, nor are the ethics committees vigilant enough, to make us sanguine. By failing to police itself, Congress has not elevated itself above suspicion. A critical observer can hardly take heart at the number of congressmen and staff who have been caught. There are no cops regularly patrolling Capitol Hill corridors, and no law enforcement agencies devote resources to congressional crime. The luckless few are exposed more by fluke than investigation. Until the two houses put themselves in order, friends and cynics will continue to wonder not what congressmen do but how they do it.

6

Games Congressmen Play:
The Capitol Culture

*This damn place is plenary of Rotarians. The
House acts, thinks, and reacts in terms of some
stodgy old Philadelphia club.*

—A congressman

Every small town has its Elks Club or Kiwanis. But
only Washington has a club which runs the country.
Compared to any Masonic lodge, Congress is not
unusually quaint; compared to the hierarchies of the
film industry, or backdoor intrigue at the Vatican, its
rituals of power are not particularly occult. In most of
its ways, Congress is, as one senator put it, "just like
living in a small town." Just as their executive relations
and the committee system say something about the way
they govern the country, so do the congressmen's customs and folkways.

The Politics of Deference

When the Constitutional Convention was hammering
out new provisions in 1787, its members did not have
to worry that their comments would be flashed back to
local voters on the evening news. With a candor that
modern publicity makes hardly possible, Pennsylvania's
Gouverneur Morris said at the convention that he hoped
the Senate "will show us the might of aristocracy."
Poorly as this seems to fit normal ideas of representation
and democracy, it comes closer to catching the Senate's
spirit than many other definitions. Spectators watching
from the Senate galleries understand Morris's meaning;
while members of the House scurry in and out like har-

ried businessmen or tired farmers, the senators emerge from the cloakroom doors and glide onto the floor with the weighty tread of men who know they are being recognized. House members make fun of the Senate for this difference; but both houses pay extraordinary attention to rituals designed to boost prestige.

On first glance, the most noticeable feature of congressional proceedings is the antique language and minuettish courtesies which encase them. Before beginning an attack on another congressman's proposal, a member will hang garlands of "my distinguished friend" around his neck. Former House Speaker John McCormack, for example, warmed up for an attack on a Gerald Ford position by noting that "we are all very happy in the justified and deserved recognition that our distinguished friend, the gentleman from Michigan [Ford], received yesterday . . . when the city of Grand Rapids set aside a special day in recognition of such an outstanding legislator and in recognition of such a great American." To make sure that no one missed the point, McCormack's sidekick, Majority Leader Carl Albert, chimed in, "I wish to join our distinguished and beloved speaker in the tribute paid to our distinguished minority leader." Then, like boxers who had completed the ritual glove touching, they dug in.

After sitting through one too many of these syrupy prefaces, Massachusetts Senator Edward Brooke suggested that if the word "distinguished" were eliminated from the proceedings, the legislators could save 10 percent of their time. To which Majority Leader Mike Mansfield replied, "I appreciate the remarks of the distinguished senator from Massachusetts for his views."

The model for this behavior is, of course, the world of diplomacy (what Adlai Stevenson once called, in words also evocative of Congress, a place of "protocol, alcohol, and Geritol"). There, each delegate represents a nation, and a little ceremony is in order. Congressmen emulate other parts of the diplomatic procedure as well. While the Pope or the English queen might get away with saying "We" instead of "I," congressmen prefer third person references to themselves. When he was majority leader, Lyndon Johnson couched one opinion in the following cumbersome prose: "The senator from Texas does not have any objection and the senator from Texas wishes the senator from California to know that the senator from Texas knew the senator from California did not criticize him." In the haste of quick-moving debate, congressmen may even forget "the senator," and refer to themselves as states.

To keep the rituals up, congressmen have developed a number of unwritten social rules. One of the most basic is that no one must poke holes in the delicate fabric of congressional frill. In private, congressmen may call each other (as they did to some of our interviewers) "screaming idiots" or "jackasses." In public, this would provoke outrage. There are strains involved—"It's hard not to call a man a liar when you know that he is one," said one senator—but most keep themselves under control. If their resolve slips, they can remember the case of Congressman John Hunter—who in 1867 was formally censured by the House for saying of a colleague's comment, "So far as I am concerned, it is a base lie." *

Since freshman congressmen are inexperienced in political deference when they arrive, careful instruction is necessary. In the first few weeks, freshmen from both

---

* Occasionally, breaking political etiquette goes even further —into the realm of physical violence. Just as a prim Victorian England encouraged a very racy pornographic subculture, so the constant constraint of deference can at times lead to its opposite. During heated debate over the Compromise of 1850, Senator Henry S. ("Hangman") Foote brandished a pistol at Thomas Hart Benton; before Foote could fire, other senators subdued him. Six years later, during the Kansas debates, a South Carolina representative bludgeoned Senator Charles Sumner so severely that he could not return to the Senate for three years. Today's violence is not nearly so serious, but it still at times exists. Congressmen Bert Podell and James Delaney of New York City got into a shoving match at a luncheon after Delaney dressed Podell down for defeating him for a seat on their party's steering committee. And Senator Strom Thurmond, a physical culturist, engaged in a lengthy wrestling match in the Senate Office Building with former Senator Ralph Yarborough when Yarborough tried to dragoon Thurmond into attending a committee hearing.

parties put aside political differences to attend briefings. There they learn, according to a *New Yorker* profile of Allard Lowenstein, "the special political etiquette of favors that members expect from each other and should be prepared to repay." In addition, they learn the wisdom of Sam Rayburn's maxim, "To get along, you've got to go along."

The freshmen must also learn their special role in this hierarchy of deference. The more florid levels of posturing are reserved for their seniors; like children, the freshmen are meant to be seen and not heard. When they do make a sound—in their maiden speeches—they are urged to be concise, modest, and well prepared. In this they follow the advice George Washington gave in 1787 to a nephew who was about to enter the Virginia House of Delegates: "Should the new legislator wish to be heard, the way to command the attention of the House is to speak seldom, but to important subjects . . . make yourself perfectly master of the subject. Never exceed a decent warmth, and submit your sentiments with diffidence."

Slow learners get reminders. In the 1950s, a freshman senator found himself sitting next to Walter George, who as longest surviving senator had earned the title of "Dean." Wishing perhaps to show George that he was eager to learn, the youngster leaned over and asked how the Senate had changed during George's countless years as a member. George paused, then icily responded, "Freshmen didn't used to talk so much." And the late Carl Hayden used to recall his first speech in the House in 1913. He had kept quiet for many months until a matter unimportant to the House but very important to his native Arizona came up. Hayden spoke to the chamber for only a minute, and returned to his seat next to a more senior member, who turned to him and angrily said, "Just had to talk, didn't you?"

This system is tolerated only because its victims know that someday they will be on the other end of the sneer. It is perpetuated with a powerful system of informal sanctions. "They can give you the silent treatment," said one representative, "and the real whip is delayed

action. You may think you are not going to be punished for your failure to stay in line because there is
no immediate penalty. Months later, however, something happens which makes you realize they were just
waiting for the proper moment to strike. There is no
doubt about it," he ruefully concluded, "if you are going
to be independent around here, you are going to pay a
steep price for it."

As in so much else, the senior members of Congress
can take liberties that no freshman would wisely dare.
Senator Bob Kerr of Oklahoma could call Senator
Homer Capehart "a rancid tub of ignorance" over a
decade ago precisely because he was Bob Kerr, one of
the most powerful men in the Senate. In 1972, Senate
Minority Leader Hugh Scott knew he would not suffer
for saying that the investigating of ITT's affair with the
Republican National Committee was Democratic "jack-
assery." But there is a line which even the powerful
cross with hesitation: charges that impugn a congressman by name. In the mid-sixties, Senator William Fulbright made just that mistake. Other senators did not
mind his usual charges that the "military industrial complex" influenced policy in Vietnam, but they were unhappy when he named Richard Russell, Scoop Jackson,
and Mendel Rivers as its operatives. And so, even
though his charges were truer than much of what passes
on the floor, and despite his seniority, Fulbright later
had to apologize formally for "any embarrassment" he
had caused. William Proxmire—less senior than Fulbright, but usually less impressed by rituals—was forced
into the same position. Proxmire sent a letter to Alabama's John Sparkman, chairman of the Banking Committee, complaining about delays in a consumer bill.
Sparkman could stand complaints—but not the public
airing of them that followed when Proxmire's letter
leaked to the Jack Anderson column. The code broken,
Proxmire had to go through the ritual of contrition and
forgiveness. On the Senate floor he said, "In the fourteen years I have been on the committee, I have never
known the senator from Alabama to stop legislation."
Knowing that it would wash away the stains, Proxmire

went on: "There has been no stalling, no delay—never."

If these indiscretions become chronic—or if they are not followed by repentance—they eventually push their authors into a special class within the congressional society. The newspaper-reading public may think of these congressmen as colorful or frank; but within Congress, they are pariahs. If they please their constituents enough to stay in office and gain seniority, they may eventually get some power in Congress. But such exiles can forget about the many stepping stones open to those who follow the rules.

Congressman Ronald Dellums, who as a black "radical" was already suspect in the eyes of many colleagues, earned the opprobrium of the House when he told a reporter that most senators and congressmen "are mediocre prima donnas who pass legislation that has nothing to do with the reality of misery in this country. The level of mediocrity of the leaders in the country scares the hell out of me." For this comment, Dellums was challenged by Congressman Wayne Hays on the floor:

> *Hays:* Did the gentleman [n.b.] make that statement?
> *Dellums:* Yes. Do you want me to explain it?
> *Hays:* No, I do not need you to explain it. I just wonder if you then want a bunch of mediocre prima donnas to pay more serious attention to your amendment?
> *Dellums:* If I don't, then my statement has double merit. I would simply say that [congressmen] go around strutting from their offices to the floor of the Congress and do not deal with the human misery in this country.
> *Hays:* You may strut around from *your* office to the floor and to God knows where . . . but do not measure, as my father used to say, everybody's corn in your own half-bushel.

Congressman Sam Steiger, a conservative Republican from Arizona, made a different escape from the same predicament. On a television program, Steiger had answered the question "Is it true that some members of Congress show up drunk?" by saying, "I have never seen them drunk on the floor. I have seen them drunk during the day. . . . Some members [are] assisted to their offices during the morning." When asked if some were "dumb clucks," Steiger said, "Oh yes. I think there are members of Congress that you wouldn't hire to wheel a wheelbarrow." In retribution, the House later initially killed Steiger's bill to transfer some federal land to the government of Steiger's home city—a routine measure usually passed without comment. Since then, Steiger has worked hard to overcome his gaffe and rewin his friends. One sign of his success came in mid-1971, when Bella Abzug delivered a two-minute speech against the war. As she took her seat, Steiger yelled "Right on, right on," to the chortles of his friends. Cajoling his way back into favor, Steiger has now become one of the boys again.

Congresswoman Bella Abzug probably could have guessed that her reception in Congress would be cool, despite her hats. She has followed few of the codes of etiquette, tongue-lashing the House ("I'm tired of listening to a bunch of old men who are long beyond the draft age standing here and talking about sending our young men over to be killed in an illegal and immoral war") and tongue-lashing Speaker Carl Albert ("Now you listen to me, Carl. I'm sick and tired, because it's about time this Democratic caucus went on record against the war. . . . What's the matter with you?"). She so dominated the proceedings of the Democratic caucus with her views that it soon became difficult to find a quorum. Congress stores up its vengeance silently. Whenever Abzug offers a measure, it gets 20–30 fewer votes than the same bill would under someone else's name. On September 30, 1971, she learned about more blatant retaliations. Shortly before noon, she began walking to the House floor, ready to present a resolution to force the State Department to reveal how deeply the United States was involved in South Vietnam's presidential elections. Although the House formally convenes at noon, routine trivia usually postpone the serious business till 12:30 or later. But on this day, at 12:01, Albert cracked his gavel and quickly called on Tom Morgan. Fighting hard to suppress guffaws, the House listened to Morgan say, "Mr. Speaker, I intended to yield to the gentlewoman from New York for ten minutes for debate only, but I do not see the gentlewoman on the floor." Within seconds, Albert and the House agreed to table the motion. It was all over by the time Bella strolled in at 12:03.

Congressman Don Riegle, a liberal Republican from Michigan, learned early that his ambitious peers cannot stand those who voice their ambitions openly. Riegle revealed his own daydreams, announcing in 1969, at age 31, that he hoped to be president in fifteen years and then retire to a university presidency. Riegle had not been in Congress long enough to read the invisible banner which flies atop the Capitol: Know Your Place. With help from men like Congressman Chuck Teague, who coos "How are you today, Mr. President?" each time he passes Riegle, Riegle has now learned. He now admits that his announcement was naïve, but he still hammers out a place for himself with antiwar statements and his recent and frank book, *O Congress.*

Senator Fred Harris, Oklahoma Democrat, was elected senator in 1964, at age 34, and a mere four years later was chairman of the Democratic National Committee. The normal pattern—that of Hubert Humphrey or Lyndon Johnson—would have been to settle for another twenty years of slow progress upward. Instead, Harris began to feel other pulls. His perspective shifted from the all-excusing "long run" view—which would have let him go along on many issues he could not stomach—to a more immediate concern with economic and social problems. He resigned from the National Committee and began a brief, luckless run for the 1972 presidential nomination. He began to push too hard in the Senate. On July 7, 1971, for example, he stood alone against sixty-four other senators. The Senate was voting on whether it should allow South Africa a sugar quota; it was nine at night, and all but Harris wanted to get home. In order to delay a second vote on the issue, Harris began to threaten a series of spurious quorum calls and amendments. Falling back on form rather than substance, Majority Leader Mike Mansfield made a final attempt to pull Harris back within the code. He accused Harris of having promised earlier that he would not introduce any amendments. "In the Senate," he said, "a senator's word is the only thing we have to rely on and that word ought to be something sacred." Harris wouldn't listen. He won his legislative point that night, but not before he was slapped on the wrist for it. On an amendment of his—to apply a form of economic discrimination against countries who exploit sugar workers under "inhuman conditions"—the Senate voted No by 78–14, largely out of pique.

Senator Mike Gravel, even more than Harris, has applied external standards of morality and propriety to the workings of the Senate. As Gravel thought more deeply about the horror of the Asian war, and compared it to the daily pleasantries on the Senate floor, he began to doubt that the "antiwar" senators were doing as much as they could. The cracking point came in 1971, with the appearance of the Pentagon Papers. While his colleagues were torn between consternation at what the papers showed, and irritation at the improper and possibly illegal publication of them, Gravel devoted himself to making the information public. He first tried to read then-unpublished portions into the *Congressional Record.* Blocked because there was no quorum, he then called a hasty meeting of the Senate Public Works Committee, of which he is a member. For three and a half hours he read, tears pouring down his face. With passion rare for its sincerity, he concluded, "The greatest representative democracy the world has known, the nation of Jefferson and Lincoln, has let its nose be rubbed in the swamp by petty warlords, jealous Vietnamese generals, blackmarketeers, and grand-scale dope pushers."

Like banqueters who see a starving child staring in through the window, the Senate turned away, angry at the intrusion. What mattered about Gravel's performance was not that the material was true, but that he had broken the rules in releasing it. Republicans Scott and Dole mumbled something about sanctions; Majority Leader Mansfield instead had a "friendly talk" with his erring ward. Managing a measure of contrition, Gravel later said, "Perhaps I did not approach the matter with the same degree of delicacy another would employ. What I did, I felt and continue to feel, will bring credit to the United States Senate, not embarrassment. I would never be party to any act that would not bring credit to this august body." To other senators, this last sentence was ludicrous: by bringing the starving child into the hall, Gravel had humiliated them all.

For those who can adapt to the folkways of the congressional society, there is a reward far different from the exile endured by Gravel and Abzug. This is membership in the "Club"—the informal roster of those who meet the Senate's and House's standards. Some degree of personal submission is required. Ambitious John and Robert Kennedy never learned this lesson, and were never popular among senators. Other traits can offend as well: Wayne Morse was too belligerent and waspish, Eugene McCarthy too detached and cerebral, Joseph Tydings too aloof. Those who best qualify have power (Lyndon Johnson and Robert Kerr), dignity (Richard Russell and Paul Douglas), homespun friendliness (Warren Magnuson), or seniority (the Southern patriarchs, living emblems of the motto Longevity Is Power).

Although Club perquisites come more naturally to older members and to conservatives than to young liberals, there is no ironclad age or ideological test for those who seek entrance. No clearer proof can be given than the case of Allard Lowenstein, one-term representative from New York. Before his election in 1968, his career as a political organizer and architect of the "Dump Johnson" movement placed him well to the left of most congressional liberals. But on his arrival—unlike Ms. Abzug—Lowenstein managed to play by House rules. Other

congressmen "found that he is not the wild-eyed maverick most people thought him to be," said one colleague. "He's quietly doing his homework, and as a
result he's gaining much respect in the House." When
first introduced to Mendel Rivers—grand promoter of
the defense industries Lowenstein fought—Lowenstein
said, "Mr. Chairman, I have relatives who are constituents of yours"—adding that their name was Rivers.
"Well," rumbled Rivers, "there's been a lot of inter-
marriage down there." After that, the two would call
each other "cousin." He also managed to charm Carl
Albert, who told Lowenstein, "You're not a long-hair-
and-beard type at all." After he had served a few weeks
in the House, Lowenstein won the unusual privilege
for a freshman of presiding over the floor for a few
minutes in Albert's absence.

Another freshman who is trying hard to win the club-
men's hearts—and who has a better chance than Lowenstein of staying to reap the rewards—is Republican
Senator Charles Mathias of Maryland. In his first two
years, Mathias has established himself to such an extent
that one colleague says, "On those quickie votes on
amendments, you waltz on the floor and the first things
you ask are 'What is it?' and 'Whose is it?' If it is
Mathias, that's worth about ten votes."

Called Mac (a boyhood name) by all factions,
Mathias has struck the right mixture of dignity and
affability. "He's always got that cherubic smile and sort
of twinkle in his eye," says one senator. Another adds,
"He doesn't take himself so serious as to be ponderous."
Mathias deftly displayed a due courtesy toward the
Senate's demigods in response to questions about his
future goals. He replied that the ideal senator was someone like Robert Taft, Sr., of Ohio, "whose word and
position were respected in the areas in which he was
a leader."

Congressional Cliques

President Nixon has Bebe Rebozo and Vice President
Agnew has Bob Hope, Harvard has the Porcellian Club

and Yale has Skull and Bones—and the American Congress has, among others, the Chowder and Marching Society, the Doormen's Society, the Prayer Breakfast Group, the Sundowners, the Monday Morning Meeting, the Tuesday Morning Breakfast Club, the Wednesday Group, and the Southern Caucus.

As in any tradition-ridden society, these clubs play a crucial part in the social structure of Congress. Any implication at all of frivolity or lightness is usually deserved. Like girls at camp, boys at college, or adults in bowling leagues and stag clubs, congressmen just can't resist high jinks and good clean fun. Like basketball players on the court, or collegians coming home after heavy dates, congressmen "don't just speak to one another," Riegle writes. "They punch each other on the arm, slap each other on the knee, grab each other's jackets and—occasionally—give each other the goose." The main difference between the congressional club system and university fraternities is that while the members give allegiance to the rules and habits of the group, only in Congress does the fraternity atmosphere make a difference in the way the rest of us live. In trying to understand some of the inexplicable outcomes of our legislative process, it is important to note the roles of three kinds of social clubs.

The first category is made of the purely good-times groups. Congressmen, like the rest of us, want to relax when the day is over. For some, the best way to do this is with their colleagues. Current social clubs include the Doormen's Society, which meets each year for a "Knight's Night." Last year, Gerald Ford was finally made a member; not really joking, he said, "It took me 16 years to become minority leader, but it's taken me 23½ years to become a Doorman, which I take as a measure of its prestige." Older members meet in the Sundowners Club, while former members make up the Former Members of Congress. This is one of the largest groups—its ranks boosted after each election—and has 370 members. At its annual reunion in 1971, members offered long speeches (Walter Judd), short speeches (101-year-old Earl Haley, who said, "I'm happy to be here today—and that's no lie"), and ribald speeches (Carl Bachman). Frank Chelf, a former Kentucky Democrat, said that whenever he felt a speech coming on, he tried to resist and play the harmonica instead, at which point he whipped out his harmonica and played a rendition of "My Blue Heaven."

When these recreational activities are loaded with political overtones, they lead to the second category of congressional clubs. In these, business is pleasure; votes are traded over card games and glasses of gin; good joke-telling or expert arm-wrestling may make the difference between success and failure for an education or defense bill. They descend from the nineteenth-century School of Philosophy Club, where it was hard to separate the poker from the politics. An equally misnamed group, Sam Rayburn's "Board of Education," used to meet in the late afternoons in Mr. Sam's hideaway office in the Capitol to sip whiskey and play politics. Today the Chowder and Marching Society gives its fifteen members the chance to talk intimately with Gerald Ford or Defense Secretary Melvin Laird. On his admission to the club, Congressman Thomas Railsback said, "It was the best thing that has happened to me from a political standpoint." Members even got to go to a special White House dinner with President Nixon. Another Republican group, SOS (allegedly for "Save Our Souls") includes all the upper stories of the GOP power structure. "The groups do groom people for leadership," says a Chowder man, "perhaps not by a conscious effort but as a result of the close relationships the members form." *

The third type of group fits more closely the textbook

---

* A variant of this type of group is the Prayer Breakfast Club. About thirty to forty-five members meet weekly for prayer and fellowship, creating bonds which appear later in legislative cooperation. Since 1955, a room has been set aside in the Capitol for their prayer and meditation. "Normally used sparingly at the beginning of a session," writes Charles Clapp in *The Congressman: His Work as He Sees It*, "the room is much frequented when critical complex issues are before the House."

model of what congressmen do with their spare time. These clubs—like the Democratic Study Group or the Black Caucus—are purely political alliances, the structural manifestations of congressional allegiances and blocs. The first one began in 1957, when eighty House liberals began a study group. Alternately named "The Young Turks," "The Liberal Manifesto," and "McCarthy's Mavericks" (after founder Eugene McCarthy, then a representative), the group finally settled on the bland title of "Democratic Study Group" (DSG) in order to discourage the press from referring to them as insurgents. In its early days, the group remained intentionally loose and informal; to do more, McCarthy said, "might be construed as a direct challenge to [House speaker] Rayburn's leadership." In the last decade the DSG has become more active, providing much-needed information on bills to members and lining up votes with its own "whip" system It also produces fact books for the public, including recent ones on the defense budget and tax reform The group reached a peak membership of 180 during the Eighty-ninth Congress (1965–66), the heady days of Lyndon Johnson's Great Society. Since then its membership has fallen to 140.

Two other ideological groups are the Black Caucus and the Members of Congress for Peace through Law (MCPL). The thirteen black congressmen who make up the caucus use the group as an organizing center for congressional action on issues of importance to black Americans. By holding unofficial hearings, issuing press releases, and developing legislation, the group puts pressure on resistant points in Congress. Because it represents a national constituency, and because its members are usually from safe districts, the caucus can afford to be less reverent toward other congressmen. "There are many congressmen whose constituencies are 35 to 40 percent black who consistently vote against the interests of their black constituents," says Congressman William Clay of the caucus. "We are going to expose the records of those congressmen." Such direct affronts to other members' security are rare elsewhere.

The MCPL is one of the few beneficial products of

the war. It began as a series of informal luncheon discussions in 1967, and now includes 134 members. Unlike most of the other clubs, it contains members from both houses and parties. Its slant, however, is clearly liberal—especially on defense questions. The organizers of MCPL show an acute perception of Congress's weakness. Realizing that Congress can hardly challenge defense budgets when congressmen know so little about any of the items requested, MCPL members have tried to correct that problem by making individual members into specialists on missile policy or tank programs. "Essentially, it's a rebel organization," says member Pete McCloskey. "We're rebelling against the close tie between the administration and committee chairmen, who have a monopoly on information."

A Little Bit of Pomp

Buckingham Palace would probably run without its guards; the American judicial system would probably not suffer if it had no clerks to yell "Oyez, oyez, oyez . . . God save the United States of America and this honorable court." Congress, too, would survive, shabbier but no less efficient, if its quaint customs and rituals were streamlined away. But Congress would be poorer for the loss—as would forests without their beautiful hummingbirds or envelopes without colored stamps.

Like a foreign city which unveils its treasures only slowly, Congress has more arcane, implausible traditions than are at first apparent. It has a Capitol architect who is rarely an architect; it declares a national emergency after each summer vacation to comply with a moldy statute permitting autumn meetings only at time of crisis. The most obvious tradition in daily performance is the emphasis on parliamentary decorum. There are tales from pre-War Germany of Jewish families who dined on in controlled calm as storm troopers burst through the front door. Congress, too, gives that impression of order in the face of adversity. In 1932, a department store clerk leaned from the House galleries waving a gun and demanding a chance to speak. Panic broke out below, and congressmen fled for cover. But as Congressman Thomas S. McMillan, then in the presiding officer's chair, decided that his life, too, was worth saving, House parliamentarian Lewis Deschler told him solemnly, "You can't leave. You're presiding." Deschler, who is still the parliamentarian, was proud of the resolve displayed several years later by Congressman Joe Martin. As four Puerto Rican nationalists began to rain shots down at congressmen from the gallery, Martin managed to blurt, "The House stands recessed," before running for his life.

Beneath this crust of decorum, some customs have a more important effect on how well Congress gets its work done. One obscure ritual devours more congressional time than items like "legislating" or "attending to the nation's problems." This is the quorum call—the parliamentary device of making sure there are enough members on the floor to conduct business. In practice, it is a stalling technique. When congressmen want to check the arrangements for an upcoming bill, look over the draft of a speech they're making, or head off an upcoming vote, they say, "Mr. Chairman, I suggest the absence of a quorum." Then the whole machinery of government grinds to a halt, and buzzers ring throughout the Capitol buildings. Members drop what they are doing —holding committee hearings, listening to constituents—not because there's anything important on the floor, but because they want to have a good attendance record. Most members know precisely how long it takes from the ring of the first buzzer until their name is called, and they time their arrival so they can stride onto the floor, answer "Present," and head back without breaking stride. "Two minutes after its conclusion," says writer Larry King, "one couldn't find a quorum with bloodhounds." In the meantime, an average of twenty-five minutes for each congressman has been wasted.

At the other end of the efficiency spectrum is the custom of the Capitol flagpole. With a spirit that would have made early Yankee traders proud, Congress has devised one more way of marketing its prestige. Two congressional employees, James Reed and Walter Childress, go to work each morning knowing that by the time they quit they will have added several hundred more artifacts to history. These two fellows run American flags up and down the Capitol flagpole, so that members can mail certain constituents a genuine "United States flag flown over the Capitol." To the unwary, this might suggest a tattered Old Glory, buffeted by winds but still proudly flying, returning to some safe resting place after a long career aloft. In 1937, for example, only six flags flew the whole year. Today's instant mementos spend only a few seconds atop the Capitol. "When I get going, I'll be running them up and down every three minutes," Reed says. In 1971, he and his associate worked fast enough to get 27,649 up and down. His pace is slowed down days when the flags must fly at half-staff, and he also is encumbered by the requirement that the flags actually "fly" at the top of the pole. There is no precise definition of "flying," but direct observation of the flagpole on August 9, 1972, showed that the 86 flags processed spent an average of seven seconds aloft. Eight hit the top and then immediately began their descent. In its report on the day's operation, however, the Capitol architect's office somehow reported that 128 flags were ready to be distributed by congressmen.

In the same spirit of giving everyone a little dab of government, congressmen also spend inordinate time naming days after local groups. During 1968 and 1969, more than five hundred special days or weeks were proposed—including Service Station Operation Day, Date Week, Break-No-Law-Today Day, National Jewish Hospital Save Your Breath Month, and standard items like Mother's Day and Flag Day. Political maneuvering can be as sharp here as in weightier matters. When Wilbur Mills asked Lyndon Johnson's White House to proclaim National Duck Day on behalf of a duck-calling contest in Arkansas, LBJ proclaimed Migratory Waterfowl Day to emphasize protecting ducks, rather than shooting them.

Few of these charades would be possible or worthwhile without the help of the *Congressional Record*—which is, in its way, the greatest charade of them all. In purely technical terms, the *Record* is an impressive operation: each day, within thirteen hours of the close of debate, the congressional presses have turned out 49,000 copies of another thick edition of the *Record*. As congressmen arrive for their morning's work, they find tall stacks of the *Record*, still glistening with printer's ink, waiting outside their door. But while the production of the *Record* may be impressive, its content is not. The *Record* is a subsidiary Xeroxing service for congressmen, producing by the thousands whatever item they choose. The back section of the *Record*—often half or two-thirds of its bulk—is made of various insertions: articles from *Reader's Digest*, speeches boosting some favored constituent, clever items from the home-town paper which have caught the member's eye. One day, shrewd doctors and dentists will learn to stock their waiting rooms with copies of the *Record*, knowing that their anxious patients may relax with items like the following:

> *Sen. Marlow Cook:* Mr. President, the more than 38,000 dry cleaners in America are proud of their role as one of the active forces that help Americans maintain their status as the best groomed people in the world.
>
> Representatives of the drycleaning industry are located in every community in the United States and employ over 300,000 persons. Thanks to this industry, Americans may go to work, to school, to church, or to social gatherings in clean freshly pressed garments composed of a variety of materials and styles. . . . I hope that all my colleagues will join with me in supporting the joint resolution that I introduced which is so necessarily desired by the drycleaning industry as a tribute to all Americans who recognize the importance of good grooming habits in their everyday life, and in doing so, convey a most favorable impression of the American people to the rest of the world.

Rep. Thomas Ashley: Mr. Speaker, it is with great pride that I take this opportunity to congratulate the Whitmer High School debate team of Toledo, Ohio, for winning its second consecutive national debate championship in the National Forensic League tournament held at Wake Forest University in Winston-Salem, N.C., from June 19 to June 22.

Even the parts of the *Record* which appear to be chronicles of the day's debate are far from accurate. Under a ritual known as Privilege to Revise and Extend, members are able to edit their remarks into coherence —or delete them—before they are committed to print. Without this review, said one congressman, the *Record* "would be really sad reading the next day—the best comic book you ever saw." What this says about the caliber of actual floor debate does not seem to sink into the congressmen. Instead, knowing that only the handful of people in the galleries know what they really said, they are content to make a garbled statement so long as they later make the *Record* precise. "After you fix your senator's mistakes," says one aide, "you may have to call the staff of the other senator and say, 'How about changing your guy to saying something else so my guy will make sense?' You're not supposed to change the contents of the *Record,* but we do." The benefit of revision can lead to sloppy habits. One congressman complained that something he had said in an interview with the Nader Congress Project was used (accurately) in his profile; "I'm used to amending my remarks," he lamented. But even worse, changes in content can mean changes in the law, since courts trying to determine "legislative intent" may turn to the congressional debate to see what Congress had in mind.

The final twist on the revise and extend privilege is the power it gives congressmen to insert "speeches" which were never delivered. To give the insertions roughly the same authenticity as the seven-second flags, the chair will call on the missing representative, pause, and then say "The time of the gentleman has expired."

Into the gap goes the written speech, looking exactly as if it had been spoken. Congressman Ken Hechler poked fun at this ruse by "saying":

> I do not want to kid anyone into thinking that I am now on my feet delivering a stirring oration. As a matter of fact, I am back in my office typing this out on my own hot little typewriter. . . . Such is the pretense of the House that it would have been easy to just quietly include these remarks in the *Record,* issue a brave press release and convince thousands of cheering constituents that I was in there fighting every step of the way, influencing the course of history.*

To put the appropriate close on these congressional customs, we should note the tradition of prayer. Strict rules govern the prayer which begins each morning's session: the House chaplain emphasizes the bipartisan tone of his calling by sitting first on the Democratic side, then with the Republicans, after his speech; he cannot favor any denomination over another; he can give no spiritual guidance on upcoming votes.

At times visiting ministers are permitted to deliver the

---

* However deceptive the *Record* may be, pornographic it is not. In October, 1921, the House censured Thomas Blanton, a Democratic representative from Texas, 293–0, for inserting profane language into the *Record*. He had included an angry letter from a government employee who wrote the following to someone who had fired him, according to the way the *Congressional Record* now reports the proceedings of October 22, 1921: "You are a G-d d-mn liar, you low-down son of a b----."

The *Record* cannot be accused of sensationalism either. When Puerto Rican Nationalists shot five congressmen from the galleries on March 1, 1954, the *Record* for that day dryly notes that "at approximately 2 o'clock and 30 minutes P.M. a demonstration and the discharge of firearms from the southwest House Gallery (No. 11) interrupted the counting of the vote; the Speaker, pursuant to the inherent power lodged in the Presiding Officer in the case of grave emergency, after ascertaining that certain Members had been wounded and to facilitate their care, at 2 o'clock and 32 minutes P.M. declared the House in recess, subject to call of the Chair."

prayer. The member who represents the minister's district invariably rises afterwards to congratulate the guest speaker, which naturally pleases him and, the member hopes, his flock. One visiting prayer became a classic when the minister decided to incorporate parliamentary jargon into his talk:

> O Supreme Legislator . . . Make seniority in Your love ever germane to their conduct. Make them consistently vote yea in the cloakroom of conscience that at the expiration of life's term they may feel no need to revise and extend. . . .
>
> When the Congress of life is adjourned and they answer the final quorum call, may the eternal committee report out a clean bill on their lives.

Perquisites: Nice Work if You Can Get It

Congress has rarely had a problem recruiting members to fill its seats. But—as part of the sad irony that loads most benefits on jobs that would be satisfying anyway and gives least reward to tasks of dull drudgery —the side benefits (called "perquisites") of being a congressman have steadily risen. Some are small but meaningful: cheap, tax-free meals in House and Senate restaurants; a tax deduction of $3,000 annually for living costs in Washington; free plants from the botanical garden; unduly cheap taxi rides in Washington (a privilege shared with other residents of the District of Columbia, who must endure rule by congressional committees); medical care at a flat rate of $58 per day at any military hospital; twelve free trips home per year; free travel abroad if an official reason can be found.

Other privileges are invisible on the record books, but can take the breath away when seen at first hand. Policemen spread their arms to part the traffic on nearby streets when congressmen pass. Special elevators are marked "Senators Only" or "Members Only," and whisk their occupants away while the masses stand waiting for the unrestricted cars. They park their automobiles (with their prestigious license plates) at special, nearby garages. Clerks at Washington's National Airport delay planes for tardy congressmen and bump paying passengers to make way for senators. The phone company puts "Honorable" before their listing in the directory.

Then there is the pay—$42,500, up 42 percent since 1965—which is a sensitive issue for congressmen, who fear voter resentment over its scale. When Congress voted in 1816 to raise its salary to $1,500 per year, there was a voter backlash which defeated many members. The newly elected Congress promptly repealed the increase. A century and a half later, shortly before voting to approve its present salary, a member admitted, "My lips say No, No, but my heart says Yes! Yes!" The $42,500, comfortable as it sounds, actually disappears quickly when applied to the expenses of holding office: the costs of printing newsletters; trips home beyond the twelve at public expense; the ornaments of gracious living, such as memberships in stylish clubs or donations to home-town causes, which the constituents expect of their elected. Many congressmen, therefore, complain that the $42,500 is not enough to live on, as does Congressman Louis Frey (who regularly votes against unemployment compensation for migrant workers).

For both the taxpayers and the congressmen, the most financially important congressional perquisite is the office and staff allowance. For a government that runs on paper, the congressman has ample free allowances at the government stationery store; there is an ample budget for office equipment. Senators are allowed between $295,938 and $477,978, depending on the size of their states, to hire secretaries and professional staff; representatives get $141,492 to $148,896. The staff payrolls have swollen dramatically in the past decade; because of this, together with higher congressional salaries, increasing mounds of franked mail, and other rising expenses, the cost of running Congress has more than quadrupled within ten years, from $135.4 million in 1962 to $557 million in 1972.

Members and their staffs work out of official offices, which themselves become a next level of perquisites; or, as it is said, where a man stands depends on where he sits. Like so much else, allocation of office suites depends on seniority. In order to get a three-room suite in the new and spacious Rayburn Office Building, one has to be at least a five-term representative. (You can also get three rooms in the older Longworth Building, but "the third room may be down the hall or upstairs," says House Building Superintendent A. E. Ridgell.) So freshmen like Congressman Les Aspin or Senator John Tunney get located in obscure corridors far from the center of activity. As suites open up, the most senior members get first pick. Former governors like Harold Hughes and Mark Hatfield, accustomed to a state mansion, chauffered car, and #1 license plate, have the most difficult time adjusting to their lowly freshman status.

Only the very most senior can get a crack at one of the seventy-five secret hideaways within the Capitol Building itself. These provide quiet retreats from the bustle outside, and have been used for pastimes ranging from office dictation to partying to Sam Rayburn's "Board of Education." Lyndon Johnson, before moving to 1600 Pennsylvania Avenue, had seven of these rooms, together known as "LBJ Ranch East." To distribute the other rooms, Johnson "put together rooms like a subdivided building or tract," said a senator's aide. "When you wound up in one of those windowless basements where the walls sweated all day, you got a pretty good idea of where you stood with LBJ." More recently, the most splendid secret room belonged to the late Allen Ellender. It had two huge chandeliers, a built-in stove, and a freezer stocked with oysters and Louisiana shrimp.

To house these offices, stately and lowly, and to give a final perquisite, Congress has sponsored a building boom inspired by the judgment and tasteful restraint of Albert Speer and Ramses II. As recently as 1900, congressmen had no formal "offices." If they couldn't do their work at their desk on the floor, they took it back to their boardinghouse room. As business expanded, and as the committee system added a new bureaucratic order to congressional operations, both houses decided in the early years of the century to outfit themselves with adequate offices. In 1903, the first House building was completed, and a year later the Senate moved into its office building.

The need for working space was certainly acute, but there is reason to doubt that the enormous piles of marble on Capitol Hill are the appropriate remedy. The recent buildings include the New Senate Office Building (1958), the extension of the east front of the Capitol (1960), the Rayburn Office Building (1965), and the pending plan to extend the west front of the Capitol by 88 feet.

The plans for the west front extension—one of many campaigns overseen by Capitol architect George Stewart, who died in 1971—have been quite controversial. The current western façade is shaky and needs work; but, as the *New York Times* editorialized, "According to the Capitol architect, the only way to prop up the crumbling west front is with two restaurants, two cafeterias, two private dining rooms, conference, committee, and document rooms, offices, a barber shop, a visitors' center—at a cost of $45 million. . . . This is not exactly a bargain. It is, in fact, an outrage."

For precedent, critics of the west front plan need only glance across the Capitol lawns to the glistening edifice known as the Rayburn Office Building. As the construction costs rose from the early estimates of $40–$65 million to the eventual record-setting $122 million, so did the grandiose dreams of its designers. The same people who call the dead the "dear departed" or bombing raids "interdictment," refer to the building's style as "simplified classic." In more straightforward language, it has been called "Mussolini Modern" or "Texas Penitentiary." Within its 720 feet of frontage and 450-foot depth, it contains 50 acres of office space, 25 elevators, 23 escalators, garage space for 1,600 cars, a swimming pool, a gymnasium, and several overnight rooms. In sum, in the words of architectural critic Ada Louise Huxtable, it is "a national disaster. Its defects range from profligate mishandling of 50 acres of space to elephantine esthetic brutality at record costs. . . . It is quite possible that this is the worst building for the most money in the history of the construction art. It stuns by sheer mass and boring bulk."

But it makes congressmen feel important, the way pyramids made pharaohs feel godlike. When the buildings and the offices and the staffs combine with the less ostensible emoluments of citizen deference to the member's station, what one observer has called the "elevator phenomenon" sets in. A new congressman may arrive with humility intact, but when he gets instant elevator service while others are kept waiting, he begins to realize that he is, well, different. For the perquisites and their general status create a gigantic congressional ego, a state of self-reflection which has a serious influence on how the members relate among themselves and to outsiders. "On the hustings they are all good Joes," said a Senate staffer, "but when they are here [in Washington] a good many of them try to play God."

Love and Marriage

Washington, Mrs. Oliver Wendell Holmes once told Teddy Roosevelt, is "a place full of famous men and the women they married when they were young." One result, especially recently, has been the breakups of politicians' marriages. Nearly all congressmen arrive married; the current Congress includes only thirteen bachelors. But the tensions of political life apply strains that some marriages cannot endure. Mrs. William Proxmire, separated from her husband, bemoaned the difficulties of "living in a fishbowl and the long separations." "Everyone else has first claim on the senator," says Mrs. George Aiken (who should know, since she has been, as well, Aiken's staff aide for years). Consequently, their marriages and family lives often take a second seat to the fulfillment of the spouse's political career. When Mrs. Albert Quie called her husband to say that her baby was about to arrive, Quie replied, "Well, I've got to make a speech against Secretary Freeman first." He did, and was still in time to get to the hospital.

Another burden on marriages is the sexual temptations public officeholders face. Using power as a love potion, mixing with the glamorous, some congressmen put aside marital loyalties as carelessly as they shed other duties. There is not much discussion of this in print, since it is unfair to single out a congressman or congressmen as a group for something not unique to Washington. But at the same time it would be naïve to assume that only fidelity flourishes on Capitol Hill.

Congressional sexual activity varies in aim and intensity. Most innocently, there is the kind of leering indulged in by high school students. Don Riegle reports that a Republican colleague once nudged him on the House floor and said, "Look up there—in the third row," motioning toward the visitors' gallery. According to Riegle, "Sitting there was an attractive redhead in a green dress. What my colleague was directing my attention to was the fact that one of her thighs was fully exposed. He had already tipped off several other members, all of whom were casting appreciative glances at the gallery. Some, in fact, had moved to other locations on the floor to get a better view. Thigh watching is one of the most popular diversions in the House."

There can also be the old-fashioned, direct proposition. *Washington Post* reporter Sally Quinn describes how "one senator offered me a ride home from a party and it was raining and so I accepted. On the way he mentioned his wife was out of town, and put his hand on my head, then on my neck, and pulled me close. I pulled away from him. 'I thought you were offering me a ride home,' I said. He looked at me and said, 'What do you think I'm running, a taxi service?'" Or there can be something seamier. Congressman Thomas Steed, annoyed with the Senate's stance against free junk-mailing privileges for House members, threatened a sexual exposé unless the Senate changed its mind. After Senator Everett Dirksen ridiculed Steed as "the white charger from Oklahoma," Steed retaliated with his "exposé": "I personally know of a senator who keeps two call girls on his payroll." Steed eventually apologized for making the charges, but did not retract them. Such alleged practices are undoubtedly rare, since they contain the makings of a Profumo-type scandal. At the same time, there was the observation of Arthur Marshall, state's attorney for a county near Washington, D.C., who said there had not been many prosecutions for prostitution in his area since they arrested a call girl "who had a substantial index file containing the names of many important men, including members of Congress."

Wives react differently to all the marital strains. The largest number simply "fulfill" themselves through their famous husbands. Others contribute directly to their husbands' work: Marvella Bayh and Eleanor McGovern are political confidants as well as spouses. A few wives chart their own lives: Jane Hart has become a peace activist, with several arrests on her record, while Mrs. Herman Talmadge runs a thriving business back home in Georgia.

But some marriages cannot withstand the tension of wives tending the households, alone, while their husbands politick. In the last few years, William Proxmire, Eugene McCarthy, and Pete McCloskey have all separated from their wives; Robert Dole was divorced in January, 1972, and John Tunney's wife filed for divorce a few months later. Formal divorces—as opposed to dead but unburied marriages, of which there are many—have become more frequent in recent years, as national taboos have relaxed and as politicians like Nelson Rockefeller have shown that a broken marriage need not end a political career.

Relatively few congressmen seem to have considered one other alternative: sacrificing their political hopes. Two who did—Congressmen William Curlin and Patrick Coffery—voluntarily retired from Congress in 1972 rather than subject their families to the inevitable pressure. "You pay a price in terms of family life if you pursue a congressional career," said Curlin.

At Play

Mike Mansfield relaxes in his garden, Hugh Scott is one of the country's leading collectors of Chinese art of the T'ang dynasty, Congressman James Symington thinks karate is "a great conditioner," and 69-year-old

Senator Strom Thurmond jogs, lifts weights, and performs calisthenics. All is not intrigue in cloakrooms or debate over issues of national moment. Congressmen, too, know how to relax.

Even before Richard Nixon became *de facto* coach for the Washington Redskins, sports have been popular on Capitol Hill. Senators Javits and Percy are both adept tennis players, rising at daybreak to get in a few swings before starting work. Senator Alan Cranston, 58, is a serious sprinter, the former holder of the world record for 55-year-olds in the 100-yard dash (12.6 seconds). An admitted "track nut," Cranston wakes up at 6 A.M. most mornings to work out.

Many members of the House work out in the Rayburn pool and gym, two places forbidden to visitors. Congressmen regularly swim naked in the 20-by-60-foot pool—except on the three mornings a week when congresswomen get their chance. Perhaps the most popular Capitol Hill sport is paddleball, a cross between squash and tennis. It is rumored that some members will ask for quorum calls so they can sneak down to get a choice court when the paddleball players scatter for the floor. Congressman Guy Vander Jagt is the president of the paddleball players and was a winner of the annual Bullshot of the Year award. While nominally awarded to the congressman who cheats and argues most during a game, it is actually a reflection of peer esteem. (The only responsibility it carries is to preside over the gym's annual dinner, which invariably ends with congressmen dipping their napkins into water pitchers and hurling wetballs at each other in athletic romp.) Don Riegle has gone so far as to call paddleball "sacrosanct." Once, during one of the few House debates on the war, an irritated Riegle said, "And where are those members who minutes ago voted to cut off debate? They're down in the House gym playing paddleball!" For this he was roundly criticized by his colleagues. "You know damn well we need a House gym," said Congressman Elford Cederberg. "Members just don't get enough exercise."

In part to insure that they get good exercise, Democratic and Republican congressmen play each other in an annual summer baseball game at RFK Stadium in Washington. In 1971, the Republicans won their eighth straight game, 7–3, provoking a series of explanations from the losers. "We're doing well," said Congressman James Symington, "it's merely a question of our hitting and fielding, which are terrible." Congressman Morris Udall soothed his teammates, saying, "We've been losing these games for eight years and winning all of the important elections." But jokes aside, the game is played in earnest, as Congressman James Mann found out when he dislocated his shoulder while sliding into home plate —and catcher Barry Goldwater, Jr.

A different "sport" practiced by some congressmen is drinking, which is indulged in, although not publicly talked about. Titillating novels about political Washington probably exaggerate its extent, but not its existence. If there are five million alcoholics in America, and many million more who drink heavily, it is understandable in as pressured and fast-paced a world as Washington that not all congressmen are teetotalers. There is a rule that liquor cannot be brought onto the floor of either chamber. This was reportedly laid down in March of 1865, after Vice President Andrew Johnson reeled into the Senate to take his oath of office and triggered a scandal as well. Nevertheless, many members' offices contain well-stocked liquor cabinets which swing open at the end of a long day. Its effect on their daily responsibilities is largely a matter of conjecture, but Congressman Richard Bolling did reveal in an interview that, as part of the strategy for passing the 1961 plan to expand the House Rules Committee, it was necessary to get one key congressman drunk before the voting.

A more open way that congressmen play is to party. Washington has come a long way since a French envoy said upon his arrival there in 1803, "My God! What have I done to be condemned to reside in this city?" If anything, there is a surfeit of partying. There are some 100 embassies which throw two parties a year. There are 262 national associations, 50 state delegations, and of course 535 senators and representatives, many of whom throw bashes. One could spend every night simply going from one to the other, but this is not as much fun as it seems. After a bit, they can become quite similar and boring. Of course, going to hostess Perle Mesta's is different from a night at the Icelandic embassy, but not by all that much. The posh and stylish Georgetown used to be *the* place for *au courant* parties, but its Kennedy glamour has faded in a socially drab Republican administration. Night life does, at least, enable you to know colleagues and their spouses in a way the House and Senate do not facilitate. When Birch and Marvella Bayh first came to Washington from the Midwest in the early 1960s, they were invited to a typical party. "I wondered how I'd fit in," Mrs. Bayh admitted. "But everybody was so nice and so helpful and I realized that almost everybody in Washington had the same experience. . . . I remember one night sitting next to Senator Estes Kefauver of Tennessee and he turned and asked me if he could finish my dinner if I wasn't going to eat it and I thought then how these are just people like us."

7

Work Congressmen Do

> *My father served in Congress from 1909 to 1919 from the state of Texas. . . . A representative got about fifteen letters a week. Only at rarè intervals would a constituent come to see him. He had no pressure groups to contend with. Because Congress enacted only a few bills each session, legislation got the deliberative attention it deserved. . . . A good debater had no trouble getting a large audience in the chamber. Most of the member's time was spent on legislation. There was little else for him to do.*
> —Congressman Martin Dies, 1954

As the newly elected congressman heads off in glory to Washington, he knows that power, duty, and a hand in the nation's future lie ahead. But he may be puzzled by the same question that John Kennedy asked himself as he settled behind the Oval Office desk after his inauguration: Just what am I supposed to *do* all day?

In the early years of the Republic, the answer would have been "Not much." A member of the First Congress, Senator William Maclay, recorded the events of April 3, 1790, in his diary: "We went to the Hall. The Minutes were read. A message was received from the President of the United States. A report was handed to the chair. We looked and laughed at each other today for half an hour, then adjourned."

Today it's a different story. Starting early and sometimes working into the night, he or she goes to committee meetings and listens to hearings; answers mail and woos constituents; fields phone calls and courts

government agencies; gives speeches and prepares legislation; seeks out campaign monies and rushes to roll
calls; returns to the district and speaks wherever two
or more are gathered. "I'm absolutely swamped with
work," Clark MacGregor said during his days in Congress. "After the long day, I must do an additional two
to four hours of research at home." Across the range of
ideologies, from conservatives like William Poage to
liberals like Bella Abzug, fourteen-hour days are common. Congress used to convene on March 4 and adjourn
by July 4. Now it convenes the first week in January
and doesn't go home until sometime in the late fall.

Although most congressmen do work long and hard,
it is still impossible for them to accomplish more than a
small fraction of what is expected of them. Which is
why every member has a staff. As used in Washington,
"the staff" refers to one of the great cryptic institutions
of government, the administrative assistants and legislative aides who make up a congressman's alter ego.
Ranging in number from ten to fifty per member (depending on whether one is a representative or a senator,
whether from a small or large state), staff assistants
can be as important as the members they work for. As
Nicholas I once lamented, "Not I, but ten thousand
clerks rule Russia."

The staff person's duties are identical to the textbook
listing of a congressman's duties. In each stage of the
legislative process—from opening the mail to drafting a
bill—the staff does most of the legwork. This is a curious institution—in which talented people pour their
efforts anonymously into another man's performance
and prestige. But it has also become a necessary one as
Congress's workload has grown. Someone must answer
the four thousand letters Senator Jacob Javits receives
each week. And someone must assist Javits since he
serves on seven committees and nineteen subcommittees
and since he may be scheduled for half a dozen hearings
in any one morning. Because the number of senators
has not expanded to keep pace with the Senate's volume
of business ("Our most precious commodity," a staff
man has said, "is senators"), Javits could not hope to

keep up with the work without the help of his staff, which numbers about fifty in Washington. Thus, when Javits gives a Senate speech on civil rights legislation, Pat Shakow whispers key facts into his ear; when Senator Philip Hart holds a press conference on antimonopoly legislation, Buck O'Leary, who directed the drafting of the bill, gives him answers to reporters' questions. It was excellent staff work which prepared Senator Fulbright's famous 1964 "Old Myths and New Realities" talk, Robert Kennedy's seminal statement on Latin America in 1966, and Senator Tom Eagleton's recent battle against the Pentagon's MBT-70 tank.

Less grandly, congressional assistants must gauge what to feed their employer, and when. Too much information is as bad as too little. One aide to Senator Hart said, "You can walk down the hall with Hart or Humphrey and say, 'These are the six things you have to remember—tick, tick, tick, tick, tick, tick,' And they'll remember every detail. But it wouldn't have done a damn bit of good to give them information a week ahead." And they must do what their boss would rather avoid. "You need them for protection," said former Senator Eugene McCarthy, "to go to lunch for you."

The ideal staff must be like the ideal hairpiece: effective but unobtrusive. One man runs their show, and at no time should they entertain loyalties to anyone besides "the Senator" or "the Representative." What lures them to perform this uncelebrated work? Partly it is money; a good administrative assistant may be earning $30,000 after a few years in Washington. Even more, it is the sense of power that comes from intimacy with the mighty. Although the senator's name is attached to a speech or bill, the staff man who wrote it can always think of it as his. The natural danger is, as one put it, "You begin to think you're brighter than your boss. Some people even start acting as if they're really the senator or congressman." But whatever the benefit to the staff assistant, the benefit to the representative or senator is obvious. As one staff person put it, "A good administrative assistant can make or break his boss. If he's good he can make an ordinary guy look great. In all the years I worked there, the only times I ever heard of a congressman or senator getting into real trouble came from one of two reasons. His administrative assistant let him down, or there was hanky-panky in his office."

Even with a capable staff, however, all the work still cannot get done. There were approximately the same number of members fifty years ago, but the population was only half as large and the problems of society far less complex. Workload has recently been increasing: in just the area of legislation, while there were 7,845 measures introduced in the Seventy-eighth Congress (1943–45), in the Ninety-first Congress (1969–1971) there were some 29,040. Consequently, congressmen and their staffs must carefully choose just where to invest their time and energy. Following are a number of areas of possible focus.

Servicing Constituents

Greenhorn congressmen may imagine that they will spend all day thinking great thoughts and making them into laws. This is far from the way it is. "I thought I was going to be Daniel Webster," said one disillusioned representative, "and I found that most of my work consisted of personalized work for constituents." A 1965 study by John Saloma III found that fully 41 percent of all staff time and 28 percent of a member's time was devoted to servicing constituents. This included handling their correspondence, receiving visitors, answering requests for information, and doing casework.

The reason congressmen invest such effort in constituent services is evident. "My experience is that people don't care how I vote on foreign aid, federal aid to education, and all those big issues, but they are very much interested in whether I answer their letters." The politics of personal favors is not new. King Solomon regularly assisted his subjects with their personal problems—as the story of the two women who quarreled

over an infant shows—in a manner not unlike the way
congressmen help their constituents understand Social
Security laws or veterans' benefits.

"During the last year and a half," said one senator,
"I have done favors for about three thousand persons.
When you consider the word-of-mouth spread, this
amounts to a substantial number of constituents." One
representative was even more specific. "A survey indicated I had three thousand farmers in my district who
had to go over half a mile for mail, so I started a campaign [for mailbox extensions]. By the last election I
had gotten thirteen hundred extensions. They think of
me every time they go get that mail."

Answering mail is the mainstay of constituent services.
Mail is delivered five times a day on Capitol Hill, and
representatives and senators get between 5,000 to
200,000 letters a year. Offices are at times swamped by
waves of letters. The replies that go out are usually form
letters which state the member's views on something or
thank the writers for their opinions. Some of the requests
are for information—a Department of Agriculture book-
let entitled "How to Fix Potatoes in Popular Ways," a
civil service form from the Justice Department for employment—which congressmen readily forward to the
relevant agency. Most agencies try to answer congressional mail immediately, so as not to offend congressmen. The day he was confirmed, OEO chief Philip
Sanchez wrote all his staff that "response to congressional mail takes precedence over every other item of
agency business." In 1970, the Pentagon got 200,000
congressional letters, and HEW received 85,000.

In addition, there are the eccentric requests by those
who consider their congressman a glorified valet, and
there are the crank letters. One woman requested help
on replacing her broken china; another asked a representative to get President Nixon to purchase a wooden
spoon for her while he was in Europe; someone wanted
a gold brick from Fort Knox; and one citizen asked
that travel arrangements be made for his trip abroad
with his wife. The crank letters aim more to irritate
than inquire. In a classic response to one of this genre,

Congressman John Steven McGroarity of California wrote in 1934, "One of the countless drawbacks of being in Congress is that I am compelled to receive impertinent letters from a jackass like you in which you say I promised to have the Sierre Madre mountains reforested and I have been in Congress two months and haven't done it. Will you please take two running jumps and go to hell." Former Senator Stephen Young was long envied by his more cautious colleagues for his biting ripostes to crackpot critics. When one correspondent requested that his horse be transported at public expense since the First Lady's horse had been, the irascible Young replied, "Dear Sir: Am wondering why you need a horse when there is already one jackass at your address."

While there are often complaints about the level of incoming mail, many members seem eager to increase outgoing mail. Most offices have staff who pour over local newspapers for notices of weddings, births, deaths, or for Girl-Scout-of-the-Month, Million-in-Sales winners, or college queen contestants. A note of congratulations is immediately shipped out.* Even though the congressman himself may never participate in this process, it shows that he cares. It seeks good will in the short run and some votes in the long run. But it can occasionally backfire. One man in east Texas who shotgunned his wife to death and said he was glad he did it received a condolence card while in prison from Congressman John Dowdy. Due in part to such frivolous enterprises, the volume of franked mail sent by members of Congress has increased from 24 million pieces in 1938, 29 million in 1948, and 65 million in 1958, to 178 million pieces in 1968.

A more serious form of outgoing mail is the congressional newsletter. Ninety percent of all members send them. They tell constituents about important current

---

* Senator Robert Byrd goes even further. He keeps a list of 2,545 cards of key people in his small state of West Virginia. Periodically, Byrd will personally call them up to find out how they are, how the kids are doing, what's on their mind.

events, tell them what their congressman is doing, and tell them what a terrific guy he is. They range in quality from Congressman Morris Udall's literate and informative monthly newsletters to Robert Nix's once-a-year cut-and-paste job. Some congressmen include questionnaires in their newsletters. These are supposed to take the pulse of local views while flattering the voter by showing that someone is interested in him. Congressman Charles Vanik, for one, refuses to use them because he considers them statistically invalid. But others don't want to miss out on a good thing. "Polling your people with questionnaires is a greater gimmick than mailing out free flower seed," said one.

Mail is only one component of servicing constituents. Voters often visit Washington and "drop in on their congressmen." It has become a growing burden for many, as noted by an assistant to former Senator Eugene McCarthy. "In 1948, we got letters. In 1954, we started getting wires. By 1959, it was telephone calls. And around 1964, people started showing up. Now you get here in the morning and you find people waiting." To avoid wasting work time, some members enter their office through special doors to avoid person-to-person encounters. But others see it as an important part of their job, even giving visitors a tour of the Capitol, complete with a picture taken on the spot.

Personal casework is probably the most demanding component of constituent-induced work. "Casework takes a lot of time," said one representative. "When you go home you cannot go to church in safety. Every time I go, there are thirty or forty people hiding behind automobiles just waiting to bump into me, always quite by accident. Each thinks his individual problem is the most important in the world." In his study of the Senate, Donald R. Matthews observed that senators received pleas from "mental cases, unwed mothers, sufferers from venereal diseases—all kinds of lost and bewildered people who do not know where else to turn." Most of the actual casework involves claims against federal or state agencies which have been ignored or delayed.

Many congressmen view their role as red-tape cutters a critical one—to the extent that they hold office hours in their districts to hear such cases. Congressman Vanik has two offices in his Ohio district. According to Vanik, they get 125 calls a day; in 1970, he held office hours forty times and saw two thousand constituents. Each Friday, Congressman Edward Koch meets with constituents in various places around his New York City district. "Some people tell me I'm doing a good job and some of them bawl me out," he says. And many of them he helps. On one typical day in 1971, he tended to a woman who complained about the atrocious conditions of the hospital treating her cerebral-palsied child (Koch sent a letter to Governor Rockefeller), a person wanting to help a resident alien stay in this country (Koch didn't like private bills, but said he'd see), a woman complaining about criminal goings-on at her building (Koch referred her to the district attorney), another wanting to know about the availability of day care centers (Koch set up a longer appointment at his permanent office), and a woman complaining about the high taxes she had to pay on her husband's estate (Koch said he favored them and she stormed out).

Congressmen like to return to their districts just to let the people know they care. Members are allowed one free round trip each month, but most go far more frequently. As incentive, they recall the case of Senator Robert La Follette, Jr., who stayed in Washington in 1946 to manage the La Follette-Monroney Legislative Reorganization Act in Congress instead of going to campaign in his Wisconsin primary. Result: the La Follette-Monroney Act passed, but La Follette was defeated by Joseph R. McCarthy.

While most representatives and senators realize the political beliefs of constituent services, and act accordingly, most also dislike its menial tasks. "I came here to write laws and what do I do?" protested Congressman Jim Wright in his book *You and Your Congressman*. "I send out baby books to young mothers, listen to every maladjusted kid who wants out of the service . . . and give tours of the Capitol to visitors who are just as worn out as I am." Others are also worried about the ethical questions raised. What if a local union, a local bank, and a local radio station all financially support a congressman's campaign, and then (a) the union wants pressure applied to the Tariff Commission for higher tariffs, (b) the bank wants a friendly word passed on to the comptroller about their pending merger, and (c) the station wants help at the FCC to enable it to stay on the air more hours? None of these are legislative matters; all purely administrative problems. There is clearly the risk of preferential treatment if a congressman pressures a downtown agency or even if they inquire into the status of a matter. Of such constituent favors former Senator Joseph Clark noted, "There is a certain amount of wear and tear on the conscience involved in all of them."

The frequency of constituent complaints suggests that citizens should be protected against the pettiness and inefficiency of the federal bureaucracy. But in Congress—with its 535 separate agents, all concerned about individual cases—the best candidate for the job? Such servicing takes away from the legislative process, which is what the Constitutional Convention really had in mind when it formulated Congress in 1787; Congress neglects key legislation and conducts inadequate oversight over independent agencies, as chapter 4 argued, in large part because so many resources are devoted to ministerial tasks for constituents.

The informal, case-by-case pleading by so many members can also hamper efficient administration in the agencies. Two congressmen have proposed different approaches. Congressman Henry Reuss suggests the ombudsman, based on a system begun 165 years ago in Sweden. Teams of people trained in draining the administrative swamps would process the casework now bogging down Capitol Hill. Cong. Les Aspin would create an ombudsman for each local district. Trained by a federal center in Washington, they would have similar skills and parallel solutions to problems. But neither proposal has received a serious hearing. For no matter how much they may complain or hide in their

offices to avoid visitors, congressmen are unwilling to
sacrifice their brand of Personal Service Democracy.
As Cong. Richard Bolling wrote in his book *Power in
the House,* "Constituent service can help a member be
reelected, and that is the main reason it will not be
handed to someone else."

Debating and Investigating

Of the five senators that the Senate has selected as
its most esteemed—Webster, Clay, Calhoun, La Follette,
and Taft—the first three were famed as orators. School-
boys remember from their history books the Webster-
Hayne debates, the 1830 struggle over states' rights
versus constitutional sovereignty, which ended with
Webster's injunction of "Liberty *and* Union, now and
forever, one and inseparable!" Upon hearing Webster
once speak, a listener said, "I was never so excited by
public speaking before in my life. Three or four times
I thought my temple would burst with the rush of blood.
. . . I was beside myself and I am still so."

Like home canning and minor-league baseball, such
debate has been a casualty of modern times. Congressmen spend large chunks of time on the floor (26 percent
of the average congressman's working time) and talk a
lot there, but the amount of high-class debate is small.
Not until March, 1970, did the House get around to first
debating a proposal to end the war—the Nedzi-Whalen
amendment. Even then, most speakers were allowed
only one minute to make their points. In another
"debate" over the war, Congressman Richard Bolling—
who has written books about Congress's responsibility to
asserts its prerogatives—refused to yield the floor to
Cong. Robert Drinan because, as he later told Drinan,
he was afraid Drinan would ask him questions he
couldn't answer. Instead of debate, the bulk of congressional proceedings consists of small inserts for the folks
back home—items which only those from the district
could not consider trivial. Incisive debate is so rare that
the late Senator Carter Glass of Virginia, after spending
more than thirty years in both houses of Congress, said

that he had never seen a single mind changed by congressional debate.

Not surprisingly, few congressmen take floor activity seriously. "There is a theory around here . . . that to attend a debate on the floor is a waste of time," observed Congresswoman Bella Abzug. "If you're seen hanging around the floor listening to others, you're considered over-earnest. . . . To stay on the floor is to be unsuave and unsophisticated." One reason for this view is appallingly apparent to anyone watching a chamber in session for the first time. It seems more like an Elks Club (after a party) than the world's greatest deliberative body. Writer Larry King, who spent ten years as a congressman's assistant, describes the scene in the House: "Members lounge while signing mail, reading newspapers, or eyeing the visitors' galleries for familiar faces or pretty ones. Some sit with their knees propped against seats in front of them chatting or laughing; others lean on the rail at the rear of the chamber to smoke or swap jokes. Congressmen wander in and out aimlessly."

There are occasional breaks in this tranquil front. In 1954, the late William H. "Wild Bill" Langer, a frontier-type representative from North Dakota, broke the top of his desk by pounding on it during a debate on the Eisenhower farm program. In an unusually blunt 1968 speech, Senator George McGovern rebuked his colleagues:

> Every senator in this chamber is partly responsible for sending 50,000 young Americans to an early grave. *This chamber reeks of blood.* Every senator here is partly responsible for that human wreckage at Walter Reed and Bethesda Naval and all across our land—young boys without legs, or arms, or genitals, or faces, or hopes. . . . Don't talk to them about bugging out, or national honor, or courage. It doesn't take any courage at all for a congressman, or a senator, or a president to wrap himself in the flag and say we're staying in Viet-

nam. Because it isn't our blood that is being shed. [emphasis added]

But mostly it is bad form to get too strident or argumentative. The demise of debate is most obvious as House floor activity drones on toward dinner. If a bill is pending, impatient members begin to chant "vote, vote," and woe to the representative who then delays the proceedings.

The other faded glory of Congress is the congressional investigation. In earlier days, these were a sure route to headlines and reputation. The 1913 Pujo Commission investigated the concentration of wealth of the "money trust." The Nye Commission, probing the munitions industry in 1936, popularized the phrase "merchants of death," and Gerald Nye was talked up as a potential Republican nominee for president or vice president. Harry Truman won national prominence as chairman of the World War II Committee to Investigate the National Defense Program. Senator Estes Kefauver became a presidential contender (and vice presidential nominee) after widely viewed televised hearings into organized crime. Throughout the fifties, other committees investigated topics from the Communist Menace (the Hiss-Chambers and Army-McCarthy hearings) to corruption in business, labor unions, and government (rigged TV shows, disk jockey payola, teamster illegalities, and Bernard Goldfine's vicuña coat).

The excesses of those investigations may have contributed to the current decline. After watching Joe McCarthy smear reputations with secret "papers in my possession," both Congress and the public saw the danger of hearings held for their own spectacle, and not for any legislative purpose. The virulent House Un-American Activities Committee has been transformed into the House Internal Security Committee—whose blander name reflects a more cautious approach. The few senators who have made names in recent investigations have run them less as witchhunts than as seminars—for example, Philip Hart's Antitrust subcom-

mittee hearings on economic concentration; Senator
Fulbright's Foreign Relations Committee hearings on
the war; or Congressman L. H. Fountain's Intergovernmental Operations hearings on the Food and Drug Administration.

Legislating and Voting

Debating and investigating lay the groundwork for
the work most people associate with a member of congress—legislating and voting. Legislation is an art form
and a formal process occurring almost entirely within
the framework of the committee system. Although already discussed in chapter 3, it is important to stress
how small a role legislating plays in the life of an average congressman. John Saloma found that congressmen
spent 50 percent more time in committees than in legislative research and reading. Congressmen farm out their
serious legislative research to the Library of Congress,
their serious bill-drafting to the Office of Legislative
Counsel, to the executive branch, or even to private
lobbyists, and their serious thinking to committee chairmen and staff. Senator John Sherman Cooper is, by
reputation, one of the only senators who considers himself a real legislator. To escape the bustle and distrac-
tion of his office, he retreats to the Senate floor to think
and read.

Even for those who try, there are barriers. "Sometimes you get the idea that everything is managed at
the top and that the decisions are none of your business," complained one member. It is almost impossible
for a congressman or senator to have his or her piece
of legislation considered unless he sits on the committee
that would handle it. For those outside the ruling circles,
getting important bills passed is rare. One member told
author Charles Clapp that "people shouldn't have any
great expectations that their congressman will be the
author of important legislation, especially early in his
career. In my six years here I have had two bills passed,
both when I was a freshman and my party was in control. One set up an advisory committee on education

in HEW—they never bothered to implement it after we got the bill through—and the other provided free dental care to Spanish American War veterans, a bill which I don't suppose my constituents sent me here to push." Some unfortunate congressmen have even worse prospects. When Congressman Abner Mikva proposed a bill to outlaw the manufacture of pistols, it got nowhere. But, says Mikva, "colleagues thanked me for introducing it—so that they could denounce it."

The final claim on a congressman's time is voting— the expression of the congressman's will and, theoretically, that of his half-million constituents. With hundreds of bills to vote on, how does the member of Congress make his choice? A standard reply is that he or she is merely a delegate of his constituents and should mirror their views. As Abraham Lincoln put it during his campaign for the Illinois legislature in 1836, "While acting as a representative, I shall be governed by [my constituents'] will on all subjects." This sounds nice in theory, but how does one know what his constituents want? There are general indicators, like election results, polls, the mail.* But as Senator John Kennedy admitted in his 1956 book, *Profiles in Courage,* "In Washington I frequently find myself believing that forty or fifty letters, six visits from professional politicians and lobbyists, and three editorials in Massachusetts newspapers constitute public opinion on a given issue. Yet in truth I rarely know how the great majority of the voters feel, or even how much they know of the issues that seem so burning in Washington."

Such doubts led Senator Kennedy to propound the

---

* Although it is important evidence of citizen sentiment, the mail is far from a perfect barometer. Often it reflects the view of *aroused* citizens, not all citizens. When FDR proposed repealing a provision of the Neutrality Act in 1939, it led to tons of mail being sent to Congress, which ran 5 to 1 against repeal. Yet a poll showed the public for repeal 56 to 44; Congress approved it. In 1940, 90 percent of the Senate mail opposed the selective service system. At the same time, a poll showed the public 70 percent for it; Congress upheld the system.

trustee theory, that a member of Congress is a free agent who should follow his own convictions. Kennedy argued that "the voters selected us, in short, because they had confidence in our judgment and our ability to exercise that judgment from a position where we could determine what were their best interests, as a part of the nation's interests." Edmund Burke's 1774 speech to the English Parliament is considered a classic explanation of this viewpoint. "Your representative owes you not his industry, but his judgment," he said, "and he betrays, instead of serving you, if he sacrifices it to your opinion. . . . You choose a member indeed; but when you have chosen him, he is not a member of Bristol, but he is a member of *Parliament*." When representatives or senators do vote their consciences in opposition to the perceived opinion of their constituents, they become, according to Kennedy, profiles in courage. This does not happen very often, but some members do take risks: Congressman Ken Hechler of West Virginia fights his state's coal mining interests; Senator Fred Harris of Oklahoma opposes the oil lobbies; Senator Philip Hart of Michigan often tangles with Detroit's automakers; and Congressman Morris Udall, from hawkish Arizona, is vigorously antiwar.

There are still other criteria for deciding how to vote. Party leadership may demand obedience to the party line; but the current leaders, Mansfield and Albert, lack the persuasive power of an LBJ or a Sam Rayburn. Often a member will go along with a colleague on an item of no great interest to him or his district so that he can garner his colleague's vote when the situation is reversed; such horsetrading has long been decried, and it leads at times to strange alliances, but it is as much a part of the ongoing legislative process as quorum calls. Or the congressman may adopt the view of his staff, of the chamber's doorkeeper who follows the progression of a vote, of a colleague considered expert in the field, or of a persuasive friend. Senator Lee Metcalf walked out of his office on the afternoon of August 2, 1971, fully determined to vote against the Lockheed bail-out bill. No big-business slush funds, the Montana populist said to his staff and himself. But as he approached the floor he was cornered by his friend Alan Cranston of California, home of potentially unemployed Lockheed workers. Senator Cranston beseeched his Democrat colleague not to throw thirty thousand people out of work. Metcalf, weakened, finally chose employment over ideology and voted for the Lockheed loan, which slipped by the Senate 49–48.

While such methods are common, such drama is not. However constitutionally precious the vote, Congressman Riegle is less than awed: "Even your vote doesn't count for much. Since I've been here [five years] only one major bill has been decided by a single vote. If you try to evaluate your incremental impact . . . you just can't have much impact on normal congressional relations."

A Congressional Composite

In large measure congressmen become homogenized once they adapt to the institution's folkways. But there are still enough differences among the 535 lawmakers to keep journalists busy. Nowhere is this clearer than in their working habits. From the range of potential activities—legislating, handshaking, debating, investigating—each congressman focuses on a few, since there is not enough time for all. As a result, there is a rough division of labor among the members. Some, feeling the pull of national prominence, speak up on every major issue. Others, forever intent on the next election, think that the only major issues are those that affect their district. From these and many other congressmen, certain categories of work styles emerge:

The Overachievers—To them Congress is not a sinecure but an opportunity to produce the reports, release the exposés, let fly the speeches, and in general stay in the news. "As if increase of appetite had grown by what it fed on," their hunger for work is never sated.

Senator William Proxmire is one. His high school classmates at Pottstown, Pennsylvania, voted him the class's "biggest grind," and he's been pushing himself ever since. He runs five miles to his Senate office every day after doing two hundred pushups and then runs back after work. One can almost see the adrenalin pumping through his taut, hyperactive body. The *Wall Street Journal* called him "one of the Senate's busiest members." Of himself, Proxmire effuses, "I've got a great job. I look forward to nearly every day with great enthusiasm. Every aspect of the job is challenging."

Proxmire used to be saddled with a different reputation, one any overachiever risks: that of an aggressive maverick. Early in his career, his aggressive ways irritated many of his colleagues. During his freshman term, on February 22, 1958, he rebuked Majority Leader Lyndon Johnson on the chamber floor for efforts to "dominate" the Senate. "The Senate today heard two speeches: Washington's farewell address [given that day as it is once a year] and the farewell address of William Proxmire," said one veteran senator.

But with some seniority and a few successes, Proxmire has largely shaken this characterization and come into his own. In his specialty, defense spending, he has made "cost overrun" household words. In less well-known efforts, Proxmire has also pushed ethics reform, opposed the Capitol west front extension, challenged the principles behind the Export-Import Bank, and fought the nomination of SEC Chairman William Casey. In addition, during a Senate vacation in August, 1971, Proxmire and his Joint Economic Committee busily took on President Nixon's sudden Phase I freeze. As if this frenetic pace on the issues weren't enough, Proxmire has not missed a Senate roll call since 1966, and he returns home to Wisconsin nearly every weekend.

The Underachievers—To say that they are not household words puts it mildly. Their seats, usually from safe districts, are a form of Social Security to them—steady income for little or no work. Others may do the legislating; these men are content to stay out of sight. There are more of them than of the overachievers.

Former Representative Philip Philburn exemplified

this species of congressman. He was uncontroversial, uninterested, and inactive in all House affairs. His indifference extended even to the Armed Services Committee, where he became vice chairman through circumstances beyond his control (he had thirty years' seniority). The *Wall Street Journal* wrote that "the 72-year-old Democrat regularly arrives on the House floor for the day's debate, affably greets his cronies, takes a seat up front near the speaker's rostrum—and then almost always falls asleep." But Philburn was a kind and friendly fellow who won affection from other representatives and his district despite his lethargy. He exploited his charm to win fifteen terms in the House, until confronted with more energetic opposition in the 1970 primary. With his defeat, he left office long after he had retired from it.

A current example is Philadelphia's black congressman, Robert N. C. Nix. With fourteen years in Congress, Nix is the second most senior black representative, and the first ever sent from Pennsylvania. Other men might have used this as a platform for legitimate publicity. Nix has modestly remained an entire unknown, both in his district and in the Capitol. The Philadelphia political machine, rubbing salt in the wounds of democratic theory, ensures his reelection; but once in Congress, Nix does little but take up space. In the 1970 campaign, Nix's opponent kept referring to him as "the phantom congressman." He did gain some notoriety of a sort in 1964 when the NAACP opposed his reelection, saying that Nix was anti-Negro since he had failed to exert any leadership to protect civil rights protesters.

The local Philadelphia newspapers rarely cover him, for there is not much to cover. But in early 1971, a *Philadelphia Tribune* columnist managed to interview him at length one night. After the article had been written, the columnist discovered that Nix's exact words that evening on Martin Luther King, the UN, Israel, education, and income tax had come directly from his October, 1970, newsletter (he sends out one a year). Nevertheless, Nix got a fellow Philadelphia congressman to insert the article in the *Congressional Record*. And in December, 1971, an unabashed Nix reproduced copies of the *Record* pages containing the article and then sent them out as his 1971 newsletter.

The Invisible Powerhouses—They are also not household words, but should be. Quietly entrenched somewhere in the congressional bureaucracy, they control vital power—usually the power to dispose more than to propose. The invisible powerhouses are rulers over their mini-domains, and are recognized as such by their colleagues, newspaper people, and few others.

John Rooney, former district attorney, has been the crusty representative from the fourteenth district in Brooklyn for twenty-eight years. Outside of his district, few citizens have ever head of him. But, as chairman of a House Appropriations subcommittee, he oversees the appropriation of more than $4 billion annually for the State, Justice, and Commerce departments and the federal judiciary. If it bothers you that one C5-A cargo plane has cost more than the budget for the entire federal court system, or ten times as much as the budget for the Justice Department's Antitrust Division, Rooney is the man to see.

His toughness varies with the agency that is before him. He admired the late J. Edgar Hoover and has readily approved every penny the FBI has requested in the last decade—"because it's the best run agency in town administratively," says Rooney. He also has a soft spot for the Federal Maritime Administration, a division of the Commerce Department. It is no coincidence that the giant Brooklyn shipyard is in his House district. "I am interested in getting ships built," he says, overlooking the economic folly of subsidizing an inefficient merchant fleet.

Toward State, Justice, and the judiciary, however, Rooney shows only contempt. Reverting to prosecutorial ways, he berates and ridicules witnesses. When a State Department official tried to justify one $300,000-program, Rooney interrupted, "Who thought this one up? What is this all about?" After the official an-

swered, Rooney said, "I know as much now as when
I asked the question. Are you going to tell us something
about it or don't you want the $300,000?" Ramsey
Clark, when attorney general, used to complain that
Rooney "had us so cowed that if we needed a hundred
lawyers we'd ask for twenty and hope to get five."

Another powerhouse unknown to the general public
but very well known to his peers is Congressman Wayne
Hays. As chairman of a formerly minor housekeeping
committee, the House Administration Committee, he
exercises influence over a wide range of House activities.
For example, he recently refused to certify the paycheck
of an aide to another congressman who, Hays said, was
getting too pushy with one of Hays's subcommittees. In
a series of cost-cutting moves, Hays took the operators'
chairs out of the House elevators, raised the price of a
haircut from seventy-five cents to two dollars and raised
the prices in House restaurants and cut the hours. More
significantly, he has taken over the introduction of computers and electronic voting equipment in the House,
and now has the power to increase, without House approval, the size of office staff and allowances available
to members.

This may all not mean much to Racine, Wisconsin,
or Macon, Georgia, but it means a great deal to other
House members. It affects their perquisites and their
daily work lives. And it puts high in the House saddle
one of the most hostile and acerbic of congressmen.
"Getting into a debate with him is like wrestling with a
skunk," said one representative. "The skunk doesn't
care; he likes the smell." He denounces other members
in person and on the floor. Congressman Ben Rosenthal
once tried to hit him with a water pitcher, and Bella
Abzug called him a "scum" (to which Hays replied,
"That really upsets me because my father always said it
takes a scum to know a scum"). But whether he obtained
his status because of his hardbittenness or despite it,
he has, as the *Washington Post* noted, "carved out a
position of power in the daily operation of the House
unmatched by any other member except Speaker Carl
Albert."

Districters—These congressmen worry little about affairs of state. They see themselves as tribunes of the people, and their highest calling is to serve their constituents' immediate problems. And that usually means in person, not by mail.

The exemplar of the congressional tribune is William Barrett, the seventeen-term representative from southwest Philadelphia. He flies back to his district *every night* from Washington to hold office hours from 9:00 P.M. to 1:00 A.M. At the corner of 24th and Wharton Streets in south Philadelphia, in the shabby office of a building he owns, Barrett sometimes sees as many as 750 people a week, "on marital matters, child welfare, foreclosures, evictions—everything that affects the human person," he says. For this, his constituents call him "the Reverend" and the night sessions "the confessional." Stephen Isaacs wrote in the *Washington Post:* "Folks line up to tell Bill Barrett their problems. He sits behind his desk, listening, his fingertips poised—barely touching—in front of his chin. And, as he has been doing for forty years—the last twenty-six as a congressman—he does something about their problems. He gets them taken care of."

Territorialists—Given the vast range of possible subjects to master, some congressmen retreat into specialties. To know one subject well is to gain a certain prominence in an institution of prominent people.

Congressman Paul Rogers, 51, from West Palm Beach, knows that there are always two bitter sides to such issues as civil rights, war, or poverty. But health is a motherhood issue, and an important one. So in 1971, forty of sixty-one floor remarks and twenty-one of twenty-eight articles he inserted into the *Record* dealt with health. Eight of fifteen bills he introduced in the first four months of 1972 concerned health. Rogers is chairman of the Subcommittee on Public Health and Environment, and nearly all health proposals must run through his committee's filter. He diligently prepares for all committee hearings, and, further, makes proposals of his own, like the federal department of health he is now pushing. This has led R. John Zapp, HEW deputy assistant secretary for health legislation, to assert that "Rogers is the most knowledgeable man on the Hill on health issues."

The Orators—Following in the tradition of Cicero and Webster, a few congressmen try to make the chamber ring. Although a small band, they occasionally provide bright moments on the chamber floor.

Three senators have laid some claim to the mantle of Everett Dirksen, who while in the Senate was surely the most florid and mellifluous speaker there. One is Gale McGee of Wyoming, who startled and impressed his colleagues in February, 1959, when he gave his maiden speech without text or notes. He nearly always speaks off the cuff, having the rare ability to think and speak in whole sentences and whole paragraphs, without pause. McGee also has a sense of drama and history, essentials of a great speaker. One witness told writer William Honan that he once saw McGee, during a speech, "strike a dramatic pose with right foot forward and both arms outstretched, which was almost identical to that of Henry Clay pleading the Compromise of 1850 as depicted on the engraving by Robert Whitechurch that hangs in SB-15 of the Capitol."

At 5' 4" and 150 pounds, John Pastore draws attentions by the discrepancy between the size of himself and the size of his voice. A snappy dresser with a trim moustache, he jumps, prances, jerks, and, with stentorian voice, booms his way through a speech or debate. One Senate worker claims he can hear Pastore while sitting at his desk one story above the floor, across a corridor, and behind two closed doors. Pastore's golden moment of oratory was when 65 million Americans heard his typically energetic keynote speech to the 1964 Democratic Convention. "Look, maybe this doesn't read too well," he said about the speech, "but it sounds good. Maybe no one would give me the Pulitzer Prize for this, but I'm not lookin' for the Pulitzer Prize. I'm lookin' for the audience."

Finally there is Frank Church, former star of the

Stanford debating team, and a powerful Senate speaker. As a freshman in 1958, he was chosen by LBJ to deliver Washington's Farewell Address, an honor usually reserved for senior members. His electric delivery inspired applause from the gallery, a rare occurrence. Such efforts led the press gallery to call him "boy orator" in 1958 and to be the keynoter at the 1960 Democratic Convention.

Church fits the classic orator mold more closely than McGee or Pastore. He speaks from a carefully prepared text, but he does so with great emphasis and verve. After Church's speech denouncing President Johnson's Vietnam policy, the visitors' gallery (again) burst into applause. Wayne Morse called it a "great speech," and Ernest Gruening said, "I believe it ranks with the classics, with the addresses of Daniel Webster and other distinguished orators of the past." Church's speech had deftly combined epigrams, metaphors, repetition, poetic license and personification of the abstract. "I'd worked very hard over that speech," he commented afterwards. "To speak well, and think, you *have* to be the author of the text yourself. We're beyond the age of great oratory today, but the truly great orators of the past were men who wouldn't be caught dead using someone else's words."

The Outspoken—While both depend on a verbal ability, the outspoken differ from the orators in that they speak more briefly, more ideologically, more bluntly, and with fewer Latin or French words.

Although the number of orators have dwindled, the outspoken are increasing in number. In the mid-sixties, Senators Wayne Morse and Ernest Gruening were famous examples. Lowenstein, Harris, Gravel, Abzug, Dellums—the recent list is long. One of the most prominent is Congressman Robert Drinan of Massachusetts.

Drinan, a Jesuit priest, is so frank in his approach that one colleague said that without his clerical collar he couldn't get away with it. Vigorously antiwar, he is the chairman of a subcommittee of the Members of Congress for Peace through Law. Drinan supported

George McGovern early in the presidential campaign while the rest of the New England congressional delegation was supporting Ed Muskie of Maine. When told he should back Muskie as a good New Englander, Drinan replied, "What the hell does that mean?" At the 1972 Democratic National Convention, NBC reporter Garrick Utley sought Drinan out for an interview on valuable network air time. With cameras rolling, Drinan —who was caucusing with his delegation on the floor— said, "My delegation is more important to me than NBC." Utley then reported to millions of viewers, "Well, Father Drinan said he had no time for us," to which Drinan snapped back, "I didn't say that. I said my delegation is more important than NBC." And he has denounced the House Democratic leadership in a *New York Times* editorial for its reluctance to push for a Vietnam pullout date. "I try not to be ashamed to be a member of Congress," he wrote. "I must confront the fact, however, that history will conclude that the House of Representatives in the 92nd Congress acquiesced in the most brutal war in all of history. . . . My mind cannot yet look forward to the hope which may come with the 93rd Congress. I am still stunned, numbed, and dismayed."

The general danger of being outspoken was well summarized by former Congressman Clem Miller:

> The congressman may seek to take the castle by scaling the walls in open combat or by a sapping operation under the moat. Scaling the walls means making many floor speeches, getting in on every debate from railroad pensions to the color of oranges, putting on the hair shirt for the public and the press, etc. The structure of Congress consigns this course to almost certain failure. The very qualities of public show, or defiance, are looked on askance. The congressman who speaks constantly, even if cogently, cannot seem to acquire respect. Even his friends begin to avoid him.
>
> On the other hand, the congressman who consults privately with shrewdness, who has just come

from a closed meeting with somebody with information to impart, who works quietly underground, will wind up with a prize. He will, in the course of time, exert influence. He will be asked for his opinion. In a profession which makes much of handing out advice, it is being asked for it that is the greatest jewel.

Organization Men—Some men are born great, some have greatness thrust upon them—and others work their way up. In big cities, it's the wardheelers, who take care of the details for their bosses—for which they are duly rewarded. In the Senate, it's the people who aid the leadership in their daily chores—Clem Miller's "sapping operation." It may not be the most glamorous way to power, but it's one way.

It is clearly Bob Byrd's way. He has always been a climber, doing hard if uninspired work. One of his 1970 campaign leaflets is entitled, "The Bob Byrd Story: From Orphan Boy to U.S. Senator." Years ago, in a local West Virginia political race, a master of ceremonies was uncomfortable about introducing Byrd, but finally did. "I'm a candidate for high office, and he introduced me as a butcher and a fiddler," seethed Byrd. "This man's a lawyer and if it's the last thing I ever do, I'm going to try to get a law degree if for no other reason than so I can stick it under the noses of people like this, and let them know I can do it too." And he did just that. Sixteen years after finishing high school he completed college, and in 1963, while a senator, he got a law degree from Amercan University.

Once in the Senate, Byrd made himself available to do legwork for others. Robert Sherrill writes that "Byrd's strength in the Senate is made up of his loyalty to the club, his thoughtfulness or sycophancy (depending on your perspective), his willingness to do the drudgery and take care of details." Byrd inched up the ladder, until in 1967 he was chosen secretary to the Democratic party conference. By 1970 he was the indispensable man for scheduling votes, lining up supporters, undertaking small favors. If he did the work, Byrd reasoned, why not get the credit? In a coup that surprised nearly all but himself, Byrd decisively defeated Ted Kennedy for the position of majority whip in 1970.

Byrd says of his present position, "I've been 100 percent loyal to the majority leader, and I want to go on being there at his side when he needs help, and when he wants to go off the floor, I want to be there to take his place. I want to fill in for him, to do his bidding, and to help him." While Byrd plays the humble good soldier, he is lining himself up for the generalship, the top rung: to be majority leader if Mike Mansfield steps down. This will prove more difficult than his other successes, for Byrd's extreme conservatism and near racism ("We can take the people out of the slums, but we cannot take the slums out of the people," he said of blacks) naturally win him enemies among the Northern, liberal wing of the Democratic party.

Parliamentarians—If you're not keen on policy-making, you should learn the rules of procedure. If you are perennially in the minority, you must *learn the rules of procedure. For you can often win procedurally what you could never achieve substantively on the merits. It is a lesson Southern senators and representatives have memorized and taken to heart.*

Senator James Allen of Alabama is the best recent example. Elected in 1968 at the age of 56, Allen had served in the Alabama state legislature for eight years and as lieutenant governor for two terms. When he came to the Senate, he understood the importance and content of parliamentary politics better than most freshmen. Allen has won the Senate's Golden Gavel Award three times for spending the greatest number of hours presiding over the Senate. In a newsletter home, he proudly describes his role as "keeping watch in the Senate to see that our position is not prejudiced by adverse parliamentary maneuvers."

In August, 1972, Allen showed the value of picayune rules when the Senate considered the House's antibusing bill. Usually bills are read twice and referred to committee. Allen drew on an obscure rule to prevent the second reading and keep it from going to the liberal Labor and Public Welfare Committee. Instead, it remains on the calendar of the full Senate, where senators intimidated by public opposition to busing are more likely to support Allen's cause. For such legerdemain, Allen is becoming a leader of the Southern bloc in legislative activity.

Absentees and Attenders—Some children play hooky, while others never miss a day of school. And some members of Congress avoid floor activity, while others relish the chance to attend everything.

As already noted, running to and from roll calls and sitting through floor proceedings can be a bore. "It would be a delightful thing," wrote George F. Hoar in 1897, "to attend Unitarian conventions if there were not Unitarians there; so too it would be a delightful thing to be a United States senator if you did not have to attend the sessions of the Senate." Anticipating this advice, only eight of twenty-two senators showed up at the opening of the first session of Congress on March 4, 1789.

Adam Clayton Powell was, of course, the prince of the absentees. In explanation, he wrote in 1963, "I refuse to answer quorum calls. Most of them are instigated mischievously and very few of them serve any importance whatsoever. . . . To answer or not to answer a quorum call has nothing whatsoever to do with voting. It is, of course, very obvious that it is the vote which counts." (By 1966, Powell wasn't even voting, but his distinction between answering quorum calls and voting calls has merit.) Some, like Powell, fail to attend because they consider attendance on the floor unimportant, others are just lazy, while yet others have competing commitments. John Kennedy came only 39 percent of the time in 1960, Eugene McCarthy a paltry 5 percent in 1968, and George McGovern 51 percent in 1972. One representative in the early 1960s made only 17 percent of all roll calls; controlling his local party machinery and coming from a "safe" district, he felt no pressure to attend and impress the people back home.

The absentees make the attenders mad. Until her hip operation in 1968, Senator Margaret Chase Smith had made 2,941 consecutive roll calls, an all-time congressional record. (Even Lou Gehrig only played in 2,130 consecutive games.) On December 21, 1971, she attacked her colleagues who failed to show up for work. "The Senate is a club of prima donnas intensely self-oriented," she said, "ninety-nine kings and one queen dedicated to their own personal accommodation." Majority Leader Mansfield, who must attend regularly because of his job, got testy about the problem. On February 8, 1972, he lectured the floor that "none of us was drafted for this job. Every single member of this body sought this position, and with the position goes a duty . . . to attendance on the floor of the Senate. The record of this body over the past month is, to put it mildly, abominable."

What drives the attenders? A good attendance record is an easy way to impress voters. Unlike most things a member does, his attendance is quantifiable. If it's good, he can profitably display this record at home. Congressman William Natcher, for example, has made 2,705 roll calls in a row since entering Congress in 1954, and Congressman Charles E. Bennett has not missed a single vote after nineteen years and 2,242 votes in the House.

Compelling attendance on the floor is a difficult, and perhaps unwise task. During a debate over the Lower California River Project in 1927, a no-nonsense presiding officer issued "warrants of arrest" and legally dragged the necessary number of senators onto the floor. Senator Smith would expel any member who missed more than 40 percent of all roll calls. But these steps go too far. A member has many responsibilities, of which being on the floor is only one. A 100 percent or even 80 percent attendance record is no guarantee of congressional efficiency or productivity; at the same time a 50 or 60 percent attendance record may be an indication of negligence. Short of the draconian solution of arrest or expulsion, the contest between the absentees and attenders will no doubt continue, with the only effective judge being the voters themselves.

While being a senator or representative looks glamorous from the outside, it has its drawbacks and disappointments. Congress devotes itself to what it was not essentially designed to do—running small favors for complaining constituents. What Congress *is* suppposd to do—legislate—it does not do well. It is the executive that now initiates most legislation, and it is the Supreme Court that has made the major human-rights breakthroughs in the past twenty years (equal education for blacks, reapportionment, criminal justice, abolition of the death penalty). To get major legislation passed often requires a major national trauma: the 1937 and 1962 drug amendments followed the Elixir and Thalidomide scandals; President Kennedy's death gave impetus to his successor's civil rights and Medicare achievements.

But legislating from trauma can fail for two reasons. First, the crisis still cannot overcome a determined vested interest (so, after a decade of assassinations by shooting, there is still no adequate gun control law); and second, the structure of both houses ensures that a good piece of legislation can founder on one of many shoals, with only an occasional one sailing surprisingly out of the harbor. A new congressman once marveled at working conditions in the Capitol: "We work in a political environment, surrounded by lobbyists, constituents, the leadership, and jangling telephones and we virtually have no time alone to think and reflect upon the problems before us. The big miracle is that somehow all of this works. On paper, looking at the situation, you'd say it couldn't possibly work and yet the fact is that it does." So the miracle of Congress, as Sam Johnson said of a dog that could walk on his hind legs, is not that it does its task well, but that it does it at all.

But how well it works is another question. Some, frustrated by the formal ways of the Senate and House, creatively plot out new approaches to solving problems: Senator Gaylord Nelson sponsored Earth Day, which helped initiate the entire environmental movement; Congressman David Pryor worked secretly as an orderly in a nursing home and later set up a headquarters in a trailer near Capitol Hill to aid the elderly, all in an effort to focus attention on the problems of old age; Congressman Henry Reuss rediscovered the unused 1899 Refuse Act, sent out a kit of instructions on its use, and thereby encouraged a process whereby water polluters could be hauled into court; after generations of members had genuflected to Pentagon budget estimates and expertise, Senator William Proxmire and Congressman Les Aspin simply developed an expertise and expert staffs of their own and have inspired the first congressional counteroffensive against the military budget waste.

Such breakthroughs are the exception. Unless they are committee chairmen or chamber leaders, most members readily admit their powerlessness. They come to Washington in the flush of victory and with a sense of self-importance, but are then odds-on favorites to sink into oblivion. "Usually only scandal, longevity, or death distinguishes a member from the pack," writes columnist Mary McGrory. Abner Mikva entered Congress in 1968 with standard awe. Two years later he spoke bitterly of his frustrations, his inability to shape legislation, or even get a hearing for his ideas. "Here I am, in Congress, a congressman. And now I find that Congress ain't where it's at." Congressman Dante Fascell metaphorically complained that "Being in the House is sometimes like trying to push a wheelbarrow up a hill with ropes as handles."

So why do they do it? Why make less money than they could in another field, and why go to all those wienie roasts in the district every weekend? Power and prestige. They sense that fame can be more fun than money, and that an ounce of history in Washington is worth a pound of success back home. So for most, simply *being there* is reward enough. It justifies (especially for the representatives, with their trying two-year terms) always running for office instead of performing in it, being more content to service specific constituents on personal problems than to represent them all on the larger issues.

8

Staying Elected *

All members of Congress have a primary interest in being reelected. Some members have no other interest.

—Former Congressman Frank E. Smith

It was early in the campaign, and the challenger, Bill McKay, was having trouble developing a strong attack upon incumbent Crocker Jarmin in the California senate race. As he went to make a speech, news came that a forest fire had broken out in Malibu. Canceling his engagement, McKay raced to the scene to denounce the disregard for watersheds that led to such fires. As the television cameras and newspapermen crowded around the young candidate, however, a helicopter flew to the scene and Senator Crocker Jarmin jumped out. McKay stood helplessly by while the incumbent announced that he had received the president's personal assurance that federal disaster aid would be forthcoming; in addition, he would introduce a bill on the Senate floor to protect watersheds and to insure the property of those whose property was damaged by mismanaged watersheds.

The scene is from a recent movie, *The Candidate,* but the script is familiar. He who holds office also holds the powers of office and can use them to promote his own reelection. The only deviation from the script is that in *The Candidate* incumbent Jarmin eventually lost the election. It is not usually so. In the 1970 elections for

* This chapter was written by Thomas A. Stewart in collaboration with the authors.

the House, only seventeen incumbents were defeated—nine in the primaries, eight in the general election. There were fifty-four newcomers in the House, but more than twice as many succeeded a retiring representative than defeated a fighting incumbent.

The situation was not quite as bad in the Senate, where thirty-five seats were up for grabs: eleven freshmen entered, six of whom had defeated incumbents in November. The disparity between the two houses is probably explained by the facts that Nixon and Agnew devoted much of their effort in the 1970 campaign to removing "radic-libs" from the Senate, not from the House; that there are fewer "safe" states than "safe" districts; and that most of the Senate's losers had special problems: Charles Goodell faced a three-way contest and Spiro Agnew; George Murphy had to buck the reaction to disclosures about conflict of interest; Thomas Dodd faced both scandal and a three-way race; and Joseph Tydings was accused of conflict of interest by *Life* magazine. (Tydings was exonerated after the election.)

In both houses, however, the trend is clear: members of Congress are serving longer and longer, being reelected more and more often. According to *Congressional Quarterly's Guide to the Congress of the United States,* in the 1870s more than half the representatives sent to the House every two years were freshmen, and the mean length of service was just over two terms. By 1900, only 30 percent of each new crop of congressmen arrived in Washington for the first time. In 1970, the figure was about 12 percent. Meanwhile, the Senate has displayed a steady upward trend in the average length of service for senators, from four and a half years (less than a full term) in 1829, to ten and a half years in 1969. In both houses, the most striking increase occurred in the years between the Civil War and the turn of the century, as party control of politics hardened.*

* A small portion of the increase in length of service must be attributed to longer life expectancies; as fewer senators and representatives die in office, more live to complete their full terms, and to be reelected, than they did a century ago.

Nowadays more members of Congress die or retire than lose.

By comparing a member of Congress's winning margin in his first successful race to his margin in his second, we can get a rough idea of how many votes incumbency is worth. Figures compiled by the writers show that a representative gets 5 percent more of the vote the second time around than he did on his first, an increase which can frequently prove decisive. In recent Senate contests, incumbents gained three percentage points in the vote total over their first run for the roses. While the gain from incumbency is smaller in the Senate than in the House, it is equally significant, as senatorial elections tend to be closer fought than House elections.

It is distressing, or at least puzzling, that so few members of Congress are defeated when they run for reelection. In the House especially, the Founding Fathers expected a high turnover rate to reflect changing public opinion. As society changes more quickly, Congress might be expected to mirror the change. But in the Congress that took its seats after the 1970 elections, the typical representative was 52 years old and had just been reelected to his seventh term. According to Kenneth Harding, who heads the House Democratic Campaign Committee, "There's no reason a House member should ever lose, after a term or two, if he's using the tools of office properly."

The origins of this invulnerability are not difficult to find. One reason is simply that the best vote-getters tend to win, and, because they are good vote-getters, to win again and again. Whether because they are personally appealing, beneficiaries of a machine, or good politicians, incumbents by definition have already shown they can win.

But aside from the survival of the fittest, there are powerful special privileges available to incumbents that cannot be enjoyed by their challengers. The most familiar incumbent advantage is the one we saw in the scene from *The Candidate:* incumbents, unlike their opponents, are already in office and can introduce bills, take credit for bills they have merely cosponsored, take credit for federal spending in their districts or states, or preempt their opponents' ideas by putting them into effect themselves. We have already cited former Senator George Murphy's attempt to bolster his flagging reelection campaign by getting Wetlands Water Project money released.

A second key advantage that accrues to the incumbent is financial. Even before the November election, the incumbent is much less likely to have to conduct an expensive, hard-fought primary campaign than his opponent. Many have no opposition at all. In 1970, two-thirds of those seeking reelection waltzed through the primaries unopposed. (Forty-three congressmen—a tenth of the House—had no opposition in either the primary or the general election.) Counting those who had no primary challenger, 94 percent of the incumbents won their primaries with a vote margin of more than 30 percent. Incumbent senators have it just as good.

Challengers can expect a tougher battle. Many more face costly primary opposition; Richard Ottinger spent $1.8 million in a vigorous 1970 Democratic primary in New York. Also, their vote margins are considerably smaller. (It is true, however, that even in primaries where no incumbent was running, almost two-thirds of the winners had a margin of 30 percent or more.) The ability to avoid a tough primary campaign is especially valuable in one-party states or districts—still common in the South and in machine-dominated cities in the North, and by no means rare elsewhere. In these areas, the primary election is often more crucial than the general election. In 1963, a congressman from a "safe" district told a Brookings Institute study: "I spend about $1,200 [in the general election] and my opponent even less. In my state the primary is far more important than the election. When I first ran there were eight of us in the primary and I spent about $25,000."

Of course, some incumbents do lose in the primaries —nine did in 1970—but surprisingly these casualties do not necessarily come from the fierce primaries in

one-party districts. Instead, the losers are almost universally old men, beaten by younger, more vigorous
challengers. Thus, the risk of a hard primary battle is
not a threat to the vast majority of incumbents—those
who have served a few terms—but to the doddering
titans who have reaped the blessings of seniority.

Despite these automatic disadvantages, and despite
the massive free publicity they can get (of which more
later), most incumbent members of the House outspend
their rivals. According to the best data gathered so far
by the Nader Congress Project, both representatives and
their challengers spend about four cents per vote, with
the incumbent adding a bit more. Significantly, the
spending margin between the two candidates seems to
remain constant; if the challenger spends $15,000, the
incumbent will spend $16,000; if the challenger spends
$20,000, the incumbent will spend $21,500, and so on.*

If veterans can match the tenderfoot dollar for dollar,
it is because they have an easier access to outside
sources of campaign funds. Many of the sources of this
money have been spelled out in chapter 1, but it is
worthwhile to mention several points here. The first
advantage incumbents have is that they already have
been assigned to committees. A corporation or labor
union knows whether a given congressman is likely to
serve on a committee with jurisdiction over subjects
important to them. For example, if a representative has
been assigned to the House Agriculture Committee, it
is a good bet that he will continue to serve there if
reelected—which means that a farm conglomerate will
be more likely to give money to him than to his opponent, who might well be assigned to the Public Works

---

* Members of Congress complained to the Brookings Institute study that they had been outspent by their opponents
roughly four to one. This seems either to be self-serving testimony or to reflect the nature of the old campaign finance law
under which a congressman's campaign expenses could be
exorbitantly high as long as he did not know that the money
was spent. Challengers for Senate seats, on the other hand,
do outspend incumbents, probably because they must become
known throughout an entire state.

Committee. Conversely, trucking executives will sooner support a Public Works committeeman than his opponent, who may end up on Agriculture.

That is precisely what happened in the 1966 and 1968 congressional campaigns. A bill was pending before the Roads subcommittee of the House Public Works Committee that would have permitted bigger trucks to operate on federal highways—a measure that would make freeway driving more hazardous for ordinary motorists, add greatly to the wear on the roads, and thus lead to more costly maintenance work—but would help the truckers. So the trucking industry went to work, pouring nearly $30,000 in campaign funds into the coffers of key members of the committees handling the bill. The biggest contribution went to the Roads subcommittee chairman, Illinois Democrat John C. Kluczynski, and smaller sums went to twelve others on the committee, most of whom were on the subcommittee as well. Nor did the truckers stop there; they also contributed to members of the House Rules Committee, through which the bill had to pass, and the Senate Public Works Committee. The bill sailed through the House, but eventually, surprisingly, died before final passage by Congress. But the truckers had tried. As the treasurer of the Truck Operators Nonpartisan Committee told reporter Nick Kotz, who had first broken the story, "We do what we can for those on the committees who might help us. It's as simple as that." It is not impossible that a sly senator or representative will request a committee assignment precisely because a corporation or a union gave him a sizable campaign contribution, with promises of more.

A second advantage in fundraising is that incumbent members of Congress are worth more to contributors than freshmen, because they have stored up seniority and the power and influence that come with it. The advantages of seniority are recognized not only by the special private interests who give more to ranking members, but also by the House and Senate congressional campaign committees, which distribute party money.

A third advantage incumbents have is that they are

"viable candidates." They have won at least once, and they can be expected to win again. No reasonably self-interested campaign contributor wants to throw good money into a losing cause; he wants his man to win. The phenomenon applies to all aspects of campaigning, from collecting endorsements from party celebrities and campaign appearances by them to getting press coverage to getting money. The presidential campaign of George McGovern is like a typical senatorial campaign in these respects. Before he won the Wisconsin primary, party notables were notable for their absence; the media was lackadaisical in its coverage; and the money was coming in in nickels and dimes from small contributors, not from the big ones. Within a week after the Wisconsin victory, the coffers were brimming; as McGovern's momentum built up, the money built up, too. When, after the convention and *l'affaire* Eagleton, McGovern's campaign seemed again in trouble, the money again dried up, and McGovern went back to the nickel-and-dimers who had served him so well before.

As noted in chapter 1, the Republican and Democratic Campaign Congressional committees—there is one for each party in each house—can also serve incumbents by offering a convenient funnel for campaign contributions that members might not want known to their opponents or constituents. Special interests can earmark contributions to the congressional campaign committees, specifying that the money go to an incumbent who is especially valuable to them. Former Senator Joseph Clark related one such incident:

> The conservative oil and gas lobbies, which contribute heavily to the Democratic Senatorial Campaign Committee, had not the slightest interest in the reelection of Senator Paul Douglas of Illinois in 1960, he having been a staunch advocate of cutting the depletion allowance. But they were vitally interested in the reelection of the late Senator Bob Kerr of Oklahoma, who was the most articulate spokesman for the oil interests in the Senate. Quite naturally, Senator Kerr received a

very much larger contribution from the Senatorial Campaign Committee than Senator Douglas. The lobbies quietly earmarked their contribution to the committee for Senator Kerr, and the committee, as an implicit condition for receiving the money, sent it to Oklahoma, where it wasn't needed, rather than to Illinois, where it was.

Seniority and committee assignments help incumbents at the polls as well as with the finances. Democratic Congressman Mendel Davis, who was appointed to fill the seat vacated by the death of his patron, Mendel Rivers in late 1970, is running his 1972 campaign on the slogan "Building Seniority for You." Most members of Congress are not as blatant as Davis, but most do trade on seniority as a reason for their reelection. If they want to be more subtle, they may suggest to the voters that they cast their choice for the "most experienced" candidate. Of course, experience and seniority ought to make their positions on the substantive issues more responsible. It has been said of one representative, "He does terrible things. What makes him worse is that he does them *effectively!*" Most voters, apparently, don't catch on.

Committee assignments open the much-discussed pork barrel, and the scent of pork brings in votes. Members of Congress can be instrumental in getting a host of federal projects and grants for their constituents: post offices, dams, roads, airports, bridges, harbors, federal buildings, military installations, irrigation projects, shipyards, mass transit systems, sewage plants, veterans' hospitals, and grants for an infinite variety of medical, educational, social welfare, military, environmental, and other projects. These make news back home. Former Senator Joseph Clark of Pennsylvania once complained that his major speeches went unheralded by the press in his state, but his routine announcements of new post offices got banner headlines. Maryland Representative Clarence Long wrote that "a congressman is judged by the overwhelming mass of his constituents on the personal service he gives the home folks and the contracts he brings to the area." Congressmen make sure to call attention to, and take credit for, every federal project that lands in their territory. A survey of congressional press releases by the Nader Congress Project researchers disclosed that about one-fifth of all representatives' press releases were devoted to announcing projects.

How much is the pork barrel really worth in terms of votes? No one knows exactly, but it appears that it's worth more to freshman congressmen than to veterans. Congress Project researchers took a sample of first-term representatives and grouped them according to the amount of federal spending that went to their districts. Those with the least federal spending added 4.6 percent to their original victory margins when they sought reelection. The next group, with more federal spending, received a 6 percent hike in the victory margin. The lucky ones who procured the most local public works added a whopping 8.9 percent to their share of the vote. After the first term in office, however, the increase in victory margin does not fluctuate with the amount of federal spending. This suggests that a first-termer who wants to be reelected should go all out to bring home the federal bacon, but that he can relax a bit thereafter.

Not *all* is roses for members seeking another term. One representative thought he had done his people a big favor by voting for a dam in the district, only to discover that it would cause dozens of farms to be flooded out. The farmers helped send him into early retirement. Further, constituents may have unreal expectations of what their senator or representative can do, and may blame him for things beyond his control. Congressmen also complain that they are hampered because they have a record; this, they say, allows opponents to attack or distort what they have done, without having to endure similar attacks. A congressman's record is subject to infinite distortion. For example, a member who voted against a major bill to fund the Vietnam War that also contained a small provision for aid to Israel could be labeled—as George McGovern discovered—"anti-Israel" by an opponent; answering the charge is difficult, because issues quickly become complicated beyond the comprehension of the electorate, especially when the charge and the defense are condensed by newspapers and broadcasters.

Despite these and a few other disadvantages, incumbents still have far more strength than their opponents. One of the biggest advantages—though many representatives say it's their biggest headache as well—is that an incumbent representative is running all the time he is in office. His reelection campaign begins the moment he takes his oath of office, a fact that led one representative, quoted in Clapp's book *The Congressman: His Work as He Sees It,* to say, "You should say 'perennial' election rather than 'biennial.' It is with us every day."

Members of the House have complained about the two-year term—the real cause of the perennial campaign—for decades. Since Congress first met, some 120 resolutions have been introduced to lengthen the term to three or four years. (The Constitutional Convention considered a three-year term, but quickly rejected it.) Only two of them ever got out of committee, and only one ever came to a vote—and lost. Even if it somehow managed to carry in the House, such a proposal would die a certain death in the Senate. One of the advantages an incumbent senator enjoys is that the two-year House term makes it impossible for a representative to challenge him without sacrificing his House seat (since no one may run for more than one office at a time). Yet the short tenure of representatives is clearly anachronistic. As former Congressman Clem Long wrote,

> It was instituted at a time when the average congressman represented only a few thousand, instead of hundreds of thousands of constituents; when Congress met a month or two instead of nearly all year; and when the federal government confined its activities to national defense, the excise tax, and a few internal improvements, instead of pervading every aspect of personal and business life and spending a quarter to a third of all the income of the economy.

The many perquisites of office—the staff allowances, the free trips home, the cut-rate stationery, the allowances for office equipment and for setting up a district office, and, of course, the franking privilege—all help in the perennial campaign. The eight representatives who have not taken advantage of the subsidy for maintaining a district office, for example, all come from relatively safe districts, which suggests that incumbents view their district offices as a kind of off-year campaign headquarters. None of these free resources are designed specifically to serve the cause of reelection, but it is fair to say that they all do, to various extents.

Consider: the average congressman spends over 16 hours a week on service to his constituents, including letter writing, handling constituent problems, and meeting visitors from home; the average congressman's staff puts in another 142 hours per week on constituency service and correspondence. Little of this, of course, is work conducted for the sole purpose of being reelected. But much of it has at least an indirect effect—the opportunity to build good will, to do favors that will be returned at the polls, to increase visibility and voter recognition. It is revealing that freshman senators and representatives, less firmly entrenched than the old-timers, devote a greater amount of time to casework than the veterans, and that, until recently, Southerners devoted less time than Northerners. As the two-party system has been revived in the South, Southern members of Congress have become less secure in their seats and have started to devote more time to helping constituents.

Doing favors for the home folk and making use of his congressional allowances lets a congressman get a jump on his future competitor: he can campaign even before his competitor is chosen, and campaign before the voters think he is. As one representative said, "You can slip up on the blind side of people during an off-year and get in much more effective campaigning than you can when you are in the actual campaign." Some congressmen find casework personally satisfying, especially during their early years in office, when, lacking seniority, they aren't able to contribute much to the more exalted activities of the House. One such representative is Wisconsin's David Obey, who helped out a soldier who received orders that would have sent him to Vietnam two days before his long-scheduled wedding. Obey got his departure delayed a week. He feels good about it—and, as he told a *Wall Street Journal* reporter, he knows that the story of his good deed is being told over and over by the friends and families of the bride and groom.

There is one more edge, perhaps the greatest advantage incumbents have: domination of all the media of electioneering—the mails, the newspapers, radio, and television. Aside from the postage allowance, the basis of incumbent domination of the mails is, of course, the franking privilege. One new representative was told by his father (a former representative), "Son, I have three pieces of advice for you if you want to stay in Congress. One, use the frank. Two, use the frank. Three, use the frank." Franked mail is marked with a bold, florid signature that supposedly says, "This mail is my official business," but that all too often means, "I want to be reelected." The volume of franked mail goes up as elections come closer, as one might expect.

Although the frank is supposed to be used only for "official business," and not to aid a member's reelection, Congress has defined official business very broadly. The widest of the many loopholes in the law permits any excerpt from the *Congressional Record* to be mailed as official business at taxpayer expense. When this rule is combined with the custom that permits any member of Congress to stick anything he wants into the *Record,* the opportunity for abuse becomes clear. Congressman Alvin O'Konski prepared for his 1972 reelection campaign by sending a flood of material into the *Record* in December, 1971 (long enough before the election that it would not become a campaign issue)—including the "Biography of Alvin E. O'Konski" and an impressive list of his successes in supping from the pork barrel. Even as this is written, Cong. O'Konski's life story—excerpted from the *Record*—is filling mailboxes in Wisconsin's tenth congressional district. Other members insert flattering words about local businesses, scout troops, garden clubs, debate teams, and church groups, and mail them to the flattered parties. One congressional aide, whose boss indulges in the technique frequently, flatly admitted that the *Record* is "a great political gimmick."

Usually the use and abuse of the frank is done with more circumspection as congressmen ply their voters with newsletters, questionnaires, reprints of speeches on issues of interest, and the like. While helping keep the public informed, these letters and questionnaires also assist the incumbent's reelection. First, they increase the representative's visibility. Gerald Ford, the House minority leader, sends newsletters to his Michigan constituents weekly; as a result his voters are far more likely to recognize his name than other voters are to recognize their members' names. Second, the content of the newsletters, if not frankly political, often leans that way. In 1966, William C. Love analyzed the materials sent to constituents by senators and congressmen. In the House, Love found that 38 percent of the representatives could be classified as "self-promoters," 22 percent as "persuaders," and 17 percent as combination promoter-persuaders; much smaller percentages were found to be "reticent" or "educators." The Senate was worse: 44 percent were promoters, 28 percent persuaders, and 19 percent a combination of the two. What is more significant is that freshman senators and representatives were much more likely to be self-promoters than the secure veterans, who tended toward the "reticent" end of the spectrum.

Challengers, forced to rely on stamps instead of signatures, cannot hope to compete. To send one mailing to each of the 150,000 households in a typical congressional district would, at 8 cents apiece, set a challenger back $12,000 just for postage—not counting the printing (which the member, but not the challenger, can obtain at cost) or envelopes (which the member, but not the challenger, can obtain free). Twelve thousand dollars is just about half what is usually spent by congressional candidates.

One 1965 study found that about a third of the members of the House said that newspapers in their districts printed their news releases verbatim, and that another third wrote their own columns for the local press. Domination of the press is another media advantage enjoyed and gleefully exploited by incumbent members of Congress. It is the one perhaps most dependent upon the glory and trappings of office, which shroud the congressman until he doffs his statesman's gown and reenters the political fray, at election time. Typical congressmen pour out well over a hundred press releases each year; atypical congressmen, those from not-so-safe seats, pour out many more.

This formidable press barrage naturally does more good for congressmen from rural areas than those from big cities. The small-town editor, anxious to fill his columns, and having no Washington bureau to prepare stories for him, relies on the newsmaker more than, say, reporters for the *New York Times*. In Congressman David Obey's rural Wisconsin district, all the daily newspapers and half the weeklies publish his newspaper column, which appears every week. Obey and his peers are able to obtain columns and columns of free publicity that are simply not available to anyone hoping to challenge them, and at the same time these columns act as the filter through which news reaches his constituents. Exclusion of one's opponents from the relevant media can be as effective as an incumbent's domination of it.

When Murray Watson challenged William Poage in their east Texas Democratic primary, local newspapers totally ignored Watson's candidacy. "Watson's name never appeared in the paper except in ads," said Roger Wilson, his aide. The papers refused to print Poage's votes on environmental and consumer issues. "We finally ended up running them as ads," said Wilson.

Domination of the broadcast media, radio and television, follows a similar pattern. More than half of all representatives have their own regular radio or television broadcasts, which are eagerly aired by stations who must demonstrate their willingness to air public-service programming if they wish to keep their FCC licenses. The shows are taped for peanuts in the Senate and House recording studios, which have a mock congressional office, with an elegant desk and a window giving a glorious view of the Capitol dome in the background. Incumbents are also sought out whenever they make news, or whenever the station wants them to comment on the news. In 1965, members of the House told researchers that they averaged four television appearances and eight radio appearances every month while Congress was in session. Members of the Senate, who are sought out by the networks for national coverage, have it even better.

Some congressmen go to further lengths to assure themselves adequate exposure on the broadcast media. In 1969, there were fourteen members who owned more than $5,000 in stock in radio and television stations, and eight more were the owners or principal investors in them. One investor is Congressman O'Konski, the man who larded the *Congressional Record* with his own biography. O'Konski owns radio WLIN in Merrill, Wisconsin. He even keeps his district office there, and thereby pays himself the government subsidy that is given for maintaining a district office. The possibilities for conflict of interest in all these cases—when the station's license comes up for renewal, for example—are as obvious as the advantages to incumbents.

Members of Congress have to give up their free television and radio programs when they announce that they are candidates for reelection (which is one reason they delay the announcement as long as possible), but that does not mean that they give up their power in radio and television. One of the big advantages they have over their opponents is financial. The House and Senate recording studios charge members of Congress only the cost of materials when they use the studios. Everett Dirksen used the studios to record his smash-hit single, "Gallant Men," and thus got a leg up on other recording stars. The Nader Congress Project has found that to make a year's worth of weekly reports an incumbent pays $2,500, but his challenger would have to pay production costs of about $60,000.

The result of all this attention in the mails and the press and on television and radio is a much higher degree of voter recognition for the incumbent than a challenger can hope to obtain except by extraordinarily high spending. Though only half the voters know the name of their congressman, far fewer have ever heard of his opponent.

What do they know about the incumbent, besides having heard of him? Voters asked this question will usually answer, "He's a good guy," or "He does a pretty good job." Only rarely do they know what he thinks or how he votes. One remarkable survey taken by the American Business Committee on National Priorities found that "in almost every instance, between 80 percent and 100 percent" of the voters were unaware of how their representatives had voted on key issues that had drawn national attention. The Business Committee polled ten congressional districts represented by important legislators; in all of them, a majority of voters expressed opposition to continued funding of the SST. But eight out of the ten representatives voted for the SST, and apparently could get away with it, since 85 percent of the voters didn't know how they had voted and the 15 percent that thought it knew was wrong as often as it was right.

Congressmen cannot afford to ignore their constituents entirely when it comes to voting on major issues. There is at least a small group of informed citizens who follow what their member does, and cast their votes accordingly. It's unwise to alienate what political scientists call "the informed swing voter." Speaker Sam Rayburn counseled congressmen, "When in doubt, vote your district." But clearly some districts don't much care. Only this can explain some of the surprising representation sent to Congress. South Dakota, for example, has regularly returned George McGovern, a very liberal Democrat, and Karl Mundt, a very conservative Republican, to the Senate, although each represents the same constituency. Senators from Oklahoma and North Dakota are similarly contrasting—one very liberal, the other very conservative.

What all this seems to mean is that voters are more likely to vote for the image of a man than for his legislative record, and are more likely to vote for the image of a man than for the party to which he is attached. In fact, one of the reasons put forward for the recent upsurge in the trend to return incumbents indefinitely is that as party labels have less and less impact, the candidate who is best known to the public —the incumbent—will be the candidate who wins.

With the power to supervise the laws governing his own reelection, with the power to make news, with the power to determine, in many cases, what kind of news about himself filters back to his district, with the power to cater to special interests and to accept their money, the incumbent also has enormous opportunities for corruption, for unfairness, for deceit and manipulation of the public. Members of Congress have from time to time indulged in these opportunities, and stories of votes bought and sold, smear campaigns, and malicious distortion of the facts crop up in every political campaign. But there are far more important conclusions to be drawn from the advantages of incumbency than the predictable one that many congressmen and their challengers don't fight fairly. One of them is that every single member of Congress is a walking, talking embodiment of conflict of interest. On the one hand, he has an interest in staying in office, in being reelected; on the other, he has, or ought to have, an interest in serving his constituents and the nation honorably, conscientiously, and well. The congressman who lambastes the high amount of federal spending will nonetheless accept a public works project in his district, and it's difficult to see how even the most scrupulous member of Congress could refuse what may be a boon for his people, even if it's a boondoggle for the nation.

The oldest saw in politics is that a politician's first duty is to get reelected. It is comforting, at least, that members of Congress discharge their "first duty" so well. One only wishes they devoted the same amount of attention and achieved the same degree of success in the performance of other duties, duties that transcend the ambitions of self and apply directly to the hopes and problems of the people. No oath of office instructs a senator or representative to do his damnedest to get reelected.

Clearly, too, the men who framed the Constitution expected that congressmen would not get reelected as regularly as they now are; that is the whole argument behind the two-year term for members of the House of Representatives. The Senate would represent continuity, the House change. The Senate (before the Constitution was modified to provide for direct election of senators by the people) would represent the states, the House the people. Ironically, in a mass society, where each member of the House has about half a million constituents, the two-year term has come to accomplish exactly the opposite of its purpose. It was supposed to give the *people* a chance to hold their representatives accountable every two years. As George Washington wrote in a letter, in 1787, power "is intrusted for certain defined purposes, and for a certain limited period . . . and, whenever it is executed contrary to [the public's] interest, or not agreeable to their wishes, their servants can and undoubtedly will be recalled."

Now, however, the two-year term has given *special interests* a chance to hold their representatives accountable every two years. It would seem to the uninitiated that the need to seek frequent reelection would make congressmen listen more closely to the opinions of their constituents. Instead, because the costs of campaigning are so high, the perennial campaign makes congressmen listen more closely to their campaign contributors. Unlike many of the voters, the contributors know the candidate's name and how he voted.

The congressman or senator who must finance election campaigns is faced with a real and difficult ethical dilemma, which well can be illustrated by the case of former Illinois Senator Paul Douglas, one of the most conscientious, honest, and distinguished members of the Upper Chamber. Douglas had no reservoir of personal wealth to dip into when he ran for reelection. Nor did he use his office to increase his wealth. He had no outside business interests that might have posed conflicts. Every year, he made public his net worth and income. But he did have to run for reelection every six years, and he needed money to win in populous, volatile Illinois. He got a large portion of it from organized labor. And in the Senate, he voted the labor line. While Douglas generally agreed with labor anyway, the fact remains that he could not, politically, afford to offend it.

If even the most scrupulous members face this temptation, it is no wonder that those of less conscience joyfully embrace it. As former Senator Albert Gore said, "Any person who is willing to sell his soul can have handsome financing for his campaigns." The congressional Dr. Faustus who sells his soul becomes accountable to the special-interest Mephistopheles who buys it, and who is probably looking down upon him from the gallery.

The quest for reelection not only leads members of Congress into special interest dependency, but into a perversion of priorities as well. The congressman can no longer afford to come quietly into Washington, do his work, and return quietly to let his constituents judge his work; instead, he molds and manipulates and often writes the news his constituents get about him. Those who have read widely in the field of congressional newsletters will acknowledge the truth of the observation that controversial issues are usually passed over in all these reports; that the incumbent concentrates on building up a good-guy image, affable, concerned with the problems of his back-home flock and with bringing home as many public works projects as he can. What all this means is simply that congressmen distort the criteria by which they are to be judged, trivializing the work of legislation—except for lists showing how many bills they have introduced—and emphasizing the work of constituent service. There's nothing inherently wrong with servicing constituents; but dwelling on it to the virtual exclusion of more substantive legislative work not only misleads voters but encourages congressmen to pay less attention to whether more defense spending is needed than to whether the spending is going to their districts. It demeans both the issues presented to the voters and the work done by the members themselves.

The other harms of the incumbent's extraordinary advantages over his opponents are equally visible. How much respect for his constituents does a member of Congress have if he can expect them to return him unquestioningly year after year? What does it mean when a Thomas Dodd, stung by a major scandal, censured by his peers, and rejected by his party, can throw his hat again into the ring and feel he has a chance of pulling through? The electoral longevity of members of Congress—their seeming inability to lose—combines with the seniority system to keep younger, newer blood from rising high in the hierarchy of the houses. One way to change this would be to abolish the seniority system; another way would be to defeat incumbents on a regular basis.

Congress is only rarely accountable to the people. This is partly because the people do not make the effort to hold Congress accountable, do not check voting records and campaign financing information, allow themselves to be lulled into a lazy, hazy acceptance of their congressman as he is, not as he ought to be. As Adlai Stevenson once remarked, "Your public servants serve you right." But Congress is not accountable, in part becouse congressmen don't want to be held accountable and can cloud the issues and smother their opponents by virtue of the powers and privileges they grant themselves.

Citizens can make a difference. They can lobby their congressmen. They can vote them out of office. They can hold them accountable. But until they do so, the proud lords of legislation can frolic in the pool, sleep quietly at their desks, vote themselves pork barrel legislation, accept the money of special interests, capitulate to the president, obstruct important legislation, and be reassured by the knowledge that it is extremely unlikely that these pleasures and powers will ever be taken away.

9

Taking on Congress: A Primer For Citizen Action *

Liberty means responsibility. That is why most men dread it.

—George Bernard Shaw

Some citizens, peering into the chasm between congressional potential and congressional failure, may understandably shrug their shoulders in indifference. But mixed among all the cases of sloth, political hackery, insensitivity to injustice, and the dual hurdles of bureaucratic intransigence and business lobbying, are remarkable instances of citizen power. Congress has been moved by men and women with no special wealth or influence, little or no political experience, and no uncommon genius, but with the modest combination of commitment to a cause and the facts to make a case. Not often, but enough to show the way, citizen advocates have taken on industrial giants, bureaucratic inertia, public indifference, antipathy to "troublemakers"— and they have won, or at least made a difference.

Abe Bergman is one of them. He is a young pediatrician at Seattle's Children's Orthopedic Hospital, a career which is at least full time. Abe Bergman saw burned, scarred, and mutilated children—three a week, or even a day—victims of flammable fabrics, lawnmowers, and poisons alluringly packaged. He refused to shrug off what he saw, to surrender to the defeatism

---

* This chapter was written by Douglass W. Cassel, Jr., in collaboration with the authors.

that said he was powerless to affect the way corporations design and market their products. Instead he learned how laws governing unsafe products are made—who makes them and what influences their decisions. He learned that one of his senators, Warren Magnuson, as chairman of the Commerce Committee, was in a unique position to change the law. In Magnuson, he found a sympathetic response to the painful accounts of the human tragedies that daily seared his mind. Dr. Bergman became a constant and valued source of information, encouraging Senator Magnuson and the Senate Commerce Committee's staff.

His energetic and informed prodding were among the factors leading Senator Magnuson to introduce amendments to strengthen the Flammable Fabrics Act. In haughty response, the chairman of the board of one of the largest textile firms in the nation, speaking for the textile manufacturers' trade association, vowed that "blood would run in the halls of Congress" before this "unneeded" and "punitive" legislation would pass. Nevertheless, in some measure due to Bergman's testimony and Magnuson's support, the Flammable Fabrics Act Amendments did become law in 1967.

It proved to be an empty victory. For the Department of Commerce, which was to establish standards under the act, postponed their development by deferring in every imaginable way to the textile manufacturers' delays and obstructions. Unwilling to bask in the self-satisfaction of helping create a "no-law" law, Dr. Bergman persisted. In an effort to convey to the people of Seattle the intimate terror of a burn injury, he persuaded a local television station to run a half-hour film he had produced. The powerful documentary climaxed with gentle nurses and doctors changing the bandages of a scarred and frightened little girl, and it showed her suffering and inability to comprehend the constant pain. This film brought three thousand letters from the Seattle area to the secretary of commerce, insisting that he not delay or weaken the standard on children's sleepwear. At Senator Magnuson's request, the film was flown to Washington, D.C., where the secretary of commerce and his close associates saw it for themselves. Within two weeks, the secretary announced that a strict standard would take effect immediately and that proceedings would commence to raise the age limits of children protected from flammable sleepwear.

What Motivates Members?

However a case is presented, and whatever tactics are employed, it is advisable to understand initially that, above all else, *votes* motivate congressmen. A large part of their job is staying in their job, and appeals which suggest their continued tenure—such as "labor has endorsed it" or "a poll showed consumers favor it" —will be favorably received.

But pure politics is only one approach. Abe Bergman had in part based his appeal, quite simply, on the homily that "it was right." Contrary to myth, appeals to justice and fairness can ignite some kindling among the wet logs of Congress. A related appeal can be made to a member's self-esteem—that by doing right, he'll do good. A congressman likes to be known as a good guy, as a defender of democracy, rather than as a "tool of special interests." Even those who service only corporate enterprise and would barely recognize a citizen if they met one, drape their arguments with appeals to the general public interest.

If these exhortations to morality and self-esteem are attempted without the prop of actual or potential publicity, they may fail. Congressmen respond to publicity —both adverse and complimentary. For example, favorable press coverage may ease your path to a member happy to be identified with a good cause. GASP (Group Against Smog and Pollution), a local citizens' group, conducted a vigorous publicity campaign against the belching smokestacks of one of Pittsburgh's prime polluters, United States Steel's Clairton Coke Works. At one point, Pennsylvania air pollution commissioner, Dr. William Hunt, attempted to dismiss Mrs. Michelle Madoff, GASP's leader, as an "asthmatic paranoid." When a government lawsuit to stop the pollution was stalled by U.S. Steel's assertion that no adequate filter technology existed, GASP issued a thoroughly documented, expert report demolishing the claim. The press extensively reported GASP's activity, and U.S. Steel read the headlines. The firm eventually capitulated by entering negotiations for a long-range plan for air pollution abatement. Not surprisingly, Mrs. Madoff's first call to the Washington office of Congressman Joe Gaydos met a warm reception. Congressmen, like bookies, favor winners. With Gaydos's active assistance, GASP over the last few years has mobilized Pennsylvania's entire congressional delegation to intervene with state and federal air pollution officials on behalf of cleaner air in Pittsburgh.

Campaign contributions. Votes. Morality. Self-esteem. Publicity. What else motivates a congressman to act on an issue, or hide from it?

There is the simple appeal of an old acquaintance, a friend or trusted confidant. Senator Tom Eagleton showed that blood is thicker than politics by his surprise vote in mid-1972 to bury no-fault auto legislation in the Judiciary Committee. He had been lobbied by a group of his trial-lawyer father's colleagues, men that the senator, by profession and by upbringing, had come to respect. He explained ingenuously that his father had been a trial lawyer and would have "rolled over in his grave" had he voted against the tort system. The American Medical Association acknowledges the role of personal friendships in a congressman's decision. Nearly a third of its district lobbying representatives happen to be the general practitioners who delivered either the congressmen or their children.

Congressmen, like most of us, also listen to reason—but they hear many reasons. One effective way to bolster your logical argument is to cite support from a "disinterested source"—another congressman, a respected columnist, or experts. Almost universally, congressmen refused to seriously consider hazards of smoking and the need to restrict cigarette advertising until the authoritative Surgeon General's Committee on Smoking and Health delivered its grim verdict that cigarette smoking was tied to lung cancer and other disease.

Serious citizen action, with all these various approaches attempted in tandem, can succeed, even against the usual formidable odds. In 1970 and 1971, for example, the 1800-mile-per-hour Supersonic Transport appeared certain to fly unhindered through Congress. Ten years of federally funded investment and $1.1 billion already lay behind it. Three presidents (Kennedy, Johnson, and Nixon) had supported it. Its prime contractors were two giant corporations, General Electric and Boeing, and they had scattered $335 million in subcontracts across the home states of eighty-eight senators during 1967 to 1970 alone. Labor, viewing the issue as jobs, joined forces with big business to form a National Committee for the SST, headed by George Meany, president of the AFL–CIO, and Karl Harr, president of the Aerospace Industries Association. Forty-one corporations and several large unions amassed a war chest with an announced goal of $350,000 to save the SST in Congress. Big government, big business, and big labor—all combined into one giant coalition.

Opposing this colossus of economic and political power were ordinary citizens organized as the Citizens League Against the Sonic Boom—concerned about the environment and "reordering priorities." The SST, they argued, endangered the atmosphere and our health, promised noise pollution and destructive sonic booms, and diverted federal tax dollars from more pressing needs, like housing, health, and education. They won the endorsement of such groups as Common Cause, the $15-per-member national citizens' lobby chaired by former HEW Secretary John Gardner; Environmental Action, the organizers of Earth Day, 1970; the activist Federation of American Scientists; the National Taxpayers' Union; and the Sierra Club.

In April, 1970, twenty-nine of these national and local organizations joined in a Coalition Against the SST. Over the next fourteen months, their congressional effort was coordinated by George Alderson and

Louise Dunlap of Friends of the Earth, a Washington-based registered lobbying group. Enlisting the support of sympathetic scientists and economists, they prepared a thoroughly researched case, concentrating on "swing" votes: the new members of Congress, members who voted "inconsistently" on SST the previous year, and undecided congressmen. They recruited constituents to visit their congressmen in the districts and in Washington and brought experts to testify at hearings.

Member organizations, like the Sierra Club, obtained a list of the campaign contributors to key members, calling, writing, and visiting them to urge their opposition to the SST. Common Cause compiled and mailed a press kit of information about the SST to three thousand editorial writers; anti-SST editorials soon sprouted up all across the country. Newspaper advertisements, TV talk shows—every possible opportunity was taken to arouse public opinion and Congress against the SST.

No fewer than four times between December, 1970, and March, 1971, the citizens' coalition won votes on the floor of Congress—only to have each victory nullified afterward by political and parliamentary maneuvers. On one vote, Senator Clinton Anderson, chairman of the Aeronautical and Space Sciences Committee, surprised all by voting against the appropriations. He explained simply, "I read my mail"; that morning his letters and telegrams had opposed the SST by a lopsided 78–8 margin. Such citizen action persisted until a final and decisive vote in May, 1971, when the SST was grounded for good.

How to Do It

1. LEARN ABOUT CONGRESS. You begin with a problem. Your daughter is seriously ill and you've discovered that hospital care costs $100 a day, and no person of your $9,000-a-year income could possibly afford full medical insurance—unless Congress steps in. Or a gripe: Why are taxes so high? Or an idea: Why not serve nutritional food instead of glop in your child's school

lunch program? You're black, Chicano, or native American—and your state commission against discrimination drags its feet for two years before acting on complaints. Or you wonder why you can't buy a washing machine that works, or a safe car. You're a tenant in a neighborhood about to be run over by another highway or "rehabilitated" out of your price range by urban "renewal." Or you're a human being who breathes the foul exhaust of Chevrolets and Consolidated Edison plants ten miles away.

There are many ways to start acting to solve your problem. One is to write your congressmen.

Your Senator:

> The Honorable _____
> United States Senate
> Washington, D.C. 20510

Your Representative:

> The Honorable _____
> House of Representatives
> Washington, D.C. 20515

Ask what laws Congress has passed or is considering to meet your community's needs. Ask which members of what congressional committees and which federal agencies handle such laws. In fact, ask your congressman what you can do. For example:

> Dear Senator or Representative _____,
> We are two of your constituents who are concerned about hospital insurance, federal income taxes, and school lunch programs. It is important that we learn better how to be assisted by the services of Congress and how to influence and participate in congressional decisions. Although we have been doing some thinking, it seems to us that you should have a great deal more knowledge, experience, and interchange with citizens on just these issues. Would you kindly give us *guidelines*

and *details* on how we can more effectively present our concerns to you and to other legislators—local, state, and federal.

This request may take some of your time, but, if you have not already prepared such a package of advice, we are sure that many other citizens would similarly benefit from your insights and pointers. You're the expert on these matters. We look forward to your help.

Sincerely,

Fred and Martha *

But you don't need a "letter of introduction" from your congressman to "meet" Congress. You can begin with free government publications. For free copies of all House and Senate documents, including *bills, resolutions, presidential messages to Congress, most committee reports,* and *public laws,* write:

For House Documents:

      House Documents Room
      H 226
      United States Capitol
      Washington, D.C. 20515

For Senate documents:

      Senate Documents Room
      S 325
      United States Capitol
      Washington, D.C. 20510

Bills, resolutions, and laws are written in unfathomable legalese. But committee reports usually contain readable and informative descriptions of bills, presenting facts

---

* Let us know at Ralph Nader's Congress Project, Grossman Publishers, P.O. Box 19281, Washington, D.C. 20036, if you receive useful responses—or if you don't. We are preparing a *Citizens' Handbook on Congress,* and your letters will prove helpful.

and arguments for and against, though often slanted toward the committee viewpoint.

Printed hearings contain copies of all testimony offered at committee hearings on a bill. Fact-filled and mostly readable (but often a thousand pages thick), they also can usually be obtained at modest prices by writing to the U.S. Government Printing Office. For those who wish more concise summaries of the committees' findings, usually based on the entire record, a copy of the final committee report (obtainable from the same source) may be more helpful.

The *Congressional Record* is printed daily while Congress is in session and purports to be a transcript of all speeches and proceedings on the floor of the House and Senate. Despite the fact that many members hurriedly revise their speeches just before the *Record* goes to the printer, it is the most useful source of congressional activity: of roll-call votes; of committee hearings and meetings; and of the floor and committee schedule for the following week, printed every Friday. It can also provide educational insight into congressional attitudes. The *Record* can be ordered at 25¢ a copy, $3.75 a month, or $45 a year from the Superintendent of Documents, Government Printing Office, Washington, D.C. 20402; it is also located at many public university libraries.*

Once basically familiar with Congress, you can begin to act. Research your problem, organize supporters, get a bill introduced, drum up publicity, lobby, and follow through at the next election. The order of these steps will vary with the circumstances, your resources, and your resolve.

2. RESEARCH. The first response many congressmen make to any in-person citizen request is a barrage of questions: How much will it cost, next year and five years from now? What kind of tax do we use to raise the money? What does labor think about it? How many

---

* See Appendix 1 for a list of groups and publications with information on Congress.

votes will it cost me in the seventh District? How many voters benefit? Couldn't the program be better run by the states, and wouldn't loan guarantees be more effective than subsidies? Have you talked to the Banking and Currency Committee? These can wither the unprepared citizen lobbyist. To avoid trouble, first be informed; then lobby.

You can begin, of course, with information from Congress: hearings and committee reports. You can ask your congressman for information from the Congressional Reference Service on important issues. The CRS, drawing on the 60-million piece collection of the Library of Congress, answers specific questions, compiles reading lists, and discusses the pros and cons of policy issues. Do not, however, wear out your welcome on trivial requests or work you can do yourself. You can bypass the CRS and contact a governmental agency which administers federal programs that affect your community. If you seek information or help from them, your congressman can be of assistance: congressional inquiries to agencies are usually answered more promptly than your own unassisted letters, which may molder for months.

If your probing of an agency leads you to question seriously its responsiveness or performance, you can ask your congressman to call in the investigative branch of Congress, the General Accounting Office. With a staff of five thousand, led by accountants, lawyers, and other skilled professionals, the GAO has published revealing and authoritative reports on such topics as defense waste, inadequate enforcement of sanitary meat and poultry inspection, nonenforcement of pesticide safety regulations and state strip mining laws, and the financial irregularities of national political parties. Potentially one of the greatest tools for citizens and Congress, the GAO is also one of the least known. It receives only a few hundred requests for action each year by members of Congress, who alone can request a GAO investigation on your behalf.

You should also be aware of the Freedom of Information Act, which requires public access to all "identifiable records" in federal agency files (but not Congress), with certain listed exceptions. The exceptions—for national security, corporate trade secrets, internal agency memoranda, and six others—along with delaying tactics and skyhigh duplicating charges, are often purposefully used by agencies to deny information that the public has a right to know.*

Nor should you shrink from your own investigations. In April, 1972, a group of New York City neighbors, calling themselves the Upper West Side Air Pollution Campaign, conducted a building-by-building search of their community to track down polluters. Careful documentation by Campaign Against Pollution (CAP) in Chicago of how U.S. Steel underpaid its property taxes was a major factor in its plant tax reassessment and consequent higher taxes. An even more striking citizen investigation resulted from the Connecticut Citizen Action Group's study of occupational health hazards, begun in the summer of 1971. During interviews at a Connecticut plant of Colt's Firearms, a student investigator was told by outraged workers that Colt was manufacturing bent-barreled M-16's, under contract with the Department of Defense, for use by GI's in Vietnam. Not only was Colt neglecting to straighten the barrels properly, but the company was also switching parts after performance tests of the rifles, inserting untested and perhaps defective equipment. The Citizen Action Group's headline-capturing report, including sworn affidavits from the workers, was turned over to the Justice Department with a request that the FBI investigate Colt for criminal sabotage. The results of the FBI's investigation have not yet been released, but the Colt Company has suspended these practices.

Don't disband and throw away your files when you

---

* If you cannot get the records you want, contact one of the public interest lawyers who specialize in freedom of information problems. Among them are Ronald Plesser, P.O. 19367, Washington, D.C. 20036, and the University of Missouri Freedom of Information Center, Box 858, Columbia, Mo. 65201. They will supply you with advice and information.

find the information you want. Every good citizen action effort should include ongoing investigations. In fact, you will need a crack information-gathering team most in the later stages of working to get a law passed, when questions from allies and unsupported allegations by opponents arise. Also, by announcing the beginning of an investigation and by announcing the results when they later come in, you create two separate events which themselves focus attention on your issue.

Your congressman can also help obtain information from the private sector, especially giant corporations, who are far more reluctant than even government agencies to let the public peer through their screen of secrecy. At the urging of a citizen, Congressman Benjamin Rosenthal of New York sent out a letter to all domestic auto companies asking how they handle consumer complaints. The companies replied in some detail, and the letter may have stimulated them to formalize their complaint and review procedures; consumers can now at least point to these standards when they are violated. In 1966, when the information was treated like a trade secret, Connecticut Senator Abe Ribicoff successfully wrote the auto companies for a list of all models recalled for defects since 1960. A year or two later, when the National Highway Safety Administration neglected to continue gathering this data, Minnesota's Senator Walter Mondale wrote again and got more information about defective vehicle recalls by the auto firms.

3. ORGANIZE. Now that you've learned something about Congress and investigated your problem, you should be ready to take on the Capitol. But if you haven't yet organized, you should do so now.

There are several reasons why it is worth taking the time to organize a citizen action group. A group can commit more energy and resources than the most dedicated individual. An Abe Bergman could not have stopped the SST individually. A group is more likely to have the staying power to carry a seemingly interminable project through to completion. One year has already passed since the Colt investigation began, and several more years probably will pass before it ends. Finally, the results of group projects are also usually more respected than an individual's efforts.

Ordinary citizens have the capacity to organize a rudimentary group, which can grow into a powerful citizens' lobby. Take, for example, Ed Koupal, a former car salesman, and his wife Joyce. Aroused when highway incursion threatened the posh Sacramento, California, suburb where they lived, their concern spead to a range of issues. "We believe in the system, but that fools are operating it, that it can work," says Ed. He and Joyce formed the People's Lobby, whose purpose is summarized by the "Smash Smog!" on its letterhead, and which is financed by $10-membership for adults, $2 for students. "We're radical, we're militant, and we're constitutional," explains Ed. "Radical because we believe there's got to be a big change in this country. Militant because we want the law implemented. And constitutional because we operate basically through the initiative process" (a means by which citizens propose laws to be placed on a statewide ballot). "The organization," says Joyce, "is based on survival of the fittest. All these people came in, did junk work, and gradually carved out areas of responsibility. This took three or four months. Now they're department heads." And now the People's Lobby is a powerful force in California politics, organizing thousands of citizens behind smog smashing, with other goals in the mind for the future.

If you decide to form a group, you should first draft a tentative but clear statement of the scope of the group's proposed activities (such as lobbying Congress) and your purpose (such as obtaining federal mass transit development funds). Next, bring together a number of friends, acquaintances, or people in the community known for involvement in civic affairs. They might include the president of your neighborhood association, the lawyer who headed the fundraising drive for the reform candidate, or the ex-director of the free breakfast

program for Model Cities. Your first meeting will develop the core of activists for your citizen action group.

The structure of your group is important. To be
successful, you should emphasize *action* rather than
organization. Minimize such typical club activities as
regular meetings, titles, and minutes. You should divide
the following administrative posts among your members:

Group coordinator: Someone to see that there is a
person for every job and a job for every interested person. Also handles finances, calls meetings, excites the
troops. Must have telephone or be fleet of foot.

Project leader: Coordinator for each particular project.

Press contact: Someone to write press releases, call
conference, handle publicity. Should be articulate, literate, likable, and savvy, or willing to learn.

Legal adviser: Lawyer, law student, or lay person
who understands legal jargon. Useful for taxes, lobbying
laws, demonstration permits, unraveling bureaucratic
regulations, spotting congressional lawlessness, and
knowing when to bring suit.

Funding is, of course, essential to organizing. You
can get by on little money by holding meetings in homes
and similar skimping. Initial expenses can be paid by
out-of-pocket $5- or $10-contributions from the organizers. Later, money can be raised by dues, if your
membership is large, or by special fundraising events.
Monthly dues are best because people who wouldn't
dream of paying $24 to join a citizen action group will
often pay dues of $2 a month. Events like bake sales,
cocktail or wine-tasting parties, addresses by controversial speakers, newspaper recycling collections, etc.,
can raise $100 to $300 each.

But serious citizen lobbying of Congress can well drain
your coffers faster than carwashes can fill them. The
Coalition Against the SST spent more than $20,000 for
staff salaries, newspaper ads, research, phone calls,

duplicating, and mailing—not counting expenses by individual member organizations. One way to raise necessary money is to appeal to sympathetic wealthy individuals who can underwrite you with thousands of dollars. For many years, philanthropist Mary Lasker has been a one-woman bank for public health lobbyists. Her efforts deserve much of the credit for the bills which established the National Institutes of Health and Regional Medical Centers. But at the same time be careful not to be bought off: fit available funds to your goals, not your goals to the funds. Another way to raise money is by public subscription, as do GASP in Pittsburgh, and Common Cause and Public Citizen in Washington. Finally, if your citizen lobbying is nonpartisan, you may be able to obtain the support of foundations, which typically dole out $5,000 to $20,000 per worthy project.*

Once organized, your group's first project should be small, relatively easy to accomplish, cheap, and likely to arouse maximum interest and publicity. In 1969, for example, after Senator Everett Dirksen appealed on television for congressional pay hikes by arguing that "senators have to eat too," Mrs. George Cook of Idaho organized her friends to "send beans to the Senate," and received national press coverage. Other good projects are petition drives and preparing "congressional scoreboards," described below.

To be effective citizen lobbyists, group organizing should not stop at the local level. Whatever your interest, there is probably some national citizens' lobby in

---

* To learn about foundations, you can buy for $12 the *Foundation Directory,* published by the Russell Sage Foundation (most recently in 1967) for the Foundation Library Center, 444 Madison Avenue, New York, N.Y. 10022. Information about more activist fundraising can be obtained from *Action for a Change,* by Ralph Nader and Donald Ross (1971, Grossman paperback; 1972 edition forthcoming), which describes how university students fund and organize public interest research groups by levies of a few dollars per student, and it also provides illustrative consumer, environmental, and other citizen projects they can undertake; and *The Organizer's Manual* (1971, Bantam Books) which has a two-page bibliography of organizing and fundraising manuals.

Washington that shares it.* Contacting, joining, or forming a nationwide citizens' lobby with a Washington office can help you in three ways.

First, it can serve as an early warning system to keep you informed well enough and quickly enough to make your lobbying in Congress timely and effective. Newsletters and word of mouth from Washington offices can give you a head start in developing personal contacts with congressmen and their staffs. The National Welfare Rights Organization, among others, has researchers who study the mountains of documents that pile up under any welfare bill and condense them to a form that welfare recipients and interested parties have the time to read and understand. The Environmental Policy Center has hosted lobbying conferences in Washington for citizens concerned about issues like strip mining; after in-depth briefings, the citizen lobbyists from "back home" fan out to communicate with their congressmen.

Second, these Washington offices can also speed the flow of information from you to Congress. Dealing daily with congressmen and staff, Washington lobbyists can pass on the right information at the right time and become trusted advisers. This is hard to do from a purely local base.

Third, national affiliations give you at least the opportunity to lobby congressional committees. As a single local group, you can have some effect on your representative—or, if you are powerful enough, on your senators or entire state delegation. But the mem-

---

* For example, the Consumers Federation of America, the National Taxpayers' Union, Common Cause, Americans for Constitutional Action ("conservative"), Americans for Democratic Action ("liberal"), the National Women's Political Caucus, the National Tenants' Organization, the National Welfare Rights Organization, the League of Conservation Voters, Friends of the Earth, Zero Population Growth, the League of Women Voters, the NAACP, and the National Farmers Union. Their addresses can be found in a D.C. phone book, usually available at the central telephone company office in your area; at local chapters; or in the forthcoming *Citizens' Handbook on Congress,* available in 1973 from Ralph Nader's Congress Project, Grossman Publishers, P.O. Box 19281, Washington, D.C. 20036.

bers of one committee come from districts all over the country. Without a base as wide as their own, your lobbying is hampered.

As a last organizing step, you may want to align your group or national affiliation with other sympathetic organizations. Coalition building is one of the most important tasks of citizen lobbyists, as long as it doesn't become a form of mutual, bureaucratic dependence. Coalitions increase the voters and geographic base represented, as well as improve the chances that at least some members of the coalition are respected by the congressman. First look for allies in the home states and the districts of the congressmen—particularly the ranking ones—who sit on the committee you care about. A group from another state lobbying on a tax bill recently startled Wilbur Mills by encouraging picketing at his district office in Arkansas.

Some lobbyists, like the National Welfare Rights Organization (NWRO), direct more of their lobbying at other lobbyists than at Congress. Coalitions are sometimes permanent, like the Leadership Conference on Civil Rights. More often they rise and fall with each new bill in Congress, like the Coalition Against the SST.

Thus, you have now moved from a person, to a group, to a network of groups. This path is the same progressive accumulation of citizen power that impressed Alexis de Tocqueville over a century ago. "As soon as several of the inhabitants of the United States have taken up an opinion or a feeling which they wish to promote in the world," he said, "they look out for mutual assistance; and as soon as they have found each other out, they combine; from that moment they are no longer isolated men, but a power seen from afar, whose actions serve for an example, and whose language is listened to."

4. LOBBYING. To "lobby" means nothing more than to try to have an impact on the votes of lawmakers. You have a right to lobby under the Constitution, which guarantees "the right of the people peaceably . . . to petition the government for redress of grievances."

Facing you, of course, are the organized lobbies—from the National Association of Manufacturers to the AFL-CIO—discussed in chapter 2. Citizen lobbyists, however, constantly confounded the "pros" by breaking logjams of inertia and overcoming heavyweight opposition to achieve reform. There were: Dr. Isadore Buff, who carried the bitter image of black lung from the coal fields of West Virginia to the corridors of Congress; Fred Lang, a solitary engineer who unsuccessfully protested the weakness of gas pipeline safety standards to no avail, until Congress listened and enacted the Gas Pipeline Safety Law; Jeremy Stone and Jerome Wiesner and other scientists, who launched the citizen critique of our nuclear armaments policy; Warren Braren, who resigned his position in 1969 as director of the National Association of Broadcasters' code office in New York—created to regulate deceptive advertising —and appeared before a hostile House Commerce Committee to document broadcasters' lip service to self-regulation. Given such issues and such personal determination, a number of steps can be followed by the citizen lobbyist: *

• Planning. A serious lobbying organization working on a legislative effort begins with an analysis of the legislative forum in which it must do combat. Who are the key players? What role will they play? What committee or subcommittee will consider the legislation? Who chairs it? Who are the important staff members? Are there legislative assistants on the staffs of congressmen who have shown an interest in similar issues in the past? Early in the process, you should project a likely timetable of events, ranging from generating public support through introducing the bill, on to the hearing stage, committee markup sessions, floor con-

* For some, an initial, procedural step will be to file as a registered lobbyist under the 1946 Federal Registration of Lobbying Act. Registering should be as routine as renewing a driver's license. The reason for the act is not to prevent lobbying, but to keep track of who's doing it and how much is spent. (Since this is a technical area, with each situation turning on its particular facts, it is best to consult with a lawyer.)

sideration, Senate-House conference, and finally to the possibility of veto by the president. Thoughtful consideration of substance and strategy at this early stage can avoid telling delays or outright failures later.

• Timing. Assuming you are lobbying on a specific piece of legislation rather than generally to educate, your lobbying should begin early, while the legislation concerning you is still at the committee or subcommittee level. Since some 90 percent of all bills reported by committees to the House and Senate are passed exactly as written, an ounce of lobbying in committee is worth a pound of lobbying on the floor.

Lobbying in Congress can pivot around someone else's bill *or* your own bill. Do not be surprised that you can ask your congressman to introduce a bill—that's part of his job.

First write up what you want to do in plain language. You can present your proposal directly to your congressman, who can refer it to the Office of Legislative Counsel for drafting. But it's better to have your bill drafted by an attorney who advocates your point of view. One good place to look is a law-student organization at a local law school.

Even better may be one of the public interest law firms springing up around the country. "Public Interest Research Groups," staffed by lawyers and other professionals, and funded by college students who guide overall policy, already exist in fifteen states. To find out about a PIRG in your state, call your state university. To find out about public interest firms and departments near you, write Project to Assist Pro Bono Publico Programs, 1705 DeSales Street, N.W., Suite 601, Washington, D.C. 20036.

Your own congressman is probably not the best person to introduce your bill, for any bill introduced by a congressman not a member of the relevant committee is routinely passed over. Find out, therefore, which committee handles bills on your subject. But finding out can be next to impossible without help. At least thirteen committees and twenty-one subcommittees handle education bills, for example. Ask your congressman, consult a relevant national citizens' lobby in Washington, or see the forthcoming *Citizens' Handbook on Congress*.

If your congressman is not on the relevant committee, you can still urge him to introduce the bill. But beware of the token bill, introduced by the congressman to get you off his back and then left to die in a foreign committee. Most citizens are so excited by the introduction of their bill that they are easily fooled by this ploy. Ask your congressman to speak to members from your state on the committee; to write a letter to the chairman requesting hearings and to send you a copy; and to testify in favor of your bill at the hearings.

If the legislation concerning you doesn't get out of committee, chances are it will never be considered. When Emanuel Celler, chairman of the House Judiciary Committee, was asked in 1958 for his stand on a certain bill, he replied, "I don't stand on it. I am sitting on it. It rests four-square under my fanny and will never see the light of day." Of 17,728 bills and resolutions introduced to the House in 1969, for example, only 706 were reported from committee. Sometimes even the committee stage may be too late, because, as one committee staffer said, "Given an active subcommittee chairman, working in a specialized field with a staff of his own, the parent committee can do no more than change the grammar of a subcommittee report."

• Testimony and Hearings. Citizens have their best access to committees during the public hearings held on most major bills. When citizens are permitted through the large oaken doors into the hearing rooms, what they usually discover are plodding exercises in the compilation of information, views, and recommendations. Occasionally, the hearings are extravaganzas staged for publicity and the press. In either case, most experienced Capitol lobbyists find hearings serious enough—after all, they are making a public record that will last for years—so that they rarely miss an opportunity to testify.

You can find out about upcoming hearings through committee staff, or from the *Congressional Record*, which often gives more than the required one week's advance notice. Hearings are most frequently scheduled and detailed during the first five to six months of each year, before they are interrupted by the frenzy of floor activity late in the session. To testify, send your request to the committee or subcommittee chairman. If he or she refuses to schedule you, you can address your request instead to the ranking minority member, who generally can call witnesses for one day.

Testimony is an invaluable way to educate committee members, committee staff, and the press. To ensure that your position gets a fair airing, you should help recruit relevant witnesses. One good pool to tap is experts. Many experts respond to calls from lay citizens, but a request from your congressman can help. Former Georgia Congressman Jim Mackay once contacted fifty experts, many of whom peppered the House Commerce Committee with requests to testify on an auto safety bill, and the points of view they expressed prevented the hearings from being a mere whitewash. Witness recruiting is especially important on subjects so arcane— bank and tax bills, complicated housing finance laws, the El Paso Natural Gas bill—that only private interests directly affected know about the hearings. Only systematic monitoring and continuous presence in Washington can prevent defeat by default.

Yet one needn't be a professional "expert" in order to testify effectively. Often personal experience and passion count far more than learning or polish. An 11-year-old Florida schoolgirl recently testified before the Senate Commerce Committee on a study she had done of the impact of television advertising on her classmates. When Joseph ("Chip") Yablonski, son of murdered United Mine Workers insurgent Jock Yablonski, testified on UMW election irregularities before a Senate Labor and Public Welfare subcommittee, it was his intense and touching manner that etched his words onto everyone present. After the Farmington, West Virginia, mine disasters, the stricken widows of the victimized miners retained enough composure to convey the lesson of their sadness to a congressional committee.

Union rank and file on a labor bill, migrant workers on a bill to give them minimum wages, mechanics on car repairability, housewives on consumer purchases: first-hand knowledge counts.

Dramatizing your testimony with personal narration may not only stave off committee members' boredom, but can also attract press attention. During hearings on the coal mine health and safety bill, miners with severe black lung gripped the attention of congressmen by showing how they collapsed from lack of breath after jumping up and down just a few times. In the underground natural-gas pipeline hearings, Tony Mazzocchi, Washington lobbyist for the Oil, Chemical, and Atomic Workers Union, brought in the workers who repair and inspect underground pipelines in St. Louis. They showed the riddled pipe and demonstrated sloppy repairs to the members of Congress. In hearings on national health insurance, physicians performed a kidney dialysis before the wide-eyed committee members.

Before testifying, prepare a written statement and submit a number of copies to the committee a day or two in advance, depending on committee rules. After testifying, members of the committee may question you, alternately by party, down the seniority line. This is when your careful preparation and research will return dividends. But you can do more than just appear before the committee. You can contribute helpful questions for sympathetic committee members to ask of opposing witnesses.

If no hearings are being held in Congress on your concern, you can lobby to have hearings initiated. Unless your congressman is a committee or subcommittee chairman, he has no power to schedule hearings; but you can always ask him to lobby for hearings. Or if a committee chairman or the committee refuse to hold hearings, you can try to convince a friendly congressman or group of them to schedule unofficial hearings. This is precisely what Congressman Joseph Resnick did in 1967 on the secret workings of the giant American Farm Bureau.

Citizen groups can also ask members of Congress to

hold hearings where the problem is—in your community. In November, 1971, Congressman John Brademas took his subcommittee of the House Education and Labor Committee to Chicago, New York, Boston, and Miami to hear testimony on the problems of the aging. Senator Edmund Muskie trooped his subcommittee out to Gary, Indiana, to hear about alleged corporate underpayment of property taxes. Back in the fifties, Congressman John Blatnik, now chairman of the Public Works Committee, toured the country with his subcommittee looking into corruption in interstate highway construction, accumulating volumes of evidence.

You can also ask your congressman to bring unofficial hearings to your district. In the fall of 1969, congressmen from New York City held unofficial hometown hearings on one of the world's biggest air pollution problem areas. Former Democratic Congressman Allard Lowenstein from Long Island held "forums" in his district where citizens exchanged views on the Vietnam War, taxes, the ABM, campus disturbances, and how to finance education; even some Republicans came. Former Congressman Jim Mackay of Georgia topped them all: he set up a "Grass-Roots Congress" in Atlanta, with citizens' committees organized along the lines of actual congressional committees. His constituents met and proposed and discussed bills on regular schedules. He also brought cabinet officials and agency heads who discussed key legislation—and agency implementation of it—directly with the affected citizens.

• The "Markup" Sessions. After official hearings are held, staff typically prepare a draft committee bill. Committee members then meet to go over the draft bill and to propose amendments. Such "markup" sessions, even though they forge the law that eventually passes Congress, are almost always closed to the public. Having an impact on the markup session—which is essential, because it is here that the contours and details of legislation are ironed out—is more difficult than merely testifying. If you are in Washington, lobby yourself; if, as is more likely, you are far away, you can cooperate with the D.C. office of a national citizens' lobby, or ask your congressman to support you by lobbying before the markup session. Either way, if you can get through to a committee member to give him or her specific information about a bill, fine. But more commonly the people to contact are the committee staff, who have direct substantive authority over the developing legislation. "The key point of contact is usually between a highly specialized lobbyist and the specialized staff people of the standing committee," said Congressman Bob Eckhardt of Texas in 1969. "Intimate friendships spring up there—it's the rivet point. Friendships that outlast terms. They probably have a greater influence on legislation, especially if it's technical."

Your information can well prove crucial. With thousands of bills submitted and thousands considered, members and staff cannot obtain all the relevant material on each one. Even within their committees, congressmen cannot be experts. Senator Everett Dirksen, who sat on eight committees, once confessed that he couldn't keep up with every bill they handled even with "roller skates to get from one subcommittee to another." A number of congressmen respond to this information overload by concentrating their energies to become an expert in a single field. For example: Senator Sam Ervin on electronic snooping and invasions of privacy; Congressmen Otis Pike and Les Aspin and Senator William Proxmire on military waste; Cong. Ken Hechler on coal mine health and safety; Cong. Paul Rogers on health; Cong. Henry Reuss on water pollution; Senator Gaylord Nelson on marketed drugs; Senators Magnuson and Vance Hartke on auto safety —and there are many more. Try to find out if some congressman has cornered the market on your issue, since with his expertise comes greater influence. You can even ask your congressman, in effect, "Who knows what you don't?"

To have effective input into this markup stage, citizens and citizen groups should similarly stake out areas of expertise. Gain a reputation for giving honest, informative, and accurate answers. Staffers and congressmen may come to rely on your expertise. Before and during markup session it is not uncommon for committee staff to ask a trusted lobbyist how to vote on an amendment they don't understand. NAACP lobbyists assist committee staff in drafting civil rights bills for markup sessions. NWRO lobbyists have even gained admittance to markup sessions in one Senate committee.

• Lobbying for Votes. Eventually, the interested citizen will attempt to persuade a member to vote a certain way. This is the showpiece and showdown of representative democracy, where legislation comes down to a simple head count. There are various techniques to affect the vote:

You can try to *meet your congressman*. In 1965, congressmen interviewed said they spent 7 percent of their work week meeting with constituents. When you visit your congressman, write ahead to arrange an appointment. You then have a better chance of seeing him, and it is a courtesy appreciated by busy congressmen. Also, it can make your visit far more effective. If you state in your letter the precise issue you wish to discuss, the congressman can have his staff research the problem and "brief" him before your visit. Groups are even more welcome than individuals, for obvious electoral reasons.

You can also call the district office to find out when your representative will be in town, and try to arrange an appointment to see him then. Most representatives have full-time district offices, and most members are there for much of the time from October 15 to January 1 each year, as well as major holidays. Some Eastern congressmen, members of the so-called Tuesday-Thursday Club, are often in their districts Friday through Monday.

Or you can ask *a congressman to visit you and your group,* either in informal session or to give a speech followed by a question-and-answer session. Such gatherings can impress a member with your information, your issue, or your clout. Consider, for one example, Congressman Dan Rostenkowski, a Democrat from the Chicago machine. Formerly prowar, he was strongly persuaded by high school students to break with President Nixon's troop withdrawal approach. "I make a lot of speeches at high schools in my district," he explained, "and the kids ask damn penetrating questions about what useful purpose we are serving in Vietnam. As this thing has gone on, I've had more and more trouble answering them."

In personal lobbying, it is also essential to *get exact commitments*. An experienced labor lobbyist tells of the citizen group which visited its local representative to solicit federal money for schools. The congressman's response: "Why, yes, I've always been in favor of education and when the pending legislation comes up I'll certainly vote pro-education." They walked away satisfied they had a "firm commitment." In fact, the congressman was free to vote any way he pleased when the specific provisions of the education bill came up; each side could claim to be "pro" education. The lesson is to spell out exactly what you want your congressman to do. Find out and specify the bill and section number, and whether you want a yea or a nay vote.

Even if you are specific, your request may be met by a smokescreen of diversionary actions. Don't be fooled by camouflages like a public yes vote on the floor after the member has already added a crippling amendment in the privacy of committee; the introduction of a token bill which will be safely tucked away in a committee of which your congressman is not a member; or merely a nice speech inserted in the extensions section of the *Congressional Record*.

Write your congressman in the classic way to tell your member what you think. It is true that most letters from constituents never reach the congressman's desk, but they all reach his office. One vaguely written letter in an avalanche of mail may receive only a few glances from a bored clerk before being put in the pile marked "pro" or "anti," to be answered and signed by machine.

But there are letters that electrify, that counter false information, that change votes. These very often reach the congressman's attention. In the mid-sixties, when Congress had barely begun to look at unsafe automobiles, several members of the Senate Commerce Committee began to receive letters that shared common characteristics. They were written carefully, many by engineers and professional people. They were precise. Each told a similar story of the shoddy performance of tires. The committee members probably received, in all, fewer than fifty of these letters. But they had a profound impact on the members, whose staffs decided that they were unique enough and significant enough to be read by the senators themselves. Indeed, the committee cited these letters as a significant part of the evidence convincing it that tire safety legislation was needed.

Even letters which are not seen by policy-making staff or the congressman can have an important impact if there are enough of them. On important issues, many members have their clerks count their mail the way geologists read seismographs. The sample may be statistically inaccurate, but it offers understandable and numerical guidance to a member who faces conflicting views and who wants to be reelected. Form letters flooding an office will not have this impact. Many individual letters will.

Letters which demonstrate familiarity with the congressman and his record immediately evoke respectful interest. "I strongly support your efforts to amend the Housing Act by requiring the FHA inspectors to be responsible for the quality as well as the value of housing, and I was pleased to see you vote for the Morehead Amendment which would have strengthened the consumer protection bill. However, I am very much concerned . . ." This kind of opening is particularly effective because it conveys to the reader a number of facts. First, he is dealing with an informed voter, probably an opinion leader in his community. Second, this is a potential supporter, not an ideological opponent who would complain no matter what position the congressman adopted. There are other short tips which can make writing your congressman more than a futile civics exercise: always write in your own words; time your letters for maximum effect instead of wearing out the congressman's patience by writing every day; relate *local* needs to the federal legislation by describing how the bill will affect your life, family, or community; whenever possible, give first-person accounts; limit each letter you write to a single subject; include the number, title, and current status of any legislation you write about; follow up by keeping his response and referring to it at public meetings when he visits the district; if he does come through on your request, thank him by letter.

One very effective way to use the mails is to ask your congressman to explain his yea or nay on a particular vote. Few members could safely ignore, for example, a rash of inquiries asking for detailed reasons every time they vote against a consumer bill. Remember, however, that to get specific answers, you must ask specific questions.

Two alternatives to direct mail are *telegrams and telephone calls*. Early in the legislative life of a bill, when there is time to write and mail a letter, telegrams make little sense. Telegrams are attention-getters, however, and can be effective when sent just before a vote: to ask a yea or nay, and to urge the member to be present for the vote. Ducking a vote is easier when the congressman thinks no one is watching. By calling Western Union, a fifteen-word "Public Opinion Message" can be sent to Congress from anywhere in the country for a dollar. It usually arrives one day after being sent.

To phone a representative or senator, dial 202-225-3121 and "The Capitol" answers. Ask for the member of Congress you wish to reach. Whether your congressman answers usually depends on who you are. To reach him, you may have to lobby influential people in your district —the mayor, for example, or personal friends of the member, his campaign treasurer—and ask them to call. Some members, however, make themselves quite accessible by phone. Former Tennessee Congressman George Grider had a "Dial-a-Congressman" program, reserving Monday afternoons for free calls by constituents from his district office.

Pouring communications into Washington, however, is not the only way to lobby; it can and should be done in your own home district. You can contact sympathetic state legislators or city councillors to ask them to pass a resolution or ordinance requesting Congress to take action; the Massachusetts legislature passed a law attempting to immunize its citizens from unwilling service in the assertedly illegal Vietnam War. You can assist a local television station in producing a documentary on your issue. Or expose the congressman's former campaign manager to your problem and ask him to be the honorary chairman of your lobby. Or beat the corporations at their own game: instead of allowing Ford, GM, and Chrysler to enlist their local dealers as grass-roots corporate lobbyists, go to the local dealers yourself and ask them to support the stronger bumper bill. Another way to stimulate local action is to ask your congressman to inform constituents in advance whenever he introduces a bill, or even to hold advance hearings in the district on major bills. Let him spend his time in the district on the people's terms, rather than on his own terms, which tend toward backslapping, handshaking, and ribbon-cutting. Remember that getting your member committed to your cause and lobbying on your behalf is the most effective of all ways to lobby.

In lobbying, you should also take advantage of the assistance available to you from a number of sources. Black citizens, for example, should seek assistance not only from private citizens' lobbies like the NAACP, but also from the Black Caucus in Congress. It consists of all thirteen present black members of the House— expected to grow to eighteen or nineteen next year— who have pooled their hiring allowances to employ an executive director. They are attempting to serve both as the representative in Congress for the more than 22 million black citizens of the United States and as an alternative to the official processes of Congress: in July, 1972 they held highly publicized unofficial hearings on government lawlessness.

Or you may find yourself a resident of one of the growing number of states and cities which have their own full-time paid lobbyists, with offices in Washington. If you are from California or New York, for example, you can try to enlist the services of your state lobbyist to provide you information and to support your bills in Washington. State and city lobbyists can also work against you: a New York State lobbyist, Ms. Donna Mitchell, opposed amendments strengthening the water pollution bill under debate on the floor of the House in March, 1972.

5. PUBLIC COMMUNICATIONS There is no particular point in time when it becomes obvious that you have to go public with your views. At all stages, you should be seeking to educate and mobilize a wider audience than yourself or your group.

The news media is the most evident and efficient voice to disseminate your purpose and activities. You may have appealed to the press in getting your bill introduced; or in the hearings; or before the markup session. At some point, however, before a floor vote, public support becomes especially important.

The basic tool in your press kit is the *press release*. This is nothing more than a written statement by any person or group issued to the press; that is, mailed or hand-delivered to every newspaper and broadcaster in your community. It should consist of accurate, newsworthy information. The photogenic, the unusual, an event, a charge, testimony—all may be newsworthy. You should write a press release in the third person: "Herman J. Pudd, Coordinator of Citizens for Better Housing, charged today . . ." Put the most important information first. After reporters rewrite your statements, the editors may simply lop off the last paragraphs, one by one, until the story fits into whatever space or time is available. At the top of the first page, label it "news release" or "press release." State "For immediate release," or "For release Tuesday, A.M., June 13, 1973," if it is for morning release, and "For release Tuesday, P.M. . . ." if it is for an afternoon newspaper. Also, list the name and telephone number of someone who can be reached for further information at the upper right-hand corner.

A second tool, the *press conference*, must be used with more restraint. It may involve a public reading of a statement, a question-and-answer session, or both. To make the immediate issue interesting and concrete, you might try to accompany it with some symbolic act, such as the presentation of your voting scorecard (described below) to the congressman. Because they take newsmen's time, press conferences should be called only when there is important news. To help assure that the press will come to your conference, consider asking some community figure, such as a former elected official, to participate in the conference.

Your opponent's paid political ads on TV and radio may help you get *free broadcast time* to rebut them. Under the FCC's fairness doctrine, when a station presents advertisements on one side of a "controversial issue of public importance," it must present the other side as well. The doctrine doesn't guarantee equal time, but it can give you free time if the station itself fails to broadcast your side. When you see ads you think require rebuttal, write the station manager, identify your group as having membership in the area, refer to the ads, and offer to provide or help the station prepare counter ads from your viewpoint. If you get no reply in a week, or if the station rejects your offer, you can send a written complaint to Chief, Complaints and Compliance Division, Federal Communications Commission, 1919 M Street, N.W., Washington, D.C. 20036. Many radio stations (and some TV stations) devote program time for citizens to air their views. Whatever it is called—"Point of View" or "The Voice of the People"—local radio or television time is invaluable exposure.

The *print media* require a somewhat different approach. Letters to the editor, for example, are not usually too effectual unless part of a large, coordinated citizen lobbying effort. Their virtue is that they are free and attract potential adherents to the cause.

A more direct press approach is also possible. Often citizens complain about press apathy or favoritism. Most people don't realize that they can personally confront unresponsive editors. Just arrange an appointment, go down to their offices, look the editors in the eye, and ask them why they haven't covered the story. If you try to educate, rather than manipulate, and are candid and resolute, you may well affect the policy of previously inattentive local media. Develop personal contacts and information exchanges with reporters, photographers, broadcasters, and editors, just as you might with congressional staff. They can be valuable sources of information to you, and you to them.

Recalcitrant local press may also be jarred into action by national media coverage of a problem in your community. With the exception of the *Louisville Courier,* Appalachian media in the coal mining states did little or no reporting (except for covering disasters) on unsafe mines and black lung disease, until miners' marches and work stoppages caught the attention of NBC, CBS, ABC, the *Washington Post,* and the *New York Times.* This technique of appealing to national press to stimulate local reporting can be especially important for citizens of one-company communities, like textile and paper mill towns around the country.

Finally, groups can communicate with the public by more *direct action.* Altohugh some picketing and sit-ins aim more to intimidate than to inform their targets, most forms of public demonstrations are quite simply to demonstrate a point to the public. "The rich can buy advertisements in newspapers, purchase radio or television time, and rent billboard space," said Justice William O. Douglas in dissent to a Supreme Court decision involving Dr. Martin Luther King's 1963 marches through Birmingham, Alabama. "The less affluent are restricted to the use of handbills . . . or petitions, or parades, or mass meetings." Public demonstrations, often resorted to by those lacking formal access to the established media, can be a part of an overall publicity campaign to tell Congress about the depth of their concerns and convictions.

Tacticians differ on approaches. (Some business lobbies employ means that most citizens should not and could not emulate: backroom bargains based on surreptitious campaign gifts.) An experienced AFL-CIO lobbyist warns never to embarrass, offend, or threaten a congressman if you want to get his vote. One member of Congress, he explains, has voted against every poverty program bill since "some group" picketed his house while his wife was sick. Most lobbyists' tactics are moderate, polite, and traditional: letter-writing campaigns, friendly phone calls from the congressman's old friends, socializing with the member, visiting him, proposing bills, and testifying at hearings. Press releases and press conferences are usually cordial. Lawsuits are a last resort.

Such milquetoast manners leave a Washington organizer-lobbyist for the National Welfare Rights Organization cold. He lobbies by the "polarizing" method, using some dramatic demonstration or event to force both vacillating congressmen and other pressure groups to take clear sides. NWRO organizes sit-ins, takeovers, and demonstrations; its members picket and hold unofficial hearings. They hesitate before going to court only long enough to worry about how to pay legal fees.

If you do decide to demonstrate, you should prepare for two kinds of problems: legal and medical. For any outdoor, public demonstration, consult a lawyer to find out about permit requirements and what your constitutional rights do and do not protect. If there is any chance that disruption may occur, arrange for legal observers (law students or lawyers) to be present. Similarly, medical students, nurses, medics, or doctors, and well-marked medical stations can help.

Beyond Congress

"The biggest mistake I ever made," reports Dr. Bergman, "was thinking I had won the victory just by getting a bill through Congress. That was only the beginning."

First, the president may veto your bill.

Second, even if he signs it, he can refuse to spend all the money appropriated by Congress.

Finally, the federal agency that is supposed to carry out the program may write ineffective regulations within the broad congressional guidelines or may simply not enforce the law's provisions.

In each case, your lobbying must turn toward the agency and the White House. Tactics may have to change since, for example, appointed bureaucrats are generally less sensitive than elected congressmen to voters. One way to keep an agency alert is to persuade it to hold public hearings in your community or at its regional offices. Few agencies do. But the potential is there: George Romney of the Department of Housing and Urban Development has recently granted citizen requests for public hearings on housing problems, first in Washington and then hopefully in each of HUD's ten regional divisions across the country. Remember also that the agencies are beholden to the congressional committees which write laws governing their programs and which pass their annual budget. These committees (but not Appropriations committees) are now required by law to act as watchdogs over executive agencies, and, beginning in 1973, must issue reports every two years on their progress.

Another prevailing tactic beyond legislation is purely legal: going to court. NAACP lobbyists, for example, work arm in arm with their lawyer litigators, ready to file suit on the constitutionality of such bills as the anti-busing act. A recent lawsuit demonstrates the pressure which an embarrassing case can exert on a congressman. On August 15, 1972, Ralph Nader's Congress Project filed against Edward Garmatz, patriarch and sole proprietor of the House Merchant Marine and Fisheries Committee, and two of its clerks, for refusing to make records of committee votes available at committee offices as required by a 1970 reform law. Eight days later, Garmatz, through his chief counsel, opened the records.

Friendly congressmen can be of great assistance to you in bringing lawsuits, especially against hard-shelled executive agencies. Recently a new and potentially powerful course of action—directly resorting to the courts to tame the bureaucracy—is being pursued by more members of Congress. Twenty-eight congressmen sued the Civil Aeronautics Board (CAB) two years ago, challenging what they claimed to be an illegal airline rate increase approval. In 1972, Congressman Ronald Dellums of California joined James Ridgway, an editor of *Ramparts,* in suing to compel HEW to release information on Medicare and Medicaid; in 1971, Congressman John Murphy joined Staten Island officials in suing the General Services Administration to stop the proposed transfer of 125 federally owned acres to the owner of the Willard Hotel in Washington.

A different step beyond the Capitol corridors is to compete with Congress. For example, if you suspect that a bill you favor will not get a fair hearing in the official committee, hold your own hearings. The National Welfare Rights Organization did just that, conducting hearings at the Capitol on President Nixon's welfare program two days before scheduled Senate Finance Committee action in November, 1970. Senator Fred Harris, a member of the Finance Committee, was so impressed by testimony at the hearings that when the "real" committee met shortly afterward, he gave NWRO a one-vote margin of victory over the Nixon plan.

You can also competitively stimulate Congress by getting a state law passed which it can imitate. Then, Congress will have a proven model from which to build national legislation. After Massachusetts, for example, enacted a no-fault auto insurance plan, Congress gave serious consideration to a national no-fault plan for the first time.

How do you do it? In Michigan, a citizen campaign passed a bill to give individual citizens the legal right to file suits to protect the environment. They obtained an attentive press by attending hearings and numerous strategy meetings, flooding the governor's office with phone calls, concentrating on key legislators and the state's attorney general, and recruiting students to counter overblown charges made against the bill by the chamber of commerce. Joseph Sax, Michigan law professor who drafted the bill, then met with staff people working for Senators McGovern and Hart and Congressman Udall to draft a national bill. The Hart-McGovern bill was then introduced and is currently pending in Senate committee. When industrial polluters argued that the bill would choke the courts with too many lawsuits, its supporters could point to Michigan, where an average of only two suits a month have been filed since the law was passed. In addition, five other states have acted on Michigan's example to pass similar laws.

During the 1972 primary elections, the People's Lobby in California, organized by Ed and Joyce Koupal, collected several hundred thousand signatures to put a sweeping environmental control bill on the ballot. Although the People's Lobby initiative went down to defeat, buried by a costly public relations campaign funded by industrial interests, it has already forced some state legislators to take a more concerned stand on environmental questions. And the People's Lobby is still working to place other issues on the ballot, and to learn from the mistakes of its first attempt.*

Election Year

Your ultimate resort against unresponsive congressmen is to "throw the rascals out." But regardless of whether your congressman is vulnerable at the polls, election years and campaign months are the best times to press your issue upon the congressmen, who seem coincidentally more interested in their constituents at these times. There exist, however, several low-cost and little-used techniques by which citizens can change votes and views during critical campaign years.

---

* The states that *do* permit initiatives are Alaska, Arizona, Arkansas, California, Colorado, Idaho, Maine, Massachusetts, Michigan, Missouri, Montana, Nebraska, Nevada, North Dakota, Ohio, Oklahoma, Oregon, South Dakota, Utah, and Washington.

A congressional scorecard, to take a key approach, is a chart showing how your congressman has performed over the years on a specific issue—consumer protection, tax reform, civil rights, defense spending, environmental protection, or any other. Used creatively, this rating system can have a considerable impact in an election year. In 1970, for example, Environmental Action prepared environmental scorecards for members of Congress. The twelve worst performers were labeled the "Dirty Dozen," and Environmental Action focused attention on the campaigns against those twelve. Seven of them lost—a much higher turnover rate than for Congress as a whole—and the scorecards played at least some role in the defeats.

In preparing your scorecards, it is best to concentrate on one issue. Select five or ten votes in which the lines between support and opposition are clearly drawn, and make sure that you choose the important stage of the voting on each bill. (Sometimes a vote on an amendment or on a procedural motion may be more important than the vote on the final bill.) Publicize the results as widely as possible within the district.

During the election, you can also play an important role by investigating your rival's campaign finances. As explained in chapter 1, the new Federal Election Campaign Act of 1972 plugs a few of the gaping loopholes in past financing laws. It limits spending from a candidate's personal funds and for TV, radio, newspaper, magazine, or billboard ads and for paid telephone banks. It requires fuller reports on where the money is coming from. The most important part of the law to a citizen action group is the chance it gives you to find out—*before the election*—who a candidate's supporters are, what interests they represent, and how much they are contributing.

Under the new law, each congressional candidate must file extensive reports on any contributor of more than $100, and political committees, like "Bankers for McClellan," must file reports, too, if they expect to spend a total of more than $1,000 for any candidate. The reports are filed, six times during an election year, with the secretary of state in the state in which the candidate is running and in Washington, D.C., with the clerk of the House and the secretary of the Senate. They are open to the public, and you may inspect them. What use do you make of the reports? Check especially for (1) failures to comply with the election law, (2) potential conflicts of interest in the areas the candidate would cover as a legislator, (3) expenditures higher than the level the law permits, (4) reported spending that is much greater than reported contributions—which suggests that some donors have secretly given cash, or (5) contributions "in kind," such as the loan of consultants who are still on salary from a corporation.

During an election year, one of the most fruitful issues to raise with candidates is reform of Congress itself. Who goes to Congress is, of course, a critical question. But so is the question: What kind of institution should Congress be? Reform and creativity cannot flourish in an unresponsive institution, no matter how good its members. In letters, in visits, or during speeches, constituents can put their representatives on record about the rules which govern their work and our Congress. What follows are suggested questions, which can hopefuly trigger a dialogue on congressional reform; each is merely a door to a roomful of detailed, follow-up inquiries. They should be pursued until the candidate has publicly committed himself, since without a commitment there can be no accountability. Will the candidate or congressman—

• Support public financing of a substantial portion of election costs?

• Promote legislation to plug all existing loopholes (described in chapter 1) in the campaign finance disclosure laws?

• Back new legislation requiring the fullest possible disclosure of organized lobbying activity, including disclosure of the original source of all funds used in lobbying, the amounts spent and received, the way the funds are spent, and the specific issues involved?

• Work actively (including promoting legislation) to expand Congress's information-gathering capability dramatically by, for example, increasing professional staff and computer resources?

• Sponsor and back legislation making it mandatory for members of Congress and professional staff to disclose their financial interests, including directorships of firms and any other associations with persons or organizations contracting with, or working to, influence the government?

• Support rules forbidding members to serve on committees having jurisdiction over any subjects affecting them financially?

• Support legislation creating an independent enforcement agency—armed with subpoena authority and the power to issue cease-and-desist orders and assess civil penalties—to oversee the campaign finance, lobbying, and conflict of interest laws?

• Work to eliminate the secrecy that serves special interests by backing legislation to open all committee and subcommittee markup and House-Senate conference sessions to the public (limited only by national security considerations) and to require the taking of transcripts to be available immediately to the public in unedited form?

• Back democratization of the rules of committee chairman power—including empowering a majority of a committee to hire or fire committee staff, convene committee meetings, report out a bill, and have it brought to a floor vote?

• Support the abolition of the seniority system, and its replacement with a method for choosing committee chairmen and ranking minority members by open ballot of party caucus?

Finally, there is the election process itself. To participate effectively in a political campaign, you will need to learn more about political tactics than you can pick up from the morning paper or campaign finance reports. You can start to learn with advice from experienced people in your community who are sympathetic to your goals. You can arrange briefings by political reporters from the local newspapers, former campaign managers of reform candidates, local delegations to the state legislature, and leaders of voter registration drives.

You can then turn your efforts to old-fashioned political organizing techniques to get out the vote. As a citizen action group organized for nonelectoral purposes—for conservation or child care—you can often rally many people who would ignore the normal appeals of the political parties. Particularly since the surprise showing of Eugene McCarthy in the 1968 New Hampshire presidential primary, congressional candidates have respected the power of citizen groups and their volunteer workers.

Especially in the primaries, where a challenger's main problem may be to battle his way out of obscurity, door-to-door canvassers and street-corner leafleters can make a big difference. Canvassers are also needed for the all-important voter registration drives. New voters, of all ages, often poor or from minority groups, usually lean against the status quo. Later, volunteers can help man telephones, staple newsletters, lick envelopes, and mail literature from campaign headquarters. On election day, thousands of phone calls must go out to voters from sympathetic districts, to remind them to vote; carpools are needed to take house-bound voters to the polls; and leafleters should be at every nearby polling location. All these are within the capacity of a well-organized citizen action group.

Don't consider winning the election as your only goal. Your chances of losing are too great to risk such single-mindedness. A few losses could then thoroughly discourage your members. Remind them that your long-range objective is not superior numbers in November, but favorable votes in Congress. If you gain new access to your representatives or senator, or change his or her emphasis or views, your citizen action has won a victory. Even if you lost everything on your agenda, you've gained if you make your last mistakes your best teacher for another more effective drive.

Appendix 1

Sources of Information on Congress

In addition to the government publications listed in the last chapter, a good way for citizens to learn about current happenings is to draw on the research of Washington lobbies. Some distribute *free pocket-size directories* listing members of Congress and their committee assignments: Common Cause, a leading citizens' lobby, at 2100 M Street, N.W., Washington, D.C. 20037; or Chamber of Commerce of the United States, Legislative Dept., 1615 H Street, N.W., Washington, D.C. 20006; or the American Medical Association, 1776 K Street, N.W., Washington, D.C. 20006. Others publish *free "scorecards"* on how every member of Congress voted on dozens of major bills, selected and scored from the political perspective of each organization. The most prominent are AFL-CIO, Legislative Department, 815 Sixteenth Street, N.W., Washington, D.C. 20006 (labor and social welfare votes); Americans for Constitutional Action, 955 L'Enfant Plaza North, S.W., Washington, D.C. 20024 ("conservative"); Americans for Democratic Action, 1424 Sixteenth Street, N.W., Washington, D.C. 20036 ("liberal").

Several other sources offer summarized and detailed information. *Congressional Quarterly's Guide to the Congress of the United States* is an expensive ($35) but extremely thorough and interesting tome on the history and workings of Congress, first published in 1971. *The Almanac of American Politics*, by Barone, Ujifusa, and Matthews, a Gambit paperback (first published in 1972 and to be updated every two years), is a single 1,000-page volume (one or two pages per congressman), available at bookstores for $4.95. *Ralph Nader's Congress Project* has profiles of all incumbents who are running in the 1972 elections, and in 1973 will have in-depth studies of each major com-

mittee, and topical studies of such aspects of Congress as
campaign financing and congressional monitoring of executive departments. (Major libraries should have these materials.)

The *Congressional Directory,* often available free from
your congressman, otherwise a $3-paperback from the
U.S. Government Printing Office, lists all congressmen and
their committee (but not subcommittee) assignments, and
most congressional staff. More complete information about
staff is contained in the *Congressional Staff Directory,*
available at $13.50 from 300 New Jersey Avenue, S.E.,
Washington, D.C. 20003.

By writing most committee offices (same address as
your congressman), you can obtain at no cost their 100–
300-page committee *Legislative Calenders.* They list every
bill referred to the committee and what action has been
taken, as well as descriptions of committee work, members,
history, rules, etc. They are typically issued from one to six
times a year, depending on the committee, and are therefore usually weeks or months out of date.

Two periodicals are especially informative on current
legislation and, though expensive, are available in some
large public and college libraries. The $400-per-year
Congressional Quarterly Weekly Report is mailed every
Friday from 1735 K Street, N.W., Washington, D.C.
20006, and is indexed by subject. The *National Journal,* a
$200-per-year subscription, is published weekly by The
Government Research Co., 1730 M Street, N.W., Washington, D.C. 20036. Each issue includes behind-the-scenes
reports on legislative progress, pressures, and personal
profiles, indexed every three months.

Finally, thousands of documents, directories, and reports
can be obtained from the U.S. Government Printing Office.
You can find out what may be helpful in the *Monthly
Catalogue of U.S. Government Publications,* carried in
many major public and university libraries; periodic GPO
catalogues are mailed free on request.

Appendix 2
House of Representatives

Members: Democrats in roman; Republicans in *italic*

A

Abbit, Watkins M. (Va.)
Abernethy, Thomas G. (Miss.)
Abourezk, James (S. Dak.)
Abzug, Bella S. (N.Y.)
Adams, Brock (Wash.)
Addabbo, Joseph P. (N.Y.)
Albert, Carl (Okla.)
Alexander, Bill (Ark.)
Anderson, Glenn M. (Calif.)
Anderson, John B. (Ill.)
Anderson, William R. (Tenn.)
Andrews, Mark (N. Dak.)
Annunzio, Frank (Ill.)
Archer, Bill (Tex.)
Arends, Leslie C. (Ill.)
Ashbrook, John M. (Ohio)
Ashley, Thomas L. (Ohio)
Aspin, Les (Wis.)
Aspinall, Wayne N. (Colo.)

B

Badillo, Herman (N.Y.)
Baker, LaMar (Tenn.)
Baring, Walter S. (Nev.)
Barrett, William A. (Pa.)
Begich, Nick (Alaska)
Belcher, Page (Okla.)
Bell, Alphonzo (Calif.)
Bennett, Charles E. (Fla.)
Bergland, Bob (Minn.)
Betts, Jackson E. (Ohio)
Bevill, Tom (Ala.)
Biaggi, Mario (N.Y.)

Biester, Edward G., Jr. (Pa.)
Bingham, Jonathan B. (N.Y.)
Blackburn, Ben B. (Ga.)
Blanton, Ray (Tenn.)
Blatnik, John A. (Minn.)
Boggs, Hale (La.)
Boland, Edward P. (Mass.)
Bolling, Richard (Mo.)
Bow, Frank T. (Ohio)
Brademas, John (Ind.)
Brasco, Frank J. (N.Y.)
Bray, William G. (Ind.)
Brinkley, Jack (Ga.)
Brooks, Jack (Tex.)
Broomfield, William S. (Mich.)
Brotzman, Donald G. (Colo.)
Brown, Clarence J. (Ohio)
Brown, Garry (Mich.)
Broyhill, James T. (N.C.)
Broyhill, Joel T. (Va.)
Buchanan, John (Ala.)
Burke, J. Herbert (Fla.)
Burke, James A. (Mass.)
Burleson, Omar (Tex.)
Burlison, Bill D. (Mo.)
Burton, Phillip (Calif.)
Byrne, James A. (Pa.)
Byrnes, John W. (Wis.)
Byron, Goodloe E. (Md.)

C

Cabell, Earle (Tex.)
Caffery, Patrick T. (La.)
Camp, John N. Happy (Okla.)
Carey, Hugh L. (N.Y.)

Carney, Charles J. (Ohio)
Carter, Tim Lee (Ky.)
Casey, Bob (Tex.)
Cederberg, Elford A. (Mich.)
Celler, Emanuel (N.Y.)
Chamberlain, Charles E. (Mich.)
Chappell, Bill, Jr. (Fla.)
Chisholm, Shirley (N.Y.)
Clancy, Donald D. (Ohio)
Clark, Frank M. (Pa.)
Clausen, Don H. (Calif.)
Clawson, Del (Calif.)
Clay, William (Bill) (Mo.)
Cleveland, James C. (N.H.)
Collier, Harold R. (Ill.)
Collins, George W. (Ill.)
Collins, James M. (Tex.)
Colmer, William M. (Miss.)
Conable, Barber B., Jr. (N.Y.)
Conte, Silvio O. (Mass.)
Conyers, John, Jr. (Mich.)
Córdova, Jorge L. (P.R.)
Corman, James C. (Calif.)
Cotter, William R. (Conn.)
Coughlin, Lawrence (Pa.)
Crane, Philip M. (Ill.)
Culver, John C. (Iowa)
Curlin, William P., Jr. (Ky.)

D

Daniel, W. C. (Dan) (Va.)
Daniels, Dominick V. (N.J.)
Danielson, George E. (Calif.)
Davis, Glenn R. (Wis.)
Davis, John W. (Ga.)
Davis, Mendel J. (S.C.)
de la Garza, Eligio (Tex.)
Delaney, James J. (N.Y.)
Dellenback, John (Oreg.)
Dellums, Ronald V. (Calif.)
Denholm, Frank E. (S. Dak.)
Dennis, David W. (Ind.)
Dent, John H. (Pa.)
Derwinski, Edward J. (Ill.)
Devine, Samuel L. (Ohio)
Dickinson, William L. (Ala.)
Diggs, Charles C., Jr. (Mich.)
Dingell, John D. (Mich.)
Donohue, Harold D. (Mass.)
Dorn, Wm. Jennings Bryan (S.C.)

Dow, John G. (N.Y.)
Dowdy, John (Tex.)
Downing, Thomas N. (Va.)
Drinan, Robert F. (Mass.)
Dulski, Thaddeus J. (N.Y.)
Duncan, John J. (Tenn.)
du Pont, Pierre S. (Pete) (Del.)
Dwyer, Florence P. (N.J.)

E

Eckhardt, Bob (Tex.)
Edmondson, Ed (Okla.)
Edwards, Don (Calif.)
Edwards, Edwin W. (La.)
Edwards, Jack (Ala.)
Eilberg, Joshua (Pa.)
Erlenborn, John N. (Ill.)
Esch, Marvin L. (Mich.)
Eshleman, Edwin D. (Pa.)
Evans, Frank E. (Colo.)
Evins, Joe L. (Tenn.)

F

Fascell, Dante B. (Fla.)
Fauntroy, Walter E. (D.C.)
Findley, Paul (Ill.)
Fish, Hamilton, Jr. (N.Y.)
Fisher, O. C. (Tex.)
Flood, Daniel J. (Pa.)
Flowers, Walter (Ala.)
Flynt, John J., Jr. (Ga.)
Foley, Thomas S. (Wash.)
Ford, Gerald R. (Mich.)
Ford, William D. (Mich.)
Forsythe, Edwin B. (N.J.)
Fountain, L. H. (N.C.)
Fraser, Donald M. (Minn.)
Frelinghuysen, Peter H. B. (N.J.)
Frenzel, Bill (Minn.)
Frey, Louis, Jr. (Fla.)
Fulton, Richard H. (Tenn.)
Fuqua, Don (Fla.)

G

Galifianakis, Nick (N.C.)
Gallagher, Cornelius E. (N.J.)
Garmatz, Edward A. (Md.)
Gaydos, Joseph M. (Pa.)

Gettys, Tom S. (S.C.)
Giaimo, Robert N. (Conn.)
Gibbons, Sam (Fla.)
Goldwater, Barry M., Jr. (Calif.)
Gonzalez, Henry B. (Tex.)
Goodling, George A. (Pa.)
Grasso, Ella T. (Conn.)
Gray, Kenneth J. (Ill.)
Green, Edith (Oreg.)
Green, William J. (Pa.)
Griffin, Charles H. (Miss.)
Griffiths, Martha W. (Mich.)
Gross, H. R. (Iowa)
Grover, James R., Jr. (N.Y.)
Gubser, Charles S. (Calif.)
Gude, Gilbert (Md.)

H

Hagan, G. Elliott (Ga.)
Haley, James A. (Fla.)
Hall, Durward G. (Mo.)
Helpern, Seymour (N.Y.)
Hamilton, Lee H. (Ind.)
Hammerschmidt, John Paul (Ark.)
Hanley, James M. (N.Y.)
Hanna, Richard T. (Calif.)
Hansen, Julia Butler (Wash.)
Hansen, Orval (Idaho)
Harrington, Michael (Mass.)
Harha, William H. (Ohio)
Harvey, James (Mich.)
Hastings, James F. (N.Y.)
Hathaway, William D. (Maine)
Hawkins, Augustus F. (Calif.)
Hays, Wayne L. (Ohio)
Hébert, F. Edward (La.)
Hechler, Ken (W. Va.)
Heckler, Margaret M. (Mass.)
Heinz, H. John, III (Pa.)
Helstoski, Henry (N.J.)
Henderson, David N. (N.C.)
Hicks, Floyd V. (Wash.)
Hicks, Louise Day (Mass.)
Hillis, Elwood (Ind.)
Hogan, Lawrence J. (Md.)
Holifield, Chet (Calif.)
Horton, Frank (N.Y.)
Hosmer, Craig (Calif.)
Howard, James J. (N.J.)

Hull, W. R., Jr. (Mo.)
Hungate, William L. (Mo.)
Hunt, John E. (N.J.)
Hutchinson, Edward (Mich.)

I

Ichord, Richard H. (Mo.)

J

Jacobs, Andrew, Jr. (Ind.)
Jarman, John (Okla.)
Johnson, Albert W. (Pa.)
Johnson, Harold T. (Calif.)
Jonas, Charles Raper (N.C.)
Jones, Ed (Tenn.)
Jones, Robert E. (Ala.)
Jones, Walter B. (N.C.)

K

Karth, Joseph E. (Minn.)
Kastenmeier, Robert W. (Wis.)
Kazen, Abraham, Jr. (Tex.)
Keating, William J. (Ohio)
Kee, James (W. Va.)
Keith, Hastings (Mass.)
Kemp, Jack F. (N.Y.)
King, Carleton J. (N.Y.)
Kluczynski, John C. (Ill.)
Koch, Edward I. (N.Y.)
Kuykendall, Dan (Tenn.)
Kyl, John (Iowa)
Kyros, Peter N. (Maine)

L

Landgrebe, Earl F. (Ind.)
Landrum, Phil M. (Ga.)
Latta, Delbert L. (Ohio)
Leggett, Robert L. (Calif.)
Lennon, Alton (N.C.)
Lent, Norman F. (N.Y.)
Link, Arthur A. (N. Dak.)
Lloyd, Sherman P. (Utah)
Long, Clarence D. (Md.)
Long, Speedy O. (La.)
Lujan, Manuel, Jr. (N. Mex.)

M

McClory, Robert (Ill.)
McCloskey, Paul N., Jr. (Calif.)
McClure, James A. (Idaho)
McCollister, John Y. (Nebr.)
McCormack, Mike (Wash.)
McCulloch, William M. (Ohio)
McDade, Joseph M. (Pa.)
McDonald, Jack H. (Mich.)
McEwen, Robert C. (N.Y.)
McFall, John J. (Calif.)
McKay, K. Gunn (Utah)
McKevitt, James D. (Mike)
    (Colo.)
McKinney, Stewart B. (Conn.)
McMillan, John L. (S.C.)
Macdonald, Torbert H. (Mass.)
Madden, Ray J. (Ind.)
Mahon, George H. (Tex.)
Mailliard, William S. (Calif.)
Mallary, Richard W. (Vt.)
Mann, James R. (S.C.)
Martin, Dave (Nebr.)
Mathias, Robert B. (Bob)
    (Calif.)
Mathis, Dawson (Ga.)
Matsunaga, Spark M. (Hawaii)
Mayne, Wiley (Iowa)
Mazzoli, Romano L. (Ky.)
Meeds, Lloyd (Wash.)
Melcher, John (Mont.)
Metcalfe, Ralph H. (Ill.)
Michel, Robert H. (Ill.)
Mikva, Abner J. (Ill.)
Miller, Clarence E. (Ohio)
Miller, George P. (Calif.)
Mills, Wilbur D. (Ark.)
Mills, William O. (Md.)
Minish, Joseph G. (N.J.)
Mink, Patsy T. (Hawaii)
Minshall, William E. (Ohio)
Mitchell, Parren J. (Md.)
Mizell, Wilmer (Vinegar Bend)
    (N.C.)
Mollohan, Robert H. (W. Va.)
Monagan, John S. (Conn.)
Montgomery, G. V. (Sonny)
    (Miss.)
Moorhead, William S. (Pa.)
Morgan, Thomas E. (Pa.)
Morse, F. Bradford (Mass.)
Mosher, Charles A. (Ohio)

Moss, John E. (Calif.)
Murphy, John M. (N.Y.)
Murphy, Morgan F. (Ill.)
Myers, John T. (Ind.)

N

Natcher, William H. (Ky.)
Nedzi, Lucien N. (Mich.)
Nelsen, Ancher (Minn.)
Nichols, Bill (Ala.)
Nix, Robert N. C. (Pa.)

O

Obey, David R. (Wis.)
O'Hara, James G. (Mich.)
O'Konski, Alvin E. (Wis.)
O'Neill, Thomas P., Jr. (Mass.)

P

Passman, Otto E. (La.)
Patman, Wright (Tex.)
Patten, Edward J. (N.J.)
Pelly, Thomas M. (Wash.)
Pepper, Claude (Fla.)
Perkins, Carl D. (Ky.)
Pettis, Jerry L. (Calif.)
Peyser, Peter A. (N.Y.)
Pickle, J. J. (Tex.)
Pike, Otis G. (N.Y.)
Pirnie, Alexander (N.Y.)
Poage, W. R. (Tex.)
Podell, Bertram L. (N.Y.)
Poff, Richard H. (Va.)
Powell, Walter E. (Ohio)
Preyer, Richardson (N.C.)
Price, Melvin (Ill.)
Price, Robert (Tex.)
Pryor, David (Ark.)
Pucinski, Roman C. (Ill.)
Purcell, Graham (Tex.)

Q

Quie, Albert H. (Minn.)
Quillen, James H. (Jimmy)
    (Tenn.)

R

Railsback, Tom (Ill.)
Randall, Wm. J. (Mo.)
Rangel, Charles B. (N.Y.)
Rarick, John R. (La.)
Rees, Thomas M. (Calif.)
Reid, Ogden R. (N.Y.)
Reuss, Henry S. (Wis.)
Rhodes, John J. (Ariz.)
Riegle, Donald W., Jr. (Mich.)
Roberts, Ray (Tex.)
Robinson, J. Kenneth (Va.)
Robison, Howard W. (N.Y.)
Rodino, Peter W., Jr. (N.J.)
Roe, Robert A. (N.J.)
Rogers, Paul G. (Fla.)
Roncalio, Teno (Wyo.)
Rooney, Fred B. (Pa.)
Rooney, John J. (N.Y.)
Rosenthal, Benjamin S. (N.Y.)
Rostenkowski, Dan (Ill.)
Roush, J. Edward (Ind.)
Rousselot, John H. (Calif.)
Roy, William R. (Kans.)
Roybal, Edward R. (Calif.)
Runnels, Harold (N. Mex.)
Ruppe, Philip E. (Mich.)
Ruth, Earl B. (N.C.)
Ryan, William F. (N.Y.)

S

St. Germain, Fernand J. (R.I.)
Sandman, Charles W., Jr. (N.J.)
Sarbanes, Paul S. (Md.)
Satterfield, David E., III (Va.)
Saylor, John P. (Pa.)
Scherle, William J. (Iowa)
Scheuer, James H. (N.Y.)
Schmitz, John G. (Calif.)
Schneebeli, Herman T. (Pa.)
Schwengel, Fred (Iowa)
Scott, William Lloyd (Va.)
Sebelius, Keith G. (Kans.)
Seiberling, John F. (Ohio)
Shipley, George E. (Ill.)
Shoup, Richard G. (Mont.)
Shriver, Garner E. (Kans.)
Sikes, Robert L. F. (Fla.)
Sisk, B. F. (Calif.)

Skubitz, Joe (Kans.)
Slack, John M. (W. Va.)
Smith, H. Allen (Calif.)
Smith, Henry P., III (N.Y.)
Smith, Neal (Iowa)
Snyder, M. G. (Gene) (Ky.)
Spence, Floyd (S.C.)
Springer, William L. (Ill.)
Staggers, Harley O. (W. Va.)
Stanton, J. William (Ohio)
Stanton, James V. (Ohio)
Steed, Tom (Okla.)
Steele, Robert H. (Conn.)
Steiger, Sam (Ariz.)
Steiger, William A. (Wis.)
Stephens, Robert G., Jr. (Ga.)
Stokes, Louis (Ohio)
Stratton, Samuel S. (N.Y.)
Stubblefield, Frank A. (Ky.)
Stuckey, W. S. (Bill), Jr. (Ga.)
Sullivan, Leonor K.
  (Mrs. John B.) (Mo.)
Symington, James W. (Mo.)

T

Talcott, Burt L. (Calif.)
Taylor, Roy A. (N.C.)
Teague, Charles M. (Calif.)
Teague, Olin E. (Tex.)
Terry, John H. (N.Y.)
Thompson, Fletcher (Ga.)
Thompson, Frank, Jr. (N.J.)
Thomson, Vernon W. (Wis.)
Thone, Charles (Nebr.)
Tiernan, Robert O. (R.I.)

U

Udall, Morris K. (Ariz.)
Ullman, Al (Oreg.)

V

Van Deerlin, Lionel (Calif.)
Vander Jagt, Guy (Mich.)
Vanik, Charles A. (Ohio)
Veysey, Victor V. (Calif.)
Vigorito, Joseph P. (Pa.)

W

Waggonner, Joe D., Jr. (La.)
Waldie, Jerome R. (Calif.)
Wampler, William C. (Va.)
Ware, John (Pa.)
Whalen, Charles W., Jr. (Ohio)
Whalley, J. Irving (Pa.)
White, Richard C. (Tex.)
Whitehurst, G. William (Va.)
Whitten, Jamie L. (Miss.)
Widnall, William B. (N.J.)
Wiggins, Charles E. (Calif.)
Williams, Lawrence G. (Pa.)
Wilson, Bob (Calif.)
Wilson, Charles H. (Calif.)
Winn, Larry, Jr. (Kans.)
Wolff, Lester L. (N.Y.)
Wright, Jim (Tex.)
Wyatt, Wendell (Oreg.)
Wydler, John W. (N.Y.)
Wylie, Chalmers P. (Ohio)
Wyman, Louis C. (N.H.)

Y

Yates, Sidney R. (Ill.)
Yatron, Gus (Pa.)
Young, C. W. Bill (Fla.)
Young, John (Tex.)

Z

Zablocki, Clement J. (Wis.)
Zion, Roger H. (Ind.)
Zwach, John M. (Minn.)

HOUSE COMMITTEES

Agriculture
Appropriations

Armed Services
Banking and Currency
District of Columbia
Education and Labor
Foreign Affairs
Government Operations
House Administration
Interior and Insular Affairs
Internal Security
Interstate and
  Foreign Commerce
Judiciary
  Subcommittee on Claims
  Subcommittee on Immigration
  Subcommittee on Revision
   of Laws
Merchant Marine and Fisheries
Post Office and Civil Service
Public Works
Rules
Science and Astronautics
Standards of Official Conduct
Veterans' Affairs
Ways and Means {(L.H.O.B.) (Capitol)
  Hearing Room
  Minority Clerk
Select Committee on
  Beauty Shop
Select Committee on Crime
Select Committee on Parking
Select Committee on Restaurant
Select Committee on Small
  Business

LIAISON OFFICES

Air Force (R.H.O.B.)
Army (R.H.O.B.)
Civil Service (R.H.O.B.)
Executive Branch (C.H.O.B.)
Navy (R.H.O.B.)
Veterans' Administration
  (R.H.O.B.)

Senate

Members: Democrats in roman; Republicans in *italic*; Conservatives in CAPITALS; Independents in SMALL CAPS

Vice Pres. *Agnew, Spiro T.* (Md.)
Aiken, George D. (Vt.)
Allen, James B. (Ala.)
Allott, Gordon (Colo.)
Anderson, Clinton P. (N. Mex.)
Baker, Howard H., Jr. (Tenn.)
Bayh, Birch (Ind.)
Beall, J. Glenn, Jr. (Md.)
Bellmon, Henry (Okla.)
Bennett, Wallace F. (Utah)
Bentsen, Lloyd (Tex.)
Bible, Alan (Nev.)
Boggs, J. Caleb (Del.)
Brock, Bill (Tenn.)
Brooke, Edward W. (Mass.)
BUCKLEY, JAMES L. (N.Y.)
Burdick, Quentin N. (N. Dak.)
BYRD, HARRY F., JR. (Va.)
Byrd, Robert C. (W. Va.)
Cannon, Howard W. (Nev.)
Case, Clifford P. (N.J.)
Chiles, Lawton (Fla.)
Church, Frank (Idaho)
Cook, Marlow W. (Ky.)
Cooper, John Sherman (Ky.)
Cotton, Norris (N.H.)
Cranston, Alan (Calif.)
Curtis, Carl T. (Nebr.)
Dole, Robert (Kans.)
Dominick, Peter H. (Colo.)
Eagleton, Thomas F. (Mo.)
Eastland, James O. (Miss.)
Ellender, Allen J. (La.)
Ervin, Sam J., Jr. (N.C.)

Fannin, Paul J. (Ariz.)
Fong, Hiram L. (Hawaii)
Fulbright, J. W. (Ark.)
Gambrell, David H. (Ga.)
Goldwater, Barry (Ariz.)
Gravel, Mike (Alaska)
Griffin, Robert P. (Mich.)
Gurney, Edward J. (Fla.)
Hansen, Clifford P. (Wyo.)
Harris, Fred R. (Okla.)
Hart, Philip A. (Mich.)
Hartke, Vance (Ind.)
Hatfield, Mark O. (Oreg.)
Hollings, Ernest F. (S.C.)
Hruska, Roman L. (Nebr.)
Hughes, Harold E. (Iowa)
Humphrey, Hubert H. (Minn.)
Inouye, Daniel K. (Hawaii)
Jackson, Henry M. (Wash.)
Javits, Jacob K. (N.Y.)
Jordan, B. Everett (N.C.)
Jordan, Len B. (Idaho)
Kennedy, Edward M. (Mass.)
Long, Russell B. (La.)
McClellan, John L. (Ark.)
McGee, Gale W. (Wyo.)
McGovern, George (S. Dak.)
McIntyre, Thomas J. (N.H.)
Magnuson, Warren G. (Wash.)
Mansfield, Mike (Mont.)
Mathias, Charles McC., Jr. (Md.)
Metcalf, Lee (Mont.)
Miller, Jack (Iowa)
Mondale, Walter F. (Minn.)

Montoya, Joseph M. (N. Mex.)
Moss, Frank E. (Utah)
Mundt, Karl E. (S. Dak.)
Muskie, Edmund S. (Maine)
Nelson, Gaylord (Wis.)
Packwood, Bob (Oreg.)
Pastore, John O. (R.I.)
Pearson, James B. (Kans.)
Pell, Claiborne (R.I.)
Percy, Charles H. (Ill.)
Proxmire, William (Wis.)
Randolph, Jennings (W. Va.)
Ribicoff, Abraham (Conn.)
Roth, William V., Jr. (Del.)
Saxbe, William B. (Ohio)
Schweiker, Richard S. (Pa.)
Scott, Hugh (Pa.)
Smith, Margaret Chase (Maine)
Sparkman, John (Ala.)
Spong, William B., Jr. (Va.)
Stennis, John C. (Minn.)
Stevens, Ted (Alaska)
Stevenson, Adlai E., III (Ill.)
Symington, Stuart (Mo.)
Taft, Robert, Jr. (Ohio)
Talmadge, Herman E. (Ga.)
Thurmond, Strom (S.C.)
Tower, John (Tex.)
Tunney, John V. (Calif.)
Weicker, Lowell P., Jr. (Conn.)
Williams, Harrison A., Jr. (N.J.)
Young, Milton R. (N. Dak.)

SENATE COMMITTEES

Aeronautical and Space Sciences
Agriculture and Forestry
Appropriations

Armed Services
Banking, Housing and Urban
   Affairs
Commerce
District of Columbia
Finance
Foreign Relations
Government Operations
Interior and Insular Affairs
Judiciary
Labor and Public Welfare
Post Office and Civil Service
Public Works
Rules and Administration
Veterans' Affairs
Select-Small Business
Select-Standards and Conduct
Special-Aging

JOINT COMMITTEES

Atomic Energy (Capitol)
Congressional Operations
   (L.H.O.B.)
Defense Production (N.S.O.B.)
Economic Committee (N.S.O.B.)
Internal Revenue Taxation
   (L.H.O.B.)
Printing (Capitol)

LIAISON OFFICES

Air Force (S.O.B.)
Army (S.O.B.)
Civil Service (R.H.O.B.)
Navy (S.O.B.)
Veterans' Administration
   (S.O.B.)

Index

ABOUT THE AUTHORS

MARK J. GREEN graduated from Harvard Law School in 1970 and is presently the director of the Corporate Accountability Research Group in Washington, D.C. He is the author of *The Closed Enterprise System*, coeditor of *With Justice for Some* and *Corporate Power in America*, and editor of *The Monopoly Makers*, the latter two to be released shortly.

JAMES M. FALLOWS graduated in 1970 from Harvard College where he was editor-in-chief of the HARVARD CRIMSON. He then spent two years at Oxford as a Rhodes scholar. He is the author of *The Water Lords* and is an editor of THE WASHINGTON MONTHLY.

DAVID R. ZWICK is the director of the Clean Water Action Project in Washington, D.C., and wrote the book, *Water Wasteland*. He is currently on leave from the Harvard Law School and the Kennedy School of Government.

NOW—WHAT ABOUT *YOUR OWN* CONGRESSMEN?

Ralph Nader's Congress Project has completed individual profiles of almost every member of Congress in office during 1972. These profiles, on offer exclusively through Grossman Publishers, Washington, D.C., present a clear, up-to-the-minute, nonpartisan examination of every one of the U.S. senators and representatives studied. In 8½″ by 11″ magazine format, the profiles vary in length from twenty to forty pages. They include information about a member's:

- positions on important issues and votes on about ninety matters since the early 1960s
- votes in committee (generally secret until recently)
- last campaign and opponent
- sources of campaign finances and personal finances, where available
- legislative interests
- supporters in Washington, D.C., and at home
- ratings by interest groups like the AFL-CIO, Americans for Constitutional Action, Americans for Democratic Action, National Farmers Union, U.S. Chamber of Commerce, and the League of Conservation Voters
- *personal* and *political* history.

Hundreds of citizen-researchers in every state and in Washington, D.C., gathered the information contained in the profiles. Profiles were reviewed by editors and verifiers and, in most cases, by the senator or representative or his or her staff in draft form.

Only those senators or representatives in office during 1972 were profiled (senators and representatives retiring this year were not profiled).